Mediated Discourse

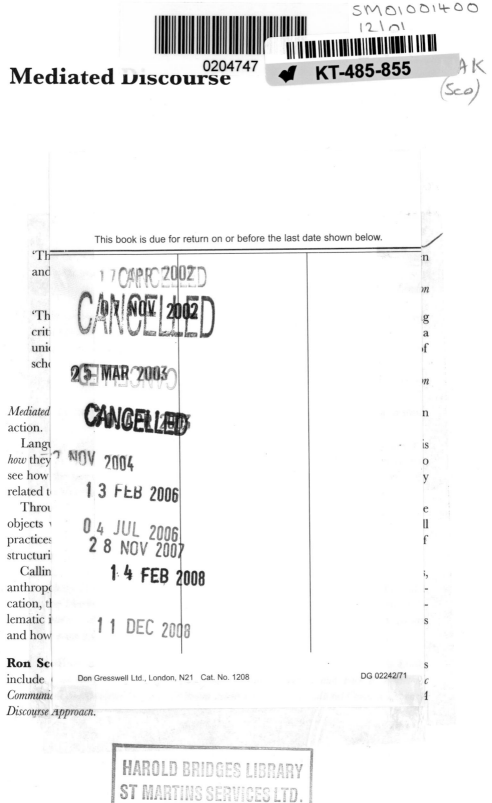

'Th   n
and   m

'Th   g
crit   a
unic   f
sch   m

Mediated   n
action.

Langu   is
how they   o
see how   y
related t

Throu   e
objects   ll
practices   f
structuri

Callin   ,
anthropo
cation, th
lematic i   s
and how

Ron Sc   s
include
Communi   c
Discourse Approach.

Ron Scollon and Brenda Wong. Photograph by Suzanne Wong Scollon.

Mediated Discourse

The nexus of practice

Ron Scollon

London and New York

First published 2001 by Routledge
11 New Fetter Lane, London EC4P 4EE

Simultaneously published in the USA and Canada
by Routledge
29 West 35th Street, New York, NY 10001

Routledge is an imprint of the Taylor & Francis Group

© 2001 Ron Scollon

Typeset in Baskerville by RefineCatch Ltd, Bungay, Suffolk
Printed and bound in Great Britain by Biddles Ltd, Guildford and
King's Lynn

British Library Cataloguing in Publication Data
A catalogue record for this book is available from the British Library

Library of Congress Cataloging in Publication Data
Scollon, Ronald, 1939–
Mediated discourse: the nexus of practice / Ron Scollon.
p. cm.
Includes bibliographical references and index.
1. Discourse analysis—Social aspects. 2. Sociolinguistics. 3. Social
interaction. I. Title.
P302.84. S3 2001
401′.41—dc21

ISBN 0–415–24882–5 (hbk)
ISBN 0–415–24883–3 (pbk)

Contents

Figures

Preface

It was a much younger researcher than this author who crawled around on his hands and knees clutching the microphone of a Sony TC110A following a one-year-old baby as she first began to work out how to find and hold her place conversationally within her world. That baby has recently finished law school and the data collected back then have been transported across oceans and continents. So it was with some mixture of hope and anxiety that I took one of the original tapes out of its box and listened to it to see if the original materials were still usable for a new study.

In discussions with colleagues, notably Ruth Wodak, during the Fall of 1999 I began to feel that social theory, particularly practice theory, was badly in need of an ontogenetic view of social practice. In linguistics, following the earlier model of psychology, it has proved to be a very rich source of insights into social process to watch the earliest development of social and psychological processes longitudinally in the opening years of life. A quick survey of the field showed me that there had been no studies which had directly taken on the challenge of studying the ontogenesis of a single social practice, which we could use to shed light on the closely related question of the aggregation of the habitus in a person in the course of living. I had hoped that I would be able to find in my original material sufficient data to say something interesting about practices of ownership and appropriation because of an ongoing interest in questions of intellectual property.

The longitudinal study of infants is a difficult kind of work which, for many cogent reasons, is often best carried out by the young parents of the children under study. With no grandchildren imminent, I had hoped and was excited to discover that my original tapes had remained in perfect condition, that the hundreds of hours of transcription of 'everything everyone said and did' had produced abundant observations which were useful much beyond the original purposes of my earlier research, and that the scores of photographs and other contextual notes taken by my colleague and wife, Suzanne Scollon, also remained in perfect condition so that I was able to undertake this new study of these archived materials. As it turned out, I found the study of the practices of ownership and appropriation far too complex to address immediately and as the file of notes grew fatter, I realized that I would have to focus even more elementally on just one single practice, the practice of handing an object from one person to another. This practice is implicated in many actions of ownership and of appropriation, of course, but I have found it enough to focus on just this one practice to develop the ideas I have presented in this book. The fuller set of questions surrounding the practices at the foundation of questions of intellectual property will have to wait for development in subsequent projects.

The primary research on which this study is based was conducted in 1972 and in the years following through 1977. I would like to thank once again the participants for their patience with me in doing this work, especially, of course, Brenda Wong. Many of the topics treated in this book were first presented to my classes in Mediated Discourse at Georgetown University. I am particularly indebted to Cecilia Castillo-Ayometzi, Sylvia Chou, Mirjana Nelson Dedaic, Ingrid de Saint-Georges, Michelle Dunne, Alex Johnston, Chris LaFargue, Philip Levine, Cecilia Magadan, Sigrid Norris, Tom Randolph, John Taylor, Jeff Young, Vicki Yung, and Chiara Zucconi who provided the stimulating environment for the discussion of these ideas in class. Tom Randolph in particular read several drafts in close detail and was most helpful in getting both words and ideas straight. Members of the Asian Sociocultural Research Projects group, also at Georgetown University, gave important feedback on many of the ideas presented here. Marilyn Merritt was particularly helpful in raising questions from a point of view outside of practice theory.

I have profited much from extended discussions of these ideas with Ruth Wodak who visited at the Georgetown University linguistics department during the Fall Semester of 1999 when the bulk of this work was being prepared. I am also grateful to Jim Wertsch, Jim Gee, and Norman Fairclough who in shorter visits stimulated much of the thinking which went into this research. Jim Wertsch and Lilie Chouliaraki also read portions of the manuscript and made very useful and insightful comments. David Barton, Gunther Kress, and Sandy Silberstein, who read the manuscript for Routledge, returned very helpful comments which have materially improved both the ideas and the presentation. As the publishing business continues to respond to market pressures for ever more textbooks, I am also very grateful to Louisa Semlyen at Routledge for being willing to support a book that addresses social theory through the analysis of the actions of a one-year-old child – surely a risk in today's market but I hope one which will prove to have been worth taking.

Chapter 1 was presented as a paper in the session on Mediated Discourse at the Sociolinguistics Symposium 2000, 'The Interface between Linguistics and Social Theory' University of the West of England (UWE) , Bristol, 27–29 April 2000. An overview of this work focused on Chapter 2 was given as a talk to the workshop on Theory and Interdisciplinarity in Critical Discourse Analysis, Institute on Discourse, Identity, and Politics, University of Vienna, 6–7 July 2000 as a pre-session to the 7th International Pragmatics Conference in Budapest (9–14 July 2000). The ideas presented here have profited much from discussions in both of these venues and I wish to thank the participants, some of whom I do not know, for stimulating commentary.

Neither the original work nor this reconsideration could have been done without the constant intellectual engagement with Suzanne Scollon. As will be clear in this analysis, she was far more than supportive in the original dissertation research – she was there to take field notes and photographs and to discuss virtually every aspect of this work as a co-researcher. Many of the ideas presented here were first developed in discussions with her and much of what one reads here first came up in discussions of her own current ethnographic project, *Pushing hands, pushing minds: Mediating transnational identity in a taijiquan group.* Our daughter Rachel, who was one of the children studied in the first instance, has now come full circle to offer highly insightful critical readings of this book in manuscript form.

With so much kind assistance and support from family, students, and colleagues one would think it difficult to fail to get it right. Nevertheless, I realize all too well that I have not been able to take into consideration all of the questions which these people have raised. They are not to be blamed for the weaknesses which have remained. It is my hope that the abundant infelicities in the argument which I have not been able to fix will only serve to stimulate new work by those younger and fresher.

1 Mediated discourse

A discursive theory of human action

Discourse and action: a cup of coffee

One morning recently in San Diego, California I had a cup of coffee at the international chain coffee shop, Starbucks®. After a short time in the queue I ordered a tall latte and another drink for my friend. I paid for the drinks and then waited a few minutes while the drinks were made and then delivered to me. We took the drinks and sat down to drink them and have a conversation. As linguists and perhaps only linguists do, in and among the other topics of conversation we talked about what was printed on the cup.

Mediated discourse analysis is a framework for looking at such actions with two questions in mind: What is the action going on here? and how does discourse figure into these actions? In a sense there is nothing very new or different about mediated discourse analysis in that it is a program of linkages among other well-established theoretical and methodological approaches. Mediated discourse analysis seeks to develop a theoretical remedy for discourse analysis that operates without reference to social actions on the one hand, and social analysis that operates without reference to discourse on the other. Virtually all of the theoretical elements have been proposed and developed in the work of others. In this mediated discourse analysis takes the position that social action and discourse are inextricably linked on the one hand (Chouliaraki and Fairclough 1999) but that on the other hand these links are sometimes not at all direct or obvious, and therefore in need of more careful theorization.

In having this cup of coffee I could say there is just a single action – having a cup of coffee as is implied in the common invitation, 'Let's go have a cup of coffee.' Or I could say there is a very complex and nested set of actions – queuing, ordering, purchasing, receiving the order, selecting a table, drinking coffee, conversing, disposing of our cups and other materials, and the rest. Likewise, I could say there is just one discourse here – a conversation among friends. Or I could say there are many complex discourses with rampant intertextualities and interdiscursivities – international neo-capitalist marketing of coffee, service encounter talk, linguistic conference talk, family talk and the rest. Mediated discourse analysis is a position which seeks to keep all of this complexity alive in our analyses without presupposing which actions and which discourses are the relevant ones in any particular case under study.

As a way to at least temporarily narrow the scope of my analysis here, I want to focus on the coffee cup. It can be called the primary mediational means by which the coffee has been produced as something transferable, delivered to me, and ultimately consumed. Without the cup there is no «having a cup of coffee» in the literal sense. Throughout all the other actions which take place, the cup figures as the material line that holds this all together. From the point of view of an analysis of mediated action (Wertsch 1998), then, we would want to consider the cup – a paper one in this case – absolutely central to both the narrowly viewed actions of delivery or drinking and to the more broadly viewed actions of consumer purchasing/marketing or of «having a cup of coffee» as a conversational genre.

If we come to this social interaction from the point of view of discourse analysis, and if we set aside for the moment all of the complexities of service encounter talk and of casual conversation between friends, we still find that the cup itself (with its protective sleeve) is an impressive semiotic complex of at least seven different Discourses in the broad sense defined by Gee (1999).

1   Commercial branding: There is a world-wide recognizable logo which appears twice on the cup and once on the cardboard protective sleeve.
2   Legal: The logo is marked as a registered property (®) and the text on the sleeve is marked as copyrighted (©). A patent number is also given. In addition, there is a warning that the contents are 'extremely hot' which derives from a famous lawsuit against another international chain where a customer had held a paper cup of their coffee between his legs while driving and been uncomfortably scorched.
3   E-commerce: A website is given where the consumer can learn more, though it does not indicate what we might learn about.
4   Consumer correctness: An extended text tells us that the company cares for those who grow its coffee and gives a telephone number where the consumer can call to make a donation to CARE on behalf of plantation workers in Indonesia.
5   Environmental correctness: We are told that the sleeve is made of 60% recycled fiber and that it uses less material than would a second paper cup. The color scheme is in natural cardboard brown with green lettering which are widely associated with environmental friendliness.
6   Service information: There is a printed roster of possibilities ('Decaf', 'Shots', 'Syrup', 'Milk', 'Custom', and 'Drink') and superimposed is the handwritten 'L' (for 'latte').
7   Manufacturing information: Under the cup around the inside rim is the information about the cup itself, its size, and product labeling and number.

On the one hand we have a fairly clear and mundane social action – having a cup of coffee in a coffee shop – and a semiotic complex of Discourses which are also, at least now at the beginning of this century, rather mundane. We have an array of analytical positions from which we can analyze this action, from seeing it as participating in a bit of micro-social interaction to seeing it as participating in the world-wide consumer practices of neo-capitalism. At the same time we have an array of analytical positions from which we can analyze the Discourses represented in these texts printed on this coffee cup. The problem that mediated discourse analysis is trying to engage is how we are to work out a way to understand the relationships among the actions – drinking the cup of coffee – and the Discourses. Ethnographic observation leads us to believe that, on the whole, except for the odd linguist, the coffee is drunk without much attention being focused on this impressive discursive array on the cup.[1] Correspondingly, the literature has many analyses of such Discourses in public places, from the products of the news industry through to the broader popular culture industry, which make scant reference at all to the actual social situations in which these Discourses are engaged in social action. Mediated discourse analysis is an attempt to theorize a way in which we can link the Discourse of commercial branding, for example, with the practice of drinking a cup of coffee in conversation without giving undue weight either to the action without reference to the Discourse or to the Discourse without reference to the actions within which it is appropriated.

A few central concepts

A mediated discourse analysis gives central importance to five concepts:

- Mediated action
- Site of engagement
- Mediational means
- Practice
- Nexus of practice

Mediated action: The unit of analysis of a mediated discourse analysis is the mediated action (not the Discourse or text or genre). That is, the focus is on social actors *as they are acting* because these are the moments in social life when the Discourses in which we are interested are instantiated in the social world as social action, not simply as material objects. We use the phrase 'mediated action' to highlight the unresolvable dialectic between action and the material means which mediate all social action (Wertsch 1998). That is, we take the position that action is materially grounded in persons and objects and that it is unproductive to work with purely abstracted conceptual systems of representation. Participation in the world-wide consumer society requires at some point the transfer of coins and cups, speaking and drinking. Conversely stated, this transfer of coins and cups and speaking and drinking inevitably entails participating in the consumer society. There is no action without participating in such Discourses; no such Discourses without concrete, material actions.

A site of engagement: A mediated action occurs in a social space which I have elsewhere called a 'site of engagement' (Scollon 1998, 1999). This is the real-time window that is opened through an intersection of social practices and mediational means (cultural tools)[2] that make that action the focal point of attention of the relevant participants. The idea of the site of engagement takes from practice/ activity theory (as well as from interactional sociolinguistics) the insistence on the real-time, irreversible, and unfinalizable nature of social action. A mediated action is not a class of actions but a unique moment in history. Its interpretation is located within the social practices which are linked in that unique moment. The cup of coffee/coffee conversation in San Diego is theoretically taken as unique and unfolding in that moment and bears only a loose, indirect, and highly problematical relationship with another cup of coffee at a Starbucks® in San Luis Obispo among the same participants a week later, if for no other reason than the first is part of the history of the second.

Mediational means: A mediated action is carried out through material objects in the world (including the materiality of the social actors – their bodies, dress, movements) in dialectical interaction with structures of the habitus. We take these mediational means to always be multiple in any single action, to carry with them historical affordances and constraints, and to be inherently polyvocal, intertextual, and interdiscursive. Further, these multiple mediational means are organized in a variety of ways, either in hierarchical structures of activities or in relatively expectable relations of salience or importance.

While I have focused on the cup in this sketch, this cup of coffee has also equally entailed the physical spaces of the coffee shop, the coins and bills exchanged, the servers, the counters, the coffee machines, the tables and chairs, the other customers of the shop, the San Diego sunshine – a significant materiality of that particular action – and our own habitus, latte for me, chai latte for my friend. The polyvocality, intertextuality, and interdiscursivity of the cup has been noted above. To this we add the Southern California décor which sets this particular shop in its place on earth and departs so radically from the 'same' company's shops in Washington, DC, Beijing, and London.

Practice and social structure: For this mediated action to take place in this way there is a necessary intersection of social practices and mediational means which in themselves reproduce social groups, histories, and identities. A mediated discourse analysis takes it that a mediated action is only interpretable within practices. From this point of view 'having a cup of coffee' is viewed as a different action in a Starbucks®, in a cafeteria, and at home. The difference lies both in the practices (how the order is made, for example) and in the mediational means (including the range from the espresso machines to the décor of the spaces in which the action is taken). That is to say, a mediated discourse analysis does not neutralize these practices and social structures as 'context', but seeks to keep them alive in our interpretations of mediated actions.

Nexus of practice: Mediated discourse analysis takes a tight or narrow view of social practice as social practices in the plural – ordering, purchasing, handing, and receiving – and so then sees these as practices (as count nouns, not as a mass noun). These practices are linked to other practices, discursive and non-discursive, over time to form nexus of practice. So we might loosely at least want to talk about an early twenty-first century American 'designer coffee shop' nexus of practice which would provisionally include such things as pricing practices (high), ordering practices (the distinctions between *caffe latte, café au lait, regular coffee with milk, cappuchino*), drinking practices (alone with newspapers, in conversation with friends), discursive practices (being able to answer to 'whole or skim?', knowing that 'tall' means the smallest cup on sale or that 'for here' means in a porcelain cup rather than a paper one), physical spacing practices (that the queuing place and delivery place are different) and the rest.

The concept of the nexus of practice works more usefully than the concept of the community of practice which was the earlier framing (Scollon 1998) in that it is rather loosely structured as well as structured over time. That is, a nexus of practice, like practices themselves, is formed one mediated action at a time and is always unfinalized (and unfinalizable). The concept of the nexus of practice is unbounded (unlike the more problematical community of practice) and takes into account that at least most practices (ordering, purchasing, handing, and receiving) can be linked variably to different practices in different sites of engagement and among different participants. From this point of view, the practice of handing an object to another person may be linked to practices which constitute the action of purchasing in a coffee shop, it may be linked to practices which constitute the action of giving a gift to a friend on arriving at a birthday party, or even to handing a bit of change to a panhandler on the street. Mediated discourse analysis takes the position that it is the constellation of linked practices which makes for the uniqueness of the site of engagement and the identities thus produced, not necessarily the specific practices and actions themselves.

This mediated action of having a cup of coffee and the concurrent and dialogically chained prior and subsequent mediated actions could be analyzed with a great deal more care than I have been able to do here. My purpose has been simply to make these five points:

- The mediated action (within a dialogical chain of such social actions as well as within a hierarchy of simultaneously occurring practices) is the focus of mediated discourse analysis.
- The focus is on real-time, irreversible, one-time-only actions rather than objectivized, categorical analyses of types of action or discourses and texts.
- An action is understood as taking place within a site of engagement which is the real-time window opened through an intersection of social practices and mediational means.
- The mediational means are multiple in any case and inevitably carry histories and social structures with them.
- A mediated action produces and reproduces social identities and social structures within a nexus of practice.

Theoretical principles

It is only with some trepidation that I suggest that mediated discourse analysis is a theory, as that word tends to evoke emotional responses only surpassed perhaps by 'patriotism' or 'plagiarism'. Nevertheless, I believe it is important to seek to make one's claims clear and then proceed with the business of discovering what is wrong with them. Here I will articulate three principles which organize mediated discourse theory. The three main principles are the principles of social action, communication, and history. I would argue that the second two are simply tautological or definitional extensions of the first principle, as are the corollaries. I make no claim that these principles are unique to mediated discourse; indeed, it is my hope that the only originality, if there is originality at all in these ideas, is in the degree of explicitness of the underlying principles I am trying to achieve.[3]

> PRINCIPLE ONE: *The principle of social action: Discourse is best conceived as a matter of social actions, not systems of representation or thought or values.*

Mediated discourse theory – to the extent it *is* a theory – is a theory about social action with a specific focus on discourse as a kind of social action as well as upon discourse as a component of social action. This principle should be recognized as an assertion of a value. That is, 'best conceived' is intended to mean 'best conceived for my purposes' which are to come to understand how action in society is possible and to what extent discourse plays a significant role in social action. A theory with an interest in the abstract formal structures of language, of which we seem to have a surplus, would be 'best conceived' as something else.

> COROLLARY ONE: *The ecological unit of analysis*

The proper unit of analysis for a theory of social action is, tautologically, the social action, or as I prefer to phrase it, the mediated action; that is, the person or persons in the moment of taking an action along with the mediational means which are used by them form the 'ecological' unit of analysis, the unit of analysis in which the phenomenon exists, changes, and develops through time (Bateson 1972).

> COROLLARY TWO: *Practice: All social action is based in tacit, normally non-conscious actions.*

'Practice' is the term most commonly used to refer to common action-in-the-world. I follow scholars such as Nishida (1958), Bateson (1972), and Bourdieu (1977 and 1990) in taking practice, not theory, as the milieu of social action.

> COROLLARY THREE: *Habitus: The basis of social action is the habitus (Bourdieu 1977, 1990) or the historical-body (Nishida 1958): an individual's accumulated experience of social actions.*

This constitutes a rephrasing of Corollary Two; a restatement or elaboration of the idea of practice. The word 'practice' focuses on the specific types of action(s); the word 'habitus' focuses on the individual's aggregate experience of practices.

> COROLLARY FOUR: *Positioning (identity claims): All social actions occur within a nexus of practice which makes implicit or explicit claims to the social groups and positions of all participants – speakers, hearers, and those talked about or in front of.*

As social action is based in habitus and habitus is the aggregation of history in concrete, sociocultural circumstances, any action which is taken reproduces (and claims, imputes, contests, and recontextualizes) the identities of prior social actions as well as negotiates new positions among the participants within this nexus of practice.

> COROLLARY FIVE: *Socialization: Because all social actions position the participants, all communications have the effect of socialization to nexus of practice.*

This is a rephrasing of Corollary Four with the focus shifted from the positioning of individuals to those positions as aspects of group membership. As I use the term, a nexus of practice is a network or matrix of linked practices which are the basis of the identities we produce and claim through our social actions.

> COROLLARY SIX: *Othering: Because of the principle of socialization, all communications have the simultaneous effect of producing 'others' who are identified by* not *being members of the relevant nexus of practice.*

Another rephrasing of Corollary Four with the focus shifted towards those who are produced as outsiders to the relevant nexus of practice.

> PRINCIPLE TWO: *The principle of communication: The meaning of the term 'social' in the phrase 'social action' implies a common or shared system of meaning. To be social an action must be communicated.*

This principle is tautologically developed from the first principle by definition.

> COROLLARY ONE: *Mediational means: The production of shared meanings is mediated by a very wide range of mediational means or cultural tools such as language, gesture, material objects, and institutions which are carriers of their sociocultural histories. 'Mediation' refers to this process. 'Mediated discourse' redundantly reminds us that all actions and all discourse are mediated.*

This corollary is terminological in that it introduces the term 'mediational means' (or the nearly alternative term 'cultural tool') for any semiotic object used to mediate social action. Language and discourse are, of course, of primary interest to mediated discourse, but there is no principled avoidance of non-verbal communication, multi-modal communication, or, indeed, architecture, urban planning, or institutions as there tends to be in language-centered theories.

> COROLLARY TWO: *Organization of mediational means: The multiple mediational means involved in a mediated action are related to each other in complex ways.*

This corollary indicates that multiple means are not just accidental aggregates, but that some mediational means will be more salient, preferred, emotionally engaging or otherwise stand in complex relations to each other as well as in relationship to the site of engagement under consideration.

> PRINCIPLE THREE: *The principle of history: 'Social' means 'historical' in the sense that shared meaning derives from common history or common past.*

This principle and its corollaries are further terminological and definitional extensions of the principle of social action. I will not comment further about them here.

> COROLLARY ONE: *Interdiscursivity: Because of the principle of history, all communication is positioned within multiple, overlapping, and even conflicting discourses.*

> COROLLARY TWO: *Intertextuality: Because of the principle of history, all communications (particular utterances) borrow from other discourses and texts and are, in turn, used in later discourses.*

> COROLLARY THREE: *Dialogicality (or conversational or practical inference): Because of the principle of history, all communications respond to prior communications and anticipate following communications.*

Why mediated discourse?

Perhaps it is obvious that many scholars in interactional sociolinguistics, critical discourse analysis, anthropological linguistics or linguistic anthropology, socio-cultural psychology, the sociology of language, new literacy studies, and practice theory as well as in yet other disciplines and research programs would find the principles I have just outlined entirely compatible with their work and with their theoretical orientation. If there is anything at all distinctive about mediated discourse theory (MDT) it is just in the attempt to find a central theoretical position and a unifying unit of analysis which can bring work in these several areas into engagement so that the particular focus will be on the mediated action. By referring to this reorganization as MDT I believe we can exploit the ambiguity in the term 'mediated discourse' to good effect. As I have suggested above, I take it in agreement with Chouliaraki and Fairclough (1999) that any social action is mediated and that it is significantly discursive. MDT seeks to keep the focus upon the concrete, real-time social action and to see these social actions as fundamentally discursive. If the theory makes any grand claim, it is simply that it will be valuable to the project of trying to understand social life and social change to organize our research around the moments in which social actions take place and to organize this research as discursive research.

In this focus on concrete, real-time social actions and social change MDT owes much to theory and practice in interactional sociolinguistics and conversation analysis. We find the concept of conversational inference particularly important to the understanding of such social actions (Gumperz 1977), though I might prefer to call this 'practical' inference to emphasize the grounding in practice and therefore the non-theoretical, non-analytical, non-conscious, non-objectivizing nature of this process of sense-making in action. At the same time, however, MDT takes the point made by Bourdieu (1977, 1990) and others that any instance of concrete, real-time social action is simultaneously the production and repro- duction of the structures of the social world and, therefore, must be conceptual- ized in a way that takes the sociocultural histories of our habitus and of our mediational means (Wertsch 1998) into account. These analytical traditions share much with Nishida's (1958) 'philosophy of nothingness', particularly the concepts of the historical-body, *rekishi-teki-shintai* (Bourdieu's habitus) and action-intuition, *koi-teki-chokkan* (Wertsch's mediated action).[4]

In this, MDT brings together practice theory on the one hand and the close linguistic analysis of social interactions on the other.[5] I take it that each of these perspectives contributes a significant strengthening of the other once the points of contention are resolved in the focus on the social action.

In any case, I would argue that interactional sociolinguistics and critical dis- course analysis (including the more general sociological practice theory of Bourdieu and even Foucault) works with an implied but not well-developed psychological theory. This has led in some cases to profound but unanalyzed differences between cognitive-based and basically rationalist analyses of social interaction and sociocultural, activity theory accounts of human learning and action. In my view sociocultural or sociohistorical psychology within the Vygotsky–Lurian tradition[6] (Wertsch 1998, Cole 1995) is highly compatible with the position taken by MDT that learning proceeds from social interaction through processes of social interaction to the reproduction on the intramental plane of human psychological structures. In my view MDT is considerably strengthened by seeking to theorize more clearly the relationship between human psychological process and social structure through the focus on mediated social action.

MDT, finally, hopes to bring to its projects insights and methodology from three often unrelated fields – anthropological linguistics/linguistic anthropology[7] new literacy studies, and intercultural communication. Work in anthropological lin- guistics has been particularly significant in the development of linguistics and discourse studies in North America beginning with the research of Boas and his students. One central issue of concern in anthropological linguistics has been the so-called Sapir/Whorf hypothesis. MDT joins with the general enthusiasm found in cultural studies and critical discourse analysis in the attempt to locate in dis- course at least some of the effective mechanisms of social and cultural change.

What is disappointing, however, is the ease with which some analysts have asserted the totalizing and determinative role of language and other mediational means in the production of social positions and actions in spite of what is now seven or eight decades of very serious and thorough anthropological linguistic research into this very question.[8] MDT takes the position that any claim for the determining role of language or discourse in social action would have to be carefully weighed against this body of research and, further, need to be theorized so that the claims would cover not just newspaper discourses of post-capitalism but also Athabaskan ritual funeral speeches, not just the policy documents in Indo-European languages of world political or corporate leaders but also the rhymes and narratives of Chipewyan and Cree children on the shores of Lake Athabaska.

Closely related to anthropological linguistics at the outset but now practiced at a considerable distance is what some have come to call the 'new literacy studies' (Street 1984, 1995). MDT takes the original concern with the technologies of literacy as a fundamental issue to be theorized in its work. In our own work (Scollon and Scollon 1979, 1980, 1981) we were concerned to study the inter-actions between the discourses – in the sense of orders of discourse – of literacy and orality and the social practices through which such discourses are produced, particularly in the developing lives of children. MDT brings from this literature an interest in the technologizations of social practice that are our current medi-ated literacies, from traditional manuscript and print literacy to the social prac-tices in the use of electronic communication and the internet. As a theoretical position based in practice theory, the contribution of MDT to new literacy studies is simply to bring together research interests in these separate areas.

Calhoun (1995) has returned to the concept of incommensurable practices introduced by Thomas Kuhn in his *The structure of scientific revolutions* (1962). MDT brings to the study of social action a concern with the development of the concept of incommensurable practices, particularly in a world where a large number of social actors find they are acting on the basis of a highly complex and internally contradictory habitus achieved through a history of life among multiple, overlap-ping, and often conflicting and contradictory nexus of practice and communities of practice. MDT is concerned that much scholarship in practice theory, while deeply concerned with social structure and the reproduction of class or group habitus, has tended to over-simplify the concept of habitus and of social practice. The concern of MDT is to come to understand how an internally complex and often contradictory set of practices and mediational means produces situations of complex identity production by social actors who are negotiating equally complex identities across overlapping nexus of practice and communities of practice.

My concern, then, with Mediated Discourse Theory is to focus my analysis on concrete, real-time social actions but from as broad as possible a range of theor-etical and methodological perspectives. In saying this, however, I do not intend to be either widely or wildly eclectic without taking into consideration serious con-flicts and incompatibilities among these different theoretical frameworks. It seems to me at a minimum, to be serious about coming to understand social action, we need to have not just a theory of discourse and its relationships to action, and not just a psychological theory of the internalization of social life, and not just a theory of the connections between language and culture or language and thought, nor just a theory of the role of technology in social life. I believe we have to see social action as being grounded in the concrete day-to-day actions which are themselves produced at the intersection of practice, discourse, technology, and analysis. 'Mediated Discourse Theory', then, seems an appropriate phrase with which to capture the complexity and ambiguity of the social actions I am interested in coming to understand.

Mediated Discourse: an ontogenetic approach

A chasm has opened up in studies of social life between those who would on the whole think of language and discourse as somewhat peripheral to social life and those who would construct all social life out of the stuff of discourse. It is ironic that among those who have been the last to take the 'linguistic turn' are linguists (Scollon 1999). One finds scholars from the discursive psychologists to art historians who would assert that all that we know and can know is constructed in discourse – that all of our social world is in fact a discursive social world. Linguists have been, at least on the whole in North America, much less ready to join in this discursive celebration of the semiotic game that the analysis of social life has become in so many other disciplines. Perhaps this is not to be entirely attributed to a deeply entrenched positivism among those who have been indoctrinated by the thoughts of Chomsky. I would argue that it represents a more fundamental skepticism about pronouncements on the relationships between language and culture based in six or seven decades of serious consideration of just these issues.

Critical discourse analysts have, on the whole, taken a moderated and, in my view, well-motivated position in contemporary scholarship focused on the social world. As Fairclough (1992; Fairclough and Wodak 1997) and others have argued, following generally within a critical theory tradition (Bhaskar 1989, 1997; Calhoun 1995), social practice is the basis of social action. They have further argued that every practice has a significant discursive element which is not just or merely a reflection upon practice but to some extent constitutive of that practice. There is much ambiguity, of course, in this phrase 'to some extent' and it is that ambiguity that I will examine in the main analysis of this book.

Chouliaraki and Fairclough (1999) have put forward a cogent and challenging statement of the foundational principles of critical discourse analysis. They argue that

> Discourse is always a significant moment because all practices are, as we have said, reflexive – constructions of that practice constitute part of a practice.
>
> (Chouliaraki and Fairclough 1999:23)

Or again they write,

> All practices have an irreducible discursive aspect . . . in the sense that all practices involve use of language to some degree.
>
> (Chouliaraki and Fairclough 1999:26)

There is much in these claims that is attractive as they provide a basis for the interaction of the analysis of discourse and action in the social world. As such claims stand, however, the ambiguity or lack of precise understanding of what constitutes a practice (as a count noun) or practice (as a mass noun) weakens the utility of such discourse analysis.

While many approaches might be taken to provide a closer analysis of discourse and practice, some of which have been taken with important success by such scholars as Fairclough, Chouliaraki, Wodak and others, I have chosen to focus my analysis in an area which is as yet largely untouched by discourse analysis working within a critical theory or practice perspective.[9] I focus on the crucial period in the life of the social actor when she/he in fact becomes such an actor – the second year of life.

Chapter 2 opens this analysis with a study of the ontogenesis of a single social practice. As I have suggested, the idea of practice is increasingly used in social and discursive theory. Nevertheless, several ambiguities have arisen in the use of this concept. At one extreme, 'practice' is used as a mass noun to contrast with 'theory' and covers virtually all of the common, day-to-day ways of being and knowing of members of society. At the other extreme, 'practice' is used as a count noun to indicate very narrowly specified repeatable social actions. In most such uses 'practice' as a mass noun is seen to be a highly complex networking among 'practices' as a count noun, but one seeks far to find either a theoretical bridging of these two ends of the practice continuum or a careful analysis of what, in fact, is practice in concrete circumstances. Most commonly 'practice' is introduced as the foundation of a theoretical perspective and then rather summarily backgrounded as being of less interest than the rest of the theoretical apparatus.

Therefore in Chapter 2, I begin by arguing that progress toward a fully articulated practice theory must proceed now from a narrowly focused analysis of practices taken in the count noun sense of the concept. It then argues that any view of practice must include a theorization of the origins of social practice in the life of the individual in the material and objective conditions within which actions take place, that is, it must include a theorization of the origins of any particular practice (an 'ontogenesis') within the life of the developing infant.

This chapter necessarily concentrates on just the question of the ontogenesis of a single, narrowly defined social practice, the practice of handing. By 'handing' I mean the simple practice of giving an object to another person. Research covering two infants in the period from birth to two years of age with a primary focus on just one of them is used to argue that (1) the social practice of handing develops out of more biological (mammalian) practices of nutrition and care (feeding, handling of the child as well as of the child's handling of the objects of care such as the mother, nursing bottles), (2) there are multiple ontogeneses, not a single developmental pathway in the development of this segment of habitus, and

(3) a significant difference across individuals in the production of the infant's habitus is the linkage or networking of several social practices, each of which is instrumental in the development of the others.

Chapter 2 concludes by observing, relevant to the question of the relationship of social practice and discursive practice, that there is no unique or necessary relationship between any discursive practice and this practice of handing which I analyze. That is to say, contrary to Chouliaraki and Fairclough's assertion that for every practice there is a reflexive, discursive practice about that practice, I have found that while there is much talk which accompanies handing, there are no fixed or concrete linkages between that talk and the practice of handing.

In Chapter 3, then, I move to the question of what sort of talk it is that we have seen. While I have argued that there is no unique or necessary link between discursive practice and the social practice of handing, I have also observed that there is, nevertheless, a lot of talk going on. To deal with this question I go back not to the specific mediated actions of handing themselves but to the practice overall. My purpose is to see if there is, overall, something that can be said about what this discourse, which is loosely coupled with handing, is doing. I look to see if there is, as Chouliaraki and Fairclough put it, any 'representation of what they do as part of what they do'.

What we see in this discourse which accompanies the practice of handing is that much of this talk is about the discursive representation of the social actor. That is, the discursive practice which accompanies handing is not focused upon the handing itself as a social practice but, rather, both the handing and the talk – the discursive practice – are focused upon the discursive construction of persons as social actors. I argue in Chapter 3 that, in the beginning of life, discursive practices which position the infant as an object in the world are notably linked to practices which ascribe social agency to the infant even when there is little behavioral possibility of this agency. I argue that by the second year of life the talk has moved predominantly into the domain of acceding agency to the child by others and by the child's increasing assertion of social agency. One might consider this a matter of using the discursive practice to 'speak through' the practice of handing to the more fundamental social issue of constructing the person as a person, that is, as a social actor enabled to engage in this (and presumably other) practices. Perhaps most significant is that much of this positioning of the infant as social actor is done through the manner (as opposed to the content) of speaking – the wide variety of the baby-talk register.

Mediated discourse is, as I have said, a discursive theory of human action. By that I mean to assert that the unit of analysis, the focus of the project is to come to understand how humans act in society. To study this I first focus on the onto-genesis of a practice – handing – which is, as I define it a chained sequence of mediated actions. There is a danger in this approach, however, of engaging in an inversion of significance. By developing such a close focus on the practice of handing, it can come to appear that humans go about doing things just for the sake of producing the practice itself over time. In Chapter 3 I argue that an analysis of the discursive practices linked to the practice of handing shows that for participants in those mediated actions, the focus is better construed as being upon the construction of the child as a social actor; that is, the focus is on the production of identities through handing, not on the handing itself, and that is why we do not find a close linkage between the discursive practices and the practice of handing.

This focus on the construction of the social actor may itself also invert the significance in many cases, at least from the point of view of the participants. It is difficult to say that this child and her mother undertake these mediated actions just so that they can produce themselves as particular kinds of social actors in the same way it would be difficult to say that every morning I buy a cup of coffee in a particular place to produce myself as a mid-morning coffee drinker (though I do do that) or to practice the handing of coins and the receipt of hot liquids (though I do do that) or to ratify, legitimate, and assist in the production of a world-wide coffee economic exchange (though I also do that). Speaking not as an analyst but as an ordinary social actor, my own view of it is that I want a cup of coffee and that I am using money and other discursive and social practices to accomplish that. That is to say, in my mind and most likely in the minds of others, I am undertaking a mediated action – buying a cup of coffee – which calls upon various social practices to accomplish this and, notably, is produced primarily through the exchange of certain objects, the money and the coffee.

Chapter 4, then, turns to the analysis of these mediational means. But this should be noted with caution as well. To refer to the money I use as a mediational means in accomplishing my purpose is straightforward enough terminologically. I am mediating the action of getting my coffee through this means. At the same time, however, mediated discourse makes no terminological distinction between the money I use and the coffee I receive in exchange. This latter is also a mediational means. In this case it mediates the action; without it I do not buy coffee but only give away money.

The complex interactions among my purposes, those of the coffee shop, of world financial and economic trade, and the social practices which link them can be made visible in such common mediated actions; when the focus of attention is an infant and the objects are crayons, fruit, a rice paddle, some pennies, or a cookie, it is somewhat more difficult to see the linkages between those objects and the actions involved in their handing and these world-wide social and institutional structures. In Chapter 4 I argue, however, that the study of how these mediational objects arise ontogenetically is central to our understanding of the objects of our material world in general.

The argument of Chapter 4 builds on the mediated action of Wertsch (1998) and others within the Neo-Vygotskian sociocultural research paradigm. I argue that it is through the construction of mediational means within the habitus of the social actor that the sociocultural and sociopolitical history are embedded in day-to-day practice. These mediational means are neither external objects nor internal psychological constructs alone but rather are a dialectical relationship between objective materiality and psychological or intramental process. In examining the mediational means which have been called upon in the practice of handing which we have seen in Chapters 2 and 3, I argue that in general these mediational means predate the social actor; that is, they arrive in the lifeworld of the social actor as objective and external givens which are, over time, appropriated into the habitus of the social actor. Thus I argue for making a distinction between the mediational means (a theoretical construct which relates external material objects to psychological intramental process within particular practices) and objects – material objects simply in the world. In this we see that mediational means, rather than being the objects in the world alone, are a class of objects or, more precisely, representations of objects within practices, as integrated with specific practices in the habitus.

I then close Chapter 4 by taking up two problems which this analysis poses. First, how is a practice related to specific mediational means? I will argue that in many cases mediational means arise as codifications and materializations of practice which I refer to as the technologization of practice. A well-known example of this is the technologization of discursive practice which takes place through literacy. This then leads to the second issue which is that such technologized practices, such cultural tools, come to exert pressure upon social practice which leads to rigidity, objectivization, and standardization. I use this set of concepts to suggest how we might come to understand the place of semiotic mediational means within a theory of mediated discourse.

Chapter 5 returns to the question of the production of the social actor in discourse which was first taken up in Chapter 3. There I argued that the central work of discursive practice in the life of the child was to produce her through this discourse, as well as through the mediated actions of handing, as a competent social actor – someone who could hand objects appropriately and to the right persons. That argument was sufficient, I believe, to show how the child was positioned as a hander and by extension I suggest that she is multiply produced through these discursive practices and other social practices as all of the other kinds of social actors of normal adult life. Now in Chapter 5 the focus turns to the question of how we can argue that she is also being produced as a member of social groups and of what social groups. We want to see to what extent we can say that she is becoming a member of her family, a middle-class child, a Japanese-Chinese Hawaiian, or a girl and not simply a universalized and objectivized social actor.

I begin by arguing that any action positions the social actor in relationship to others who are engaged in that action and practice. One might position oneself (intentionally or unwittingly) as a novice or an expert, as seriously engaged or cynical. This sort of positioning within a certain social interaction has been analyzed by Goffman (1974, 1981) and many others as well. My concern here, however, is to see to what extent or how we can say that a child who is handing an orange to her mother to peel for her is also positioning herself or being positioned as a member of a particular social group without engaging in teleological or essentialist explanations. We do not want to say, just because this child's mother was born in Japan that, therefore, this child is engaging in a Japanese action or being socialized as a Japanese child. That is, mediated discourse does not assume, as some socialization theory does, that the child is simply becoming a member of the groups which are her caregiver's groups. My purpose in Chapter 5 is to develop the argument that we must look into the mediated actions themselves. As I will argue, we must particularly look at the practices which arise from these actions and the linkages among them to see how identity within social groups is produced in practice.

Thus in Chapter 5 I first recapitulate the argument of Chapter 2 that we cannot view a practice in any single act of handing but only in the historical chained sequences of mediated actions by which the practice is constituted in the habitus (or historical-body) of the child. I then recall that we have seen that a single practice (as a historical chain of mediated actions) is not linked uniquely to any other practice, discursive or otherwise. Nevertheless, as I argue in Chapter 3, there is over time a loose linkage of discursive practice to the practice of handing which can be seen to work in the service of producing the child as a social actor. Now in Chapter 5, I argue that these linkages of practices which are multiple and interlinked themselves with other practices form what I call a *nexus of practice*. By that I mean a network or matrix of intersecting practices which, although they are never perfectly or inevitably linked into any finalized or finalizable latticework of regular patterns, nevertheless form a network or nexus which is the basis of the identity which we produce and claim through our social actions.

In Chapter 5 I specifically develop the idea of the *nexus of practice* in counter-distinction to the much more popular term, the community of practice. The focus of the nexus of practice is upon the multiple and various linkages among practices. This is distinguished from the community of practice which, although the term 'practice' is used, places the focus upon individual persons as a group which is formed within a bounded entity of membership, of inclusion and exclusion. I argue that, analogous to the social practice which becomes technologized as a mediational means or a cultural tool and then exerts pressures toward standardization and objectivization upon practice, in the same way the community of practice is best regarded as an objectivized or technologized entity which, to be sure, arises from the nexus of practice, but within which the central structural concerns have shifted to membership, identity, inclusion and exclusion – that is, the objectivization of practice and of the nexus of practice.

Chapter 6 closes the book by placing mediated discourse theory itself within this theoretical language. First I outline the four main principles for which I have argued in this book:

- Discourse and practice are mutually constitutive.
- Sites of engagement (the locus of mediated actions) are historical outcomes of the practices and habitus of social actors.
- Mediational means are constructed within practices.
- The linkage of discourse and practice is not direct but in nexus of practice; these are the source of the social identities of social actors.

Then I argue that mediated discourse theory is best seen as a nexus of practice. That is, I argue that rather than taking mediated discourse analysis as either a superordinate, encompassing – one might even say colonizing – enterprise, or as occupying a central and mediating position, I argue that mediated discourse analysis is itself a nexus of practice. That is, mediated discourse is not an objective or objectivizing structure of research practices, theory, and methodology, but a program of linkages among other research frameworks which, like the nexus of practice itself, develops over time. In this way I see mediated discourse as a nexus of practice among interactional sociolinguistics, conversation analysis, critical discourse analysis, new literacy studies, anthropological linguistics, activity theory, and practice theory in which various research projects are located at different intersections of these lines of work but are linked through these shared practices.

Finally, to close Chapter 6 I engage in a brief discussion of points that are in need of development. These I see as four: the problem of agency, the problem of representation, the problem of multimodal discourse, and the problem of social structures such as institutions and organizations, nations and cultures. While these are problems to be addressed in further work, here I argue that mediated discourse analysis is a fruitful strategy for developing our understanding of agency, representation, discourse, and social structure.

NOTES

1 I should point out that there is at least one advertising company, hotliquidmedia.com, which believes that the cardboard sleeves of such coffee cups are significant moments of contact between advertisers and their audience.

2 Wertsch uses the two terms, mediational means and cultural tools, interchangeably. Here I prefer 'mediational means' and try to reserve the term 'cultural tool' for cases in which a mediational means has been subjected to some degree of technologization or objectivization.

3 These principles are developed further in the revised edition of our *Intercultural Communication* (Scollon and Scollon 2001).

4 Nishida's work is apparently entirely unknown to Bateson, Bourdieu, or Gumperz. Certainly I have never seen any citation in their work when they have put forward quite resonant concepts. Nishida's *Philosophy of nothingness* (1958) which I read in 1959, however, was very influential in my own thinking and produced the philosophical grounding for my much later reading of Bateson, Bourdieu, and Gumperz.

5 This is not to say that it is taken *a priori* that a detailed analysis of any stretch of language will tell us anything in particular. In this case, in fact, rather little of the language on the coffee cup was of relevance to the action of having a cup of coffee. An analysis of those texts might well be beside the point in the analysis of *this action*.

6 Note that Dewey in many ways also anticipates this psychological position (Cole 1995).

7 In my view there is little to separate anthropological linguistics and linguistic anthropology beyond some contemporary institutionalization and disciplinization. I prefer to use anthropological linguistics for the work I do when it falls within this general domain.

8 Hymes (1966) is an important mid-term assessment of the state of various versions of the problem of linguistic relativity.

9 This is not to say that the ontogenetic development of language and discourse have not been studied. I rely heavily in this work on what might be glossed as Vygotskian (or

Neo-Vygotskian) psychology which is itself a practice view of psychological develop-ment. I only mean with this statement to note that critical and practice theorists who have focused on social life have rarely made any attempt to bridge the analysis of life in society and the analysis of the processes by which a social actor comes to engage in the practices of social life. I believe this is true not only of the ontogenetic development of practice and the habitus in the child but also of the development of the adult habitus as one moves from social group to social group. For an extended ethnographic study of this latter development, see S. Scollon (1996a, 1996b, 1998, 1999a, 1999b, 2000a, 2000b, 2000c, in preparation; S. Scollon and Ouyang 1998).

2   On the ontogenesis of a social practice

From dogs to gift exchanges

Each day as I walk to my office and on the way back I pass people playing with their dogs in a small park. Among the activities through which they give themselves exercise is the very common one of the human throwing an object, most often a ball, the dog chasing it, capturing it and then bringing it back to the human. The ball is transferred then from dog to human, the human throws it again, the dog chases it again. One piece of this activity routine is the transfer of the ball to the human. Each morning I also buy a cup of coffee. As part of that activity I hand money to the server and a bit later she hands me a cup of coffee. Here in Chapter 2 I address the problem of when and under what conditions I am willing to call these transfers of objects 'handing'. That is, I am concerned with not only how the social practice of handing an object from one to another is constructed, but also with the ontogenesis of this practice from a more mechanical, objectivistic notion of the transfer of an object.

When the sovereignty of Hong Kong was transferred from Britain to China, a significant moment was the lowering of the flag on Government House after which the Sergeant Major in charge handed the British flag to the outgoing Governor Patten. The BBC television coverage of that event (30 June 1997) shows Governor Patten standing erect, hands at his side, as the Sergeant Major approaches him, the folded flag held in two hands. The Sergeant Major stops a step from Governor Patten and slowly begins to transfer the weight of the flag to his left hand while Governor Patten begins to raise his right hand as if to shake hands with the Sergeant Major. The Sergeant Major, however, continues to raise his right hand to salute the Governor, and when the Governor sees this he lowers his right hand into the former position at his side to receive the salute. The Sergeant Major then lowers his right hand and shifts the flag to both hands, while the Governor then begins to raise both hands to receive the flag and finally consummate the act of handing the flag from the Sergeant Major to the Governor.

Playing catch with a dog, buying a cup of coffee, and transferring political sovereignty from one nation to another each involve the social practice of handing. In most cases this occurs without further thought. At one extreme, the human and the animal do not fully succeed in accomplishing this action, though the practice is regular and frequent.[1] At the other extreme the Governor and the Sergeant Major do not fully succeed in accomplishing this action which occurs once in history. In between are the innumerable acts of handing out of which we construct some portion of our daily lives.

Examples such as these I have just given are sufficient, perhaps, to show the range of situations in which we might examine the social practice of handing. As the centerpiece of this book, I will focus my attention on the ontogenesis of this social practice in the period from one to two years of age in the life of one child, but to do so I will have as background and from time to time call upon observations from both other children and other adults in respect to handing, and I will also call upon observations of other social practices though these latter observations will necessarily be partial. I will argue that the social practice of handing begins as a set of independent and possibly unrelated actions in which the infant is both engaged with others – notably the mother and other caregivers, and also, in this case, an older sibling – and engaged in the more 'internal' problem which Piaget refers to as 'object permanency' (Piaget 1966 [1950]). In the space of about a year these bits and pieces of socio/cognitive actions aggregate in the habitus into what we can call a social practice.

In doing this ontogenetic analysis I want to not only observe this developmental aggregation – and I specifically want to avoid calling it a sequence – but I also want to ask *how* the development from idiosyncratic action to dyadic practice to social practice is accomplished, necessarily jointly, by the child and others in her social environment. Part of the *how* will lead to arguing that this social practice of handing is linked to other social practices such as naming objects and learning their functions. Overall my purpose is to put forward the proposition that to successfully link critical social theory with social reality we need a much more concrete and carefully worked out set of notions to cover the ontogenesis of practice (as a mass noun) in practices (as a count noun) and a greatly elaborated and carefully theorized idea of the habitus as an enormously complex aggregation of practices and their linkages. This chapter, and indeed, the book does not, of course, accomplish this task; here I set out only the outline of how such work might be done.

Gift exchanges in Bourdieu's analysis: model to strategy

Bourdieu's example of gift exchanges does an important piece of work in orienting us away from a model analysis of gift exchanges toward a strategic analysis. What is crucial for Bourdieu and for us is that such exchanges irreversibly take place in real time as the lived experience of members of society. The central point of Bourdieu's understanding of gift exchanges is that at any moment in the historical sequence of exchanges the participants do not know, cannot know, and for the exchange to function meaningfully, must not know what will follow. As he puts it,

The agents practise as irreversible a sequence of actions that the observer constitutes as reversible. The observer's totalizing apprehension substitutes an objective structure fundamentally defined by its *reversibility* for an equally objectively *irreversible* succession of gifts which are not mechanically linked to the gifts they respond to or insistently call for: any really objective analysis of the exchange of gifts, words, challenges, or even women must allow for the fact that each of these inaugural acts may misfire, and that it receives its meaning, in any case, from the response it triggers off, even if the response is a failure to repay that retrospectively removes its intended meaning.

(Bourdieu 1977:5)

This is what is meant by the irreversibility of real time. In giving you a gift I must not know how you will receive it, how you will reciprocate or, indeed, *if* you will reciprocate. If all this is known, Bourdieu points out, we do not have the exchange of gifts, we have simply swapping of objects entirely devoid of their social meaning. The social meaning of giving a gift does not reside in the object or in the value of the object but in the ambiguity of interpretation. If you do not reciprocate, the meaning of my gift is very different than if you do, at some appropriate time, reciprocate. The meaning of my original gift is only brought to completion, in a sense, at that time.

Of course this is very much the same process developed by John Gumperz (1977), interestingly at about the same time as Bourdieu's book, as the concept of conversational inference. In conversation as in the more extended time periods of gift exchanges, the meanings of actions are

- ambiguous in the here and now; they are to be resolved, to the extent they are, only in subsequent actions and interpretations;
- irreversible in the sense that they do not operate by an abstract conceptual logic but rather by a moment-by-moment practical logic;
- inferential; that is, the meaning of an action is inferred not only against the act itself but against subsequent actions not only of the agent of the action but of other agents in social interaction with the agent.

The contingent nature of practice is central to our understanding of social life and in this view actions must be taken to arise out of the concrete, historical experience of agents engaged in the temporal here and now of real time.

Bourdieu comments that 'it is not easy to speak of practice other than negatively' (1990:80). That is to say, it is easier to say what practice *is not* than what it is. The question which I would like to raise here is at what level it is most useful to conceive of practice. If it is difficult to say what it is in a positive sense (that is, rather than simply what it is not) at least I will try to be definite about what I am saying so that we may get on with the study of practice, particularly as I will try to do here in its earliest, ontogenetic stages in life. The strategy I take in this case is to avoid establishing 'practice' as a higher level entity which spans a constellation of actions. I do this in spite of the argument just made that the meaning of an action is to be found not in the single action itself but in the contingencies of meaning to which an action gives rise. Obviously, any action is situated dialogically in a life-long historical sequence of acts and I would argue that at no point could one say that the right bracketing had been done to isolate just those actions in a sequence of actions which give to any one of the actions its full meaning. Following Bourdieu and Gumperz we would have to argue that the meanings of social actions are embedded in what is an unbroken chain of contingent inferences.[2]

Instead of focusing at the larger level chosen by Bourdieu, what we might call the gift exchange practice, I prefer to focus more narrowly on the much more constrained set of practices which do become achieved within the scope of the present. This is because it seems important to reground the study of social practice in the concrete and material. As the anthropologist Bray (1997) has put it,

> Paradoxically, modern marxist scholars' interest in the material world is almost always abstract and narrow, devoid of significant detail. This I find disappointing and frustrating. The materialists are not interested in the material, Foucault and Bourdieu are not interested in history.
>
> (Bray 1997: 39)

As an example I have chosen what I will call the social practice of handing. Gift exchanges could be understood to be constructed over time out of a complex network of much more narrowly constrained practices. In addition to handing there would be various discursive practices associated with gift giving: 'Here's a little something', 'I understand it's your birthday' along with the 'Thank you's' and 'You shouldn't have's' that form quite predictable sequences. These would further be associated with practices for the introduction of topics: gifts in some societies would be given upon entrance as part of the greeting practices, for example. There would further be practices of wrapping and unwrapping of gifts.

In other words, I prefer to decompose 'gift exchange practice' into a relatively large set of closely defined and relatively discrete practices such as handing, greeting, wrapping, and the like, as I believe it is at this level that practices enter into the habitus and become available as the basis for subsequent actions. As I will argue in Chapter 5, we can nevertheless maintain the concept of the gift exchange but under a different terminology as a nexus of practice so as not to fall into the confusions that arise from the simultaneous analysis of practice as real-time action and practice as social structure.

Handing as practice

One motive I have for thinking of practices rather more narrowly than Bourdieu and others have thought of them is that some practices are quite general social arrangements (structures) which are integrated into a variety of social situations (structures) almost as elements in the production of those situations. One of these practices, narrowly defined, is the handing of objects. Whether the situation under focus is paying for a cup of coffee in a kiosk, giving a gift to an old friend, or handing a marked assignment back to a student in a university class, the element of handing the object is very much of a piece in all of these situations and yet we would want to consider a commercial transaction, a gift exchange, and an academic classroom to be three rather divergent Discourses (Gee, Hull and Lankshear 1996) or universes of practice (or fields) (Bourdieu 1977, 1990). It is this unitization of practice at this rather narrow level upon which I wish to focus in what remains. I will do this because my data provide evidence that it is at this level that practices enter into the habitus and from this level practices enter into social actions.

As a minimal transaction for the study of the practice of handing we could take that of the handing and receiving of handbills in a crowded pedestrian walkway in Hong Kong (Scollon 1997, 1998). The production of this transaction relies on the intersection of several practices, the central one of which is handing but also including what we might call 'pedestrian walking'. To take up the second practice first, pedestrian walking as a practice, at least in Hong Kong, can be structurally described as moving at a particular pace – neither faster nor slower than the ambient crowd – proceeding without stopping, or if one stops doing so by stepping to one side, and moving with the flow of the pedestrian traffic, not against it. In some cases one would also want to say that the practice would include bearing to the right while passing others on the left and so forth, or in some cases doing just the opposite – walking to the left side and passing on the right. These two latter aspects of the practice are often said to distinguish Hong Kong pedestrian walking from North American pedestrian walking.

Of course I would not want to elaborate pedestrian walking as a rule-based structural system and then proceed as if walking was the playing out of a cognitive schema in action. I would prefer to see this as practice. That is, one walks without giving undue consciousness to the basis in habitus of this practice. One walks as one has walked in other cases. It is just because of this basis in habitus that a North American walking in Hong Kong rather frequently bumps into Hong Kongers. Seeing a person ahead, one does what comes 'naturally'. For the North American this is to bear toward the right to allow a bit of space for the other to pass. The other, likewise doing what comes naturally, bears *left* and rather than these two people passing with a narrow space between them they bump into each other head-on. More often, of course, they see that something is not working, each makes the tiny adjustment which practice suggests and the North American bears yet further right while the Hong Konger bears yet further left.

Often enough at this moment each works out, still largely unconsciously, that the other is moving into one's pathway and so to avoid the other one goes against social practice and lurches rather strongly in the opposite direction. When both do this they end up, yet again, directly in front of each other, doing a dance both to one side then both to the other side. The failure of practice in this case arises from a fundamental incommensurability of practice in which giving way is operationalized in opposite directions. Of course, I have labelled this incommensurability as a regional/cultural/social incommensurability – the difference between North Americans and Hong Kongers, and it remains for another study to develop an understanding of the basis for identifying different practices with different groups, although I will adumbrate that analysis in Chapter 5 when I develop the concept of the nexus of practice. What is important here is to point out that there is a very simple practice, pedestrian walking; that this practice arises, like all practice, rather unconsciously from the habitus to generate action in concrete circumstances which will reproduce the agent's history with such walking; and to suggest that this is, indeed, practice, not some human logic of action because there are ways of failing in specific circumstances which have consequences in social action.

Giving out a handbill is based in the social practice of handing as linked to pedestrian walking. Handing as a practice consists in several micro-actions. The object is held by the person offering it and the hand is extended toward the person who will receive it. That person simultaneously puts a hand forward to receive the object. At the moment both hander and receiver are in contact with the object, the object is released by one and taken up by the other so that there is neither the opportunity for the object to drop nor the feeling of resistance in releasing it by the hander. Those who have played at tossing a ball to a dog will know that the moment of transfer is negotiated with difficulty as the dog is often quite unwilling to release the object from its teeth. This very subtle negotiation of hand pressure at the moment of transfer is just one of the aspects of object transfer which leads us to call handing a social practice rather than just object transfer between mammals.

Many other details might be elaborated, but perhaps it may only be necessary to mention them. The object must be handed at a mutually agreed upon level – neither high in the chest region nor low where the arms would be stretched downward. Within some social groups (nexus of practice or communities of practice) handing is done exclusively with one hand (for small objects), in other groups with two hands. In some social groups the hand chosen for handing is normatively the right hand but this may be altered depending on the classification of the object within that group. For my analysis of social practice, what is important to observe is that, on the whole, handing as a practice is relatively the same whether the object is money in a commercial transaction, a student's paper in a classroom, or a handbill advertising electronics goods in a public street.

Handing out a handbill, then, is produced through an intersection of several social practices, notably handing and pedestrian walking, though elsewhere I have suggested that there are yet other practices involved which go beyond my argument here (Scollon 1997, 1998). This point of intersection I have called the site of engagement because of the intersection of several practices. The action itself is a mediated action. The person giving the handbill stands centered in mid-flow of the pedestrian traffic, facing the pedestrians. She – in Hong Kong it is very rarely a man – takes a handbill from the pile and extends it at the customary level and in the customary place where another would be expected to receive it. The pedestrian who is faced with this disruption of the pedestrian flow then has a choice of responding to this as a rude disruption, and that is certainly a possibility which is sometimes chosen, or as a simple matter of handing and receiving. In my observations, the vast majority of pedestrians simply put out their hands and receive the handbill and accomplish the routine social practice.

In my analysis of this social practice of handing, I have argued two further points which I will not elaborate here as they go beyond the scope of a close-grained ontogenetic analysis, which is my interest here. The first of these is that this handing entails a set of identity claims, imputations, or contestations. In Hong Kong the handbills are largely in Chinese. In the unmarked case the hand-bill is simply handed. In the case of the expatriate there is often a moment of doubt when the hander sees what she judges to be a person who cannot read Chinese and then retracts her hand and the handbill to offer it to the following pedestrian. That is, what we see in the breach is that along with the social practice of handing is an almost entirely invisible ascription of identity as 'a person for whom this is provisionally intelligible'. As I have pointed out in my earlier study (1997), when the object is not a handbill advertising electronics goods but a condom in a safe-sex campaign the imputation of identity is foregrounded and condoms are held back from children on the basis of a momentary assessment of the age of the person to whom the object is being handed. I could also argue that in the case of pedestrian walking when two pedestrians do the 'different practice' dance, imputations of identity also are a common outcome with the other person being identified as clumsy, unaware, or rude, not normally at the more accurate level of ascribing 'foreign' habitus.

The other point I have made concerning handing is terminological. I have used the term 'site of engagement' to make reference to this moment at which the social practice of handing, the social practice of pedestrian walking, and the other practices I have not described here come together to produce a moment of social action. That is, I would like to use the term 'social action' (or 'mediated action?'[3] or act) to refer to the actual, real-time, concrete here-and-now act of handing (including receiving or rejecting) the handbill. I do not want to follow either Bourdieu (1977) or Chouliaraki and Fairclough (1999) in ambiguously calling this here-and-now moment a social practice as, in my analysis, the crucial aspect of this moment is the intersection of several social practices. I would argue that there is never likely to be a particular act which is not, in fact, the intersection of or linkage of multiple practices, at least as I have defined practice here. I would also argue that to define practice more broadly as, say, handbill distribution would miss the necessary generalization that handbill distribution (as, say, an activity system) crucially involves linking one practice, pedestrian walking, with another, handing, in such a way that the contradictions between walking and handing can be exploited to force or at least encourage the walker to receive the handbill.

Handing as topic control

When a person takes up a position in a crowded pedestrian walkway, which intentionally disrupts pedestrian flow, and then exploits the social practice of handing including the deep habitus which makes it quite difficult actually to inhibit the handing/receiving practice so as not to receive the handed object, I would argue that we can see how one practice may be used to produce contradictions with another practice and that this contradiction is exploitable for further social purposes. While I would expect to find that, on the whole, social practices work through Bourdieu's principle of *genesis amnesia* (1977:79) to reproduce the world as taken for granted, in many cases a social practice may be exploited to achieve ends quite beyond any conscious or logical analysis of the practice.

Handing is a practice deeply embedded in the habitus from early in life, as I shall argue below. Among the characteristics of handing, one crucial characteristic is the successful reception of the object. A dropped object will elicit apologies and claims of clumsiness or carelessness from both parties, hander and receiver alike. That is, there is a perceived social obligation to engage in the practice smoothly. Like Bourdieu's analysis of gift exchanges on the broader level, a handed object that is dropped or refused is an affront to the person handing. It is not a delayed failure of reciprocation, however; it is an immediate rejection of the social competence and identity of the hander.

In an earlier study (Scollon 1976, 1979) of the same child I argued that when she was just two years old (at 2:0.12)[4] she exploited handing as a means of gaining topic control. I noted, following Schegloff's (1972) catalytic work, that there is a social practice for the introduction of topics which follows a sequence of a summons, an answer, and the introduction of a topic.[5] The child, Brenda, used 'Hi' seven times and 'here' twenty-two times within one hour, 'each time handing or trying to hand something to the receiver' (1976:125). As I have argued there, these uses of 'hi' and 'here' constitute a summons in the opening up of a little piece of conversation. As I have written:

> The conditions on handing will show why this should be so. Among many conditions two seem to be crucial; one is that the receiver must acknowledge that he has received the object (by taking it and usually by speech as well) and the other is that the hander is required to give further instructions. That is, in acknowledging receipt of the object the receiver grants the hander the right to interaction, specifically to say why the object was handed. In saying why the object was handed, the hander reserves the right to introduce a topic.
>
> (Scollon 1976:125)

While I would now prefer an account less based in rule structures/conditions and with less sexist pronominal reference, I believe the description of this use of 'hi' and 'here' holds as an account of a fledgling social practice for the introduction of topics in conversations so much studied in the literature on conversation analysis in the intervening years. At that time I further developed my observations about Brenda's floor-taking practices as follows:

1   When the right to talk has not been established, Brenda uses *hi, here*, or the combination of handing plus topic to initiate interactions with Suzanne and me.

2   With the mother the right to talk is permanently established.

3 With Charlotte (older sister) the right to talk may or may not be permanently established since *here* was only used a few times and when it was, it failed.
4 When the right to talk temporarily lapses but Brenda is still audience to the interaction, she regains the floor by repeating her utterance.
5 When the right to talk temporarily lapses and Brenda is excluded as participant, she becomes unintelligible until the right to talk is reestablished.

(Scollon 1976:128)

These observations describe Brenda's floor-taking practices as of two years of age. I say 'Brenda's floor-taking practices' and in doing so beg the question of whether these are social practices in the sense we would like to use the term, that is, as practices shared relatively widely within a particular group of people (nexus of practice or community of practice). They are certainly practices in the sense that they work as described within the narrowly constrained circle of her mother, father, older sister, and her two cousins.[6]

I have argued, then, that it is to paint with too broad strokes to use the term 'social practice' as a count noun to encompass whole Discourses or universes of practice (or fields), and there is much to gain by taking a narrower focus on a social practice such as handing as an element in these broader domains or, speaking concretely, in the sites of engagement within which mediated actions take place. I have suggested that it is the abrogation of the practice of pedestrian walking by disrupting it with handing that, through the contradiction or incommensurability this produces, gives the walker the urgency to accept the handbill as normal practice or, alternatively, consider the hander to be in violation of the social practice of pedestrian walking. Then I have suggested that as early as the second year of life at least one two-year-old child was able to exploit handing in a somewhat unique recontextualization of that practice to take the initiative in the control of the conversational practice by which first speaker, summonser, gains the 'right' to introduce the topic.

What I will turn to shortly, then, is the argument that in order for this two-year-old to exploit handing as a conversational practice we must first account for the construction of this practice in her habitus and in the homologous habitus (Bourdieu 1990) of the social group within which these actions are accomplished. In a return to my original data, collected over the year from one to two years of age, I will argue that handing is, in fact, not 'acquired' wholesale nor is it in any way an essential, structural characteristic of humans. I will try to show how in many social actions over the course of a year the practice is assembled. It is assembled bit by bit out of the social actions taken by the child and her caregivers. Before finally turning to this analysis, however, I will make one further departure to sketch an outline of handing as a structure of social action.

Handing as structure of social action

A structural, objectivist analysis would find in the social practice of handing at least the following dimensions:

Directionality: This distinguishes giving as opposed to receiving; this is a question of point of view to some extent, but in any case one of the participants is the 'original' possessor of the handed object.

Volition: This is partly a question of expectations but may be in response to a request: 'Please pass the salt' as opposed to 'Would you like some salt for that?' The question of interest is whether the volition lies with the giver or the receiver.

Discourse: Handbills are often handed out without saying anything; other cases have accompanying speech. That speech may attend to several aspects of the handing, the object, or the relationships among the participants:

The action: 'Here, take this.'

The object:'This is a pen.'

The expected outcome: 'You could use this.'

The relationship: 'Could I ask you to hold this for me?'

Social status: This may be indicated through discourse as 'Gimme that!' as opposed to 'Would you please hand me that?' ; Japanese verb 'agemasu' or 'kudasai' (i.e., giving 'up' or requesting 'down').

Linkage: The act of handing may be embedded in or linked to other social practices including discursive ones such as the common adjacency sequence: *Request + action + closing* as in 'Could you hand me that?' + 'Here you are' + 'Thanks.'

Object characteristics: A heavy object is handed with both hands, lighter objects with one; Athabaskan languages classify objects so that handing a cup with contents is lexicalized differently than a sheet of paper or a rope.

Manner: The style, speed, emphasis or degree of social agreement can be signalled in the manner of handing and may be lexicalized. 'Could you flip that over here?' 'Could you toss me that?' 'He didn't hand it to me; he shoved it in my face.' Food may be handled differently from dirt and, in some cases, with different hands.

Negation: No response; 'No, I won't' ; 'I'm sorry, I'm using it right now.'

I say 'at least' these dimensions would be found in a structural analysis because there is, in principle, no limit on how many features of what kind could be introduced into such an analysis. Virtually anything which might be observed as a variation on handing might be introduced as a 'feature' of the model and subsequently attributed to anyone who could be argued to be somehow a possessor of this knowledge or model or schema of handing. From a practice point of view, however, I am reluctant to attribute to the habitus of any agent any of the 'features' which are not, in fact, made manifest in particular social actions.

As I will argue in my analysis of a child's construction of handing, while we would expect to see in the adult social practice of handing that these structural 'features' are somehow 'inherent' in the social practice, it is only after an extended sequence of social actions where first one then another of these 'features' is enacted in no particular chronological, developmental, or logical order that we come to anything like the logical, structurally reversible model so central to structural analyses. As Lyra (1999) has argued, it is only the very great experience with handing that gives to an adult agent the appearance of somehow possessing the structural system which could be analyzed as I have suggested above.[7] My strategy in what follows is not to begin with a structural model of handing and see how it unfolds in the life of a child. On the contrary, it is to begin with the earliest actions which are constructed as handing by the caregivers to see how these actions cumulatively enter the habitus of one child in the course of the second year of life.

The ontogenesis of handing

The data

Beginning in February 1972 and for most of the year that followed, Suzanne Scollon and I visited the home of her one-year-old cousin, Brenda.[8] These weekly visits lasted normally from three to six hours, often including lunch or dinner. During the visit Brenda's mother and Brenda's older sister, who was four when we began, were present. On a few occasions the father was present as well. During each visit we made a one-hour tape recording with the focus of the microphone on Brenda. Within 24 hours of the visit I made detailed phonetic transcriptions of all of Brenda's utterances as well as standard orthographic transcriptions of all other speech captured in the recording. Suzanne made detailed notes of contextual matters – who was doing what at the time we were recording – and she also took photographs to further expand our noting of background and contextual objects and spaces.

The material of this study was the basis for my doctoral dissertation and was published as Scollon (1976, 1979). While the material is the same, of course, my focus has changed considerably in the intervening 25 or so years. What began in my mind as a study of the acquisition of phonology and which underwent a mutation to a study of the conversational and discursive genesis of sentence-level grammatical structure is now undergoing a further mutation into a study of the ontogenesis of a social practice. I am surprised in returning to this material to see in the first place that I have really not had reason to depart from my view established at that time that what we see as grammatical (and other formal) structures have their origins in the most basic of social interactions – those between the infant and her caregivers. I am equally surprised by how tentatively I put forward that argument then when the data, in my view, support it so strongly. I see what follows, therefore, as an extension of that work more than a reconsideration. In any event, in what follows I will not recapitulate that earlier argument as it is available in published form for those who would be interested.

The 41 examples which I use in this chapter will follow the same pattern in each case. First I will present a transcript of the action upon which I want to focus. Then I will present a short discussion of the interpretation I make of this transcript. After several transcripts I will make summarizing notes covering that sequence of transcripts. Two things should be noted: first, these transcripts have been 'cleaned up' by comparison with the original transcripts. The 'cleaning' in most cases has been to eliminate other participants who were not currently involved in that site of engagement but who were concurrently engaged in social interactions among themselves within the same situation. While I believe it is necessary for a clear exposition of my argument to have done this, the reader should remember that multiple participants were present in all of these social interactions.

In any event one should bear in mind that any construction of a body of data out of the flow of the events of life is always a construction. There is a tendency to think that somehow ethnographic constructions are more faithful in the production of context. Thus the anthropologist Bray (1997) laments:

> An anthropologist assigns social or symbolic meanings to an artifact or process on the basis of detailed ethnographic, contextual observation. But for cultures of the past, systematic fieldwork is impossible and the retrieval of context may be at best partial or distorted.
>
> (Bray 1997:17)

While I would not want to overemphasize the point, I would argue that the distinction between anthropological and historical realities is not always so great as it might be imagined. This set of tape recordings and transcriptions which were based in detailed ethnographic and contextual observation remained opaque to me in various ways until now, some 25 years after the fact, when I am equipped to see and hear in them utterances that were simply outside of my scope of knowledge and perception.

Second, I have not included every instance of 'handing' which occurred in my data but, rather, selected illustrative ones. Obviously, I have no formal record of the thousands of further instances which occurred outside of the weekly hour of my recording. From this I would want to conclude that the ontogenesis of the practice of handing would be *more complex* not *less complex* than I am able to demonstrate here. I would take this as an argument to support a practice view of the ontogenesis of handing.

In these 41 transcripts I have used the following coded abbreviations:

R	Ron Scollon, the first researcher and author of this book
B	Brenda Wong, the child upon which this research is focused
C	Charlotte Wong, B's older sister
M	The mother of the children
F	The father of the children
S	Suzanne Wong Scollon, co-researcher with R
1:0:2	Ages are given as Years:Months.Days; thus 1:0.2 indicates 'One year, (no months), and 2 days of age'
xxx	Could not be transcribed; unintelligible but audible
☺	Laughing

BRENDA I (12 months of age to 14½months)

Brenda (B) is just one year old. The handing which takes place most often is when her mother (M) gives her food or a bottle of milk or juice. At this time B cannot walk, but crawls about the house. From this point of view it is important to note that the home is organized to a considerable extent as a 'Japanese' home; that is, even though there is a sofa and there is a dining table with chairs, most activities of children and adults take place at low tables while seated on the floor.

Example 1 Age: 1:0.2

B	M	Context
[ne:ne:] [æ:pʰ] [nɛnnɛn] [nne:]	☺ Want juice? Hm? Gave you milk. You want juice now, hm? Apple? You want apple? Hm? [məman]? Yeah? ☺ You want Momma, yeah? Hm? No?	M is 'conversing' with B.

B's utterance 'nene' as well as the following two utterances are taken by M as expressions of want or need. That is to say, these linguistic actions are *heard as* requests for caregiving actions. Teleologically, we could note that later on we will find utterances such as 'I want', 'share', 'give me' in analogous functional spaces. What is important here, however, is that there is nothing in the child's utterance to cue these meanings. These are the caregiver's (M's) readings of what are really semiotically empty utterances. Finally, M's attempts to 'read' B's utterances in this case fail. That is to say, we should not make the mistake so often stated in the literature and by caregivers themselves in thinking that the mother or caregiver always knows what the child wants. It is from the beginning a negotiation of meaning in practice, which often fails. What is most important is that B's linguistic actions *are taken as discursive actions*, not as noise. There is a presumption of attemped social action, even though this presumption often fails.

Example 2 Age: 1:0.2

B	M	R	Context
{crying continuously...}	[o: əoi] [o:ho] {8x} [o:ho] {8x} [o:yo] [zə] {6x} [o:]		B falls over backwards. M picks up B, puts her on the floor sitting.

Example 2 continued

B	M	R	Context
	[æ:] [æ: zə] [o:] [zə] {4x} [o:] [ʌ:ʌʌʌ] O.K. You want pots and pans? O.K., O.K., Look at that xxx		M brings pot, spoon, and rice paddle. M bangs rice paddle in pan. B opens her eyes and suddenly stops crying, orients to the sound. B picks up spoon, bangs spoon in pan.
{crying ends abruptly}		Look how fast she stops.	

Here the handing is accompanied by banging of the pot and the wooden rice paddle. M uses first the noise and then handing the rice paddle to B, which is followed by B's own banging, to intervene in B's crying spell. One might see this as M strategizing to use a 'desirable' action (making noise with the rice paddle and pan) as a substitute for an undesirable action (crying). Handing here is instrumental in producing in Brenda a disruption of one action (crying) with a second and incommensurable action (banging on the pan). It would be too much to say that this is characteristic of socialization in general to use incommensurability of practice as a means to simultaneously introduce 'desirable' actions while blocking or disrupting 'undesirable' ones, but it is a point that needs to be considered carefully across many instances of socialization. In any case, no intentionality should be ascribed to B's actions.

Example 3 Age: 1:0.9

B	M	Context
{silent}	Yeah, what color is that? Green. Draw now. Draw?	B holds up crayon toward mother.

In Examples 1 and 2, B is the recipient of the handing, or the intended handing. Here in Example 3 is an ambiguous case where, again teleologically (see Example 4 following) it might be thought of as an attempt on B's part to hand a crayon to M. M does not construe this as handing, however, but as what we might call *pointing*. In many other cases either B or another person points to (or holds up for view) some object. This is most often accompanied by *naming*, or a request for *naming* as in Example 6. In any event, in this case M pedagogizes this action of pointing by first asking its color, answering her own question, and then dialogically moving to the third step in the *naming* practice of suggesting an action that can be taken with the object.

Example 4 Age: 1:0.9

B	C	M	Context
{silent}	Momma, look. Give me another one.	They want you to talk, Brenda. Say something. Yeah, this is yellow, yellow crayon. Thank you. Thank you. Oh. Give it to Charlotte. Thank you.	B holds out yellow crayon toward mother.

Now, about 10 minutes later, this is the same gesture as in Example 3, *pointing*, but in this case M operationalizes it as handing together with pedagogizing this handing as *naming*. In this case, however, the dialogical action suggested is not drawing but further handing in which C cooperates to bring the handing to social completion. M's 'thank you' is a pedagogical prompt to C to say 'thank you' to B. C does not cooperate in constructing this full routine.

I would like to note that M was quite conscious in this early stage of the recordings that we were interested in B's speech, and so we must take it as given that whatever else she is doing, she somehow has in mind the idea of encouraging B to talk. We can also note rivalry in the other child (C at age 4:0.13) who often tries to distract the attention of the researchers to her own projects. In many cases as in this case, M exploits these joint claims for her and our attention pedagogically.

Example 5 Age: 1:0.9

B	M	Context
[da^w] [gæ^u]	Thank you, thank you.	B hands crayon to M.

In another 10 minutes we have Example 5, an instance of 'pure' handing plus naming. In this case there is no link to pedagogical practice, or at least M does not give the color nor does she dialogically suggest a sequential action to be performed. Perhaps more interesting is that B's second utterance could be construed as 'crayon' within her current level of phonological production (Scollon 1976), though it is very difficult to establish any 'words' consistently at this time. The first utterance might be construed, equally ambiguously, as 'doll' ; there have been several attempts earlier in this session to get her to say the word 'doll'. (See Example 6 below for a subsequent attempt.)

There are two important aspects of this Example 5. First, there is nothing remarkable – it is simple handing accompanied (perhaps) by the name of the object to which an appropriate response is given. This is much like one would expect to hear among adults: 'Here's your change', 'Thanks'. The second point, however, is that we should not construe this as developmental in any way as the preceding and following examples all happen within the same stretch of 30 minutes or so. The apparent structural features are distributed among the infant, the mother, the older sister, and the analyst.

One further point by way of summary: these examples have focused on B handing to M or to C. There have been other handings of bottles of milk or juice to B but these have not been recorded. They should not, however, be forgotten.

Example 6 Age: 1:0.9

B	M	R	Context
	'Hakata' doll. Where's the hakata doll?	What d'you call that? A 'kata' doll? 'Hakata' doll.	
[da*]			
	☺ Yes, Doll. Doll. She used to giggle before but she doesn't. It's not a joke anymore. She doesn't giggle. When I say hakata doll, she used to giggle.		B looks directly at doll.
[da:: da*]			
	Doll, yes. Doll. Where's the kitty cat? Kitty cat? Kitty cat? Meow? Meow? Say something. Where's the horse? See horsie? See horsie?		

This is a case of 'pure' naming. That is, it is in response to the *pointing* of both R and M in trying to get B to say the word 'doll'. Unlike Example 5, here B's direct gaze at the doll, as well as the prior utterances of R (twice) and M (also twice), suggest that this *is* the word 'doll'. But how is it that word? Is this utterance based in practice, that is to say based in habitus, or is it a much more simple reflex imitation? I would argue that there is no meaning whatsoever to trying to create this analytical distinction. With a great deal of prompting and with abundant modeling in the immediately preceding utterances of adults, B has made a sound that can fairly easily be construed as 'the same' as that of the adults. Indeed, that is how they construct it at this time. It would be cognitivism in the extreme to seek to attribute intention to B here. But it is also very important to see that her utterance, proceeding out of habitus and imitation in the immediate circumstances, is constructed by the adults present as a meaningful and intentional utterance of the word. This process of construal was described by S. Scollon (1982) and termed 'glossing'. M ends this sequence by attempting to construct a pedagogical sequence of naming.

Example 7 Age: 1:0.9

B	M	Context
	I found candy. I found candy, Brenda. [rɛturɛtu:] (3x) Up. Up. Nice, hm? Mommy chodai, Mommy chodai. Oh. Thank you, thank you. Now. Oh, you want to open it but.	M brings box of candy, gives to B. B shakes box of candy.
[op:pʰ] [n n]	Open. So nice.	

Handing is reciprocated in this case. M hands a box of candy to B with the phrase 'I found candy' and shortly later B hands it back to M and, perhaps, says, 'Open'. This phrase of M's is yet another lexicogrammatical accompaniment to handing. It is naming to be sure, but the naming is presupposed rather than declared. B takes the box of candy without any utterance. Seeing she has difficulty with opening it, M asks B to return it. 'Mommy chodai' is Japanese[9] for 'Hand it to Mommy'. B hands it and concurrently utters what might be construed or glossed (S. Scollon 1982) as an attempt to say, 'Open'.

Social distributed action

In these transcripts handing has been seen in several forms. B's action of holding an object up to view is taken as handing without any accompanying utterance. M has initiated handing *to* B in several forms. M has requested B to hand an object to her. B has handed objects both with and without accompanying utterances. What is important to see at this stage of the analysis is that in each case we cannot assert that the structural features of 'handing' (as a generalized social practice) are present *within the habitus of the child*. In each case handing is jointly constructed in a variety of actions involving the child and others. If handing as a social practice is seen in these transcripts, it is present as a *socially distributed action*, not as the action of separate individual actors.

Example 8 Adults

M	R	S	Context
No, Auntie Marian did. I got napkins here. Auntie Ester made about a week ago. Brought it here. Nobody ate. So take that home. Seems like everybody, everybody want to give us gau.		Oh, did you make gau? Oh, Auntie Marian's funny recipe.	M is giving gau (Chinese glutinous rice cake) to R and S
	Hm.	Hm? Oh yeah?	
	☺	Yeah, that's, that's what I keep hearing. Everybody has so much gau they want to get rid of and we don't have any.	
☺	☺		

Example 8 is presented here not for any remarkable aspect of the handing in itself – M gives some *gau* (Chinese glutinous rice cake) to S (and then to R) without saying anything. S picks up the transaction by asking about the *gau*. This is followed by M giving S and R napkins in the simple declarative form. That is, the handing comprises the topic introduction in this stretch of conversation. By comparison we have seen in Example 7 M's 'I found candy', where the object of the handing is presupposed and the discursive activity focuses on talking about the object, not on the social practice of handing either ideationally ('This is *gau*') or interpersonally ('Here', 'Thank you'). I present Example 8 simply to indicate that concurrent with the handing that is going on involving the child, B, a lot of other handing is going on among the adults present in the situation.

One could analyze this handing in the presence of the child as modeling: 'This is what handing is.' While there is nothing wrong with such an analysis per se, what I would like to focus upon here is that from the child's point of view this is handing among third persons. That is, one piece of the habitus which is constructed here is *handing in one's presence* that does not involve one as either giver or receiver.

Example 9 Age: 1:0.9

R	S	Context
What is that? Thank you. (to S) Is she going to learn to write with these like a chimpanzee? It's the same kind, you know – magnetized.	 Maybe.	B hands R a green 'X' from C's magnetized letter set.

The handing we have looked at to this point is either among adults, and perhaps we can presume an *acquired* habitus for the social practice of handing, or between B and her mother. In this latter case we might want to do a bit of terminological playing and call this dyadic practice – we almost want to call it 'practice practice'. That is, in Examples 3 and 4, where B simply holds up a crayon, M constructs this as handing but there is unclear evidence in these that B herself has any intention of handing the object to M. Example 9, however, extends the practice to a non-caregiver, to R. Here we cannot argue that B and R have practiced handing between them and so can attribute some small portion of 'sociality' to this action. It is important to keep in mind that by the time this action takes place both B and R have been engaged in this social interaction (along with M, C, and S) for at least 60 minutes. Both B and R have been participants in all of the examples we have examined to this point as well as many others not recorded. Both B and R have 'learned' something here about the 'game' of handing in relationship to each other.

Homologous habitus

To adumbrate the discussion which will follow as part of my analysis, here I would like to suggest that there is some degree of integration within a person's habitus of what Bourdieu (1990) refers to as homologous habitus. This amounts to saying simply that two (or of course many more) individuals engage in the same social practice. In Bourdieu's terminology this homologous habitus would arise in the objective conditions of common class, field, or other group membership. So for two adults to hand an object from one to another without thought, comment, or consideration, that is, unconsciously undertaking this action out of habitus, would be for these two adults to engage in a social practice arising from homologous habitus. The 'test' in a sense of the presence of homologous habitus is that this unremarkable engagement in the social practice takes place between strangers. That is, the practice runs off as an action between two people whose habitus has been formed within the same social group but between whom there has been no prior social interaction.

At this other extreme we are observing here, B and M (and C, of course) engage in the construction of the social practice of handing, out of the tentative 'actions' of an infant and the highly socially constructive 'readings' of those actions by the mother. We could temporarily speak of these 'handings' as a kind of 'dyadic practice' in that they are repeated between the pairs who have practiced them, but in some cases at least, not fully social in that they may or may not 'work' with strangers. As is so often the case, we have little evidence for interactions with strangers as the social world of infants is so rarely a world which involves interactions with strangers. In this case the 'stranger', R, has been socialized into this world of B–M dyadic practice as much as B has been socialized into the world of R.

Having said this, if we return to Example 9 we can see that the 'success' of this handing is, after all, only partial. It begins as *pointing* or *naming*. That is, R seems to see this as a place to elicit some sort of nomination. B, however, says nothing. R then shifts his ground to focus on the interpersonal functioning of the action by saying, 'Thank you'. He then immediately recontextualizes this action in an aside to S which ties this to then current research with chimpanzees which used similar magnetized letters as a medium for elicitation.

Example 10 Age: 1:0.9

B	M	R	S	Context
[nanana] [ene] [xx] [na:na:nan] [nannanna]	Do you want juice? Do you want juice?			B crawls toward S's juice glass.
		You should write down that she's trying, first tried to get my taco and then tried to get your juice.		
			How can I write? ☺	B is pulling on S's juice glass in S's right hand.
[ənnannan]		I've got it now. Where can I put it so you won't get it? I don't have it. I hid it.		Left hand has taco on plate.
	☺ O.K., give it to you.	See, Suzie's got it again.		
[tɕo:da]	☺ xxx Chodai! ☺ She said, 'Chodai'.			

Example 10 continued

B	M	R	S	Context
	That means to give me please. Um hm, Yes. ☺ Did you hear that? Chodai. ☺ Yeah. Hai. You want juice? Hm? Hear what you said? You said, 'Chodai'. Hm? That's too big. Chodai. Mommy throw that.	What's that? Oh, is that right? Well I can't resist that. She just asked me like that. What can I say?		

This complex example (10) shows some degree of 'intention' on the part of B, although, as I will argue just below, it is very difficult to attribute intention to an infant of this age and stage of psychological development. The utterance [ne:ne:] in Example 1 which the mother takes as a request for juice is here queried by her in the same way. In this case, however, in addition to the utterance, B tries to grab S's juice and R's taco. This is rather definite grasping, not just gesturing toward the objects. The interesting and surprising 'chodai' (which the mother glosses as 'That means to give me please' – in Japanese) following upon the first utterance (naming?) shows some movement through the repertoire of the habitus: *naming, grasping, requesting*. What seems most interesting here is that B does show a good bit of evidence of these somehow being available in the habitus, but as we have seen, these bits of the practice of handing are separate, non-integrated, and also not entirely interpretable by others in the immediate environment. One piece of the practice, of course, is that one does not always get whatever one grabs or even asks for. An adult would be wholly in violation of practice to say, 'I want your juice, give it to me' while grabbing it at the same time. So we can see in this rather complex action bits and pieces of an aggregating habitus, but not anything like the integrated habitus of the social practice which is being constructed.

B's utterance of 'chodai' is the most surprising element of this stretch of action. The phonological form is very close to that of the adult pronunciation. This is a form used frequently by the mother (see Examples 7 above and 12, 13, 14, 18, and 19 below) when she initiates a request for B to give something to her (M); the form used in the other direction (M volunteers to give something to B) is 'Hai' (Japanese for 'yes' and used in adult handing synchronously with the moment of transfer; note that 'hai' occurs near the end of this sequence when M hands juice to B).

This utterance of B's is clearly not taken as a normal, integrated aspect of B's habitus. M first comments in imitation: 'Chodai!' followed by a laugh. She then says explicitly, 'She said, "Chodai",' and then translates this for R: 'That means to give me please.' Then, again, she draws this to R's attention: 'Did you hear that? "Chodai."' Then M turns to B to ask *her* if she had heard what she had said. This latter seems the strongest indication of the surprising nature of this utterance on the one hand and that this is not to be taken as simple utterance from M's point of view. That is, M appears to think that even B has no idea what she has 'said'. It is for this reason that I have referred to much of M's discursive activity here as pedagogizing B's utterances. B makes sounds, some of which seem much like adult utterances in both sound and position. Nevertheless, M engages in a great deal of framing of these utterances – telling B, in effect, what she has just said. To know whether or not there is intention on B's part is forever unattainable, but it is clear that for M the presumption that she makes is that there is no linguistic intention ('Hear what you said?') and that this needs to be shaped *after the fact* by her own work of pedagogization.

Finally this 'chodai' sequence ends with M now using the word to request that B hand her something. It is not clear from the transcript or the tape what this is, but M's 'Mommy throw that' indicates that it is something she plans to throw away.

Piaget's 'tertiary circular reaction'

B is one year, 9 days old as of the examples we have examined so far. She is not yet walking – at 1:1.2, about a month later, she was doing sporadic 'walking' – a few steps; a week after that, at 1:1.8, M notes that B is 'standing a long time' ; and at 1:1.27 M reports that B is 'walking now'. That is, as of Examples 1–10, walking is still more than a month and a half off.

While I am not sure how I would ultimately want to try to integrate a Piagetian cognitive analysis with a social practice analysis of a child's development, at the time of doing this research I tested B for the development of the Piagetian stages of cognitive development. A crucial stage is that of the separation of the self and the object (Piaget 1966, 1969). For B the beginning of the separation of the self and of objects was attested one week later (at 1:0.16). In the following week we see that she throws or drops objects while watching her hand release them. Two weeks later (1:0.23) B moves to the next step which is to look down to watch the trajectory of these objects once they have been released. That is, in the first move toward this separation, B appears to have focused on the releasing of the object from her hand and in the second stage moved on to watch the continued existence of the object as it moves away from her own body. At that time (1:0.23) M comments on B throwing down objects and watching the trajectory as something she does 'all the time now'.

Piaget defines stage V of the sensorimotor period as that of the 'tertiary circular reaction' (1966, 1969). This he defines as consisting of active experimentation with objects and the body with a focus on the constitution of objects and the differentiation of objects from the actions undertaken with them. Key points here are:

- permanence of the object – the object comes to be treated by the child as if having an existence independent of one's activities with it. For example, the child will continue to search for an object which has been covered or hidden.
- separation of object and action – the object is treated as being independent of the child's own actions on it. That is, the object continues to move after the action of throwing or dropping it.
- accommodation of action to object. That is, the child has to do something such as grasp the object for it to come into the hand.

On this latter point, M comments at this time that she has to put things out of reach so B cannot reach them. We have just seen in Example 10 her persistence in trying to grasp R's taco and S's juice. B is described as trying to 'get everything'.

The objects that we have observed exchanged in handing so far are: crayons (green, yellow), candy paper, pens, taco, juice (in a baby bottle), a plastic letter 'X'. The lexical items used with this handing by B are 'nene' and 'chodai'. The first is taken as meaning 'give to me' but the second is taken as a surprise even though it is a common lexical form for M to use in this same meaning.

What I would argue is crucial here is that all this handing is occurring simultaneously with this intramental constitution of 'Piagetian' cognitive operations. The first instances we have looked at occur before there is any cognitive evidence that B has achieved the separation of the self and objects. That is, in a Vygotskian framework we would want to argue that the child 'acts' in some way that is largely *not* interpretable as arising from cognitive agency in any way. M (and C and others) interpret the action as object separation (i.e., handing). This joint construction of the social action of handing occurs concurrently with the construction of the 'Piagetian' cognitive operations on the intramental plane. Therefore, I would want to argue that this opening up of the social practice of handing is concurrent with the more 'internal' development of cognitive operations. Most crucial to my argument is that what we are seeing is a piece-by-piece construction of social practice–habitus–cognition in this sequence of social interactions between B and her caregivers.

Development

Example 11 Age: 1:0.16

M	R	S	Context
Hm? O.K.? Turn around. Turn around, O.K.?			S opens can of cookies.

Example 11 continued

M	R	S	Context
Hm? ☺ Something good, hm? When it comes to food look at her. ☺			
	These are for you, Brenda. Take some.		
Oh, thank you.			
		Here, you want? This is nen.	S gives cookie to B.
Did you make it? Did you make it?			
		Yeah. She wants to take them all out of the can.	
M. Good.			
	Tell her to bring me one.	Give one to Ron. Give one to Ron. Yeah, take it to him.	
Gonna eat it first. ☺			
	No. I'm over here. Come on, you gotta bring it.		
☺ xxx Give it to Ron, hm? Give it to Ron. Ron wants it. Come and get it. ☺	Oh, I see you changed your mind.		B offers cookie but when R goes to B, she retracts it.

In Example 11 and again in the following Example 12 we see that the object which is handed is not neutral, at least for B. While during this period she is 'achieving' the Piagetian tertiary circular reaction, B seems quite unable to separate herself from a highly desired object – a cookie. While earlier in her life almost all objects which came to the hand moved quickly to her mouth whether they were food or not, now we see that she can alienate objects in the practice of handing unless they are food. In another study[10] of our own daughter, Rachel, we found that at the same stage of development, she was unable to carry a piece of fruit (lychee) from her mother to her father. She was told, 'Take this to Daddy', and began to walk across the room toward him, eyes fixed on her goal. Nevertheless, her hand quite involuntarily crept up toward her mouth, almost surprising herself to find the lychee being eaten. She could only accomplish the task when she was given two lychees – one in each hand – so that when she arrived across the room there was still one left with which to accomplish the handing.

Another not incidental aspect of this transaction here is the degree of adult contrivance to produce this action. Other observations with other children lead me to believe that at least within some social groups this high degree of adult orchestration of child performance is not uncommon (Miller, Potts, Fung, Hoogstra, and Mintz 1990; Miller, Mintz, Hoogstra, Fung, and Potts 1992; Fung 1994).

Example 12 Age: 1:0.16

B	R	S	Context
[nennen]			
		Say 'chodai'.	R trying to get B to hand him a cookie.
	Choda. Chodai. Brenda.		
			B makes gesture of handing but then takes it back.
	☺	☺	

I have already commented upon the non-neutrality of this object – the cookie. This segment is the end of a longer sequence of attempts to get B to hand a cookie to R. I have selected this little piece for comment, however, to focus on the development of the habitus of both S and R. They have now heard M say 'Chodai' in getting B to hand her things. Now, two weeks into these social events, S has begun to incorporate this discursive practice into her habitus and offers pedagogical advice to R to adopt the B/M discursive practice. R accompanies this with the vocative, 'Brenda', which in other transcripts we see is a common strategy he uses to first try to attract the child's attention before moving to a request or comment.

Example 13 Age: 0:8.23

Rachel	R	S	Context
		chodai? chodai?	Not clear what object is being requested.
xxx [riðbʊ] ('read the book') xxx xxx			
		huh?	['read the book' is 'tune before the words'.]
	xxx the book?		
xxxxxx		chodai? chodai?	
		Thank you.	

Example 13 is a different child, our own daughter Rachel. This transcript was made about two years after that in Example 12. Rachel at the time was not quite 9 months old, that is, quite a bit younger than B was in the examples we have just been considering.[11] I am producing this example here to show that from this first prompting by S to 'Say, "Chodai" ' it has now entered into her habitus as a phrase she uses in interactions with her own daughter two years later. I would argue that the putative Japanese provenance of this utterance is entirely gratuitous. I would further argue that this is, in fact, the nature of the habitus. Perhaps it could be argued that *for M in social interactions with B* there ultimately comes to be a linkage between this phrase and a language and cultural identity. For S there is possibly a much looser linkage. That is, she does 'know' that this is a Japanese phrase but, more accurately, she has learned it as a mother–child social practice that is grounded in the M–B interactions. As such it has reappeared in her own mother–child interactions two years later where the link to Japanese practice has been entirely lost.

If we return to Example 12 for a moment, there is an ambiguity here which is impossible to resolve. Has this attempt to get B to hand over the cookie failed because R is not competent or expected to say 'Chodai', or is it because, as in Example 11, the object is a cookie and B cannot separate herself from it? Here I would argue that in the first place this is impossible to resolve, and in the second place we should not be trying to resolve such issues so much as coming to understand that such failed attempts to accomplish handing are part and parcel of the production of habitus. We not only succeed, but we fail; R may learn to say 'chodai' but it is likely that this happens for adults as well as children through a succession of failures as well as some successes. What is crucial for my argument is that the success or failure of the linguistic accompaniment is best considered together with the rest of the action, including the fact that in this case it is not a neutral object being requested.

On this latter point it is also probably important to note that R is behaving *as if* it is an entirely reversible, structural objectivized system in operation here. He, and S, are acting as if the only problem is the absence of the 'magic word', 'chodai'. In this structuralist assumption they fail miserably, of course.

Example 14 Age: 1:0.23

B	M	Context
	Mommy chodai. xxx college Chodai.	M asking B to hand her an orange to peel.
		B drops orange.
	Oiyo! xxx Chodai. Chodai. Ah, thank you, thank you.	B picks up orange. B looks down toward floor.
[daa] [u]	Gone. B	
[aᵘ]		
	Orange, orange. ☺	

This example (14) is a non-unique, unremarkable case of handing with the phrase 'chodai'. One begins to feel that it is justifiable to refer to this as at least dyadic practice, if not social practice. This consists of a three-part sequence: request (with 'chodai') + handing + thank you. M requests B hand her the orange, B does so (but it falls as well), and M thanks her.

Object permanency

Apart from this somewhat uninteresting case of handing with linguistic accompaniment is the evidence of B's cognitive development. This is the first week in which B attests full separation of object. We can see this quite graphically in what happens after the orange has been dropped and picked up again. B looks at the floor, as if to confirm that the object, once in the hand, then later located on the floor is now no longer there on the floor but, indeed, back in M's hand. Perhaps more interesting than this is that M follows this conceptual work very closely and, to my mind, very accurately. She says 'Gone', which confirms what, apparently, B is checking. One might describe this as M following B's 'cognitive/social' processes of development very carefully and closely. I would prefer to describe this as M and B jointly constructing this development. Explict cases such as this show just how closely M and B are joined in this process.

B's utterances in this case are, again, quite ambiguous. The first might be construed or glossed as 'down', though we have no further evidence. The second is construed by M as 'Orange' ; this is actually quite like M's pronunciation of the word as [awrəndʒ]. It remains quite difficult to assert that B has first commented on the falling of the object and then named the object about which this process has been predicated. On the other hand she seems to have said something and this is what M is working with.

Example 15 Age: 1:1.2

B	R	S	Context
[ʊhʊ] [uhu] [u]			
			B picks up book, hands to R.
	Thank you, Brenda, thank you. Can you read this book?		
			B picks up another book, flips through.
[ti] [bu']			
		She just said, 'book'.	
	What is that, Brenda? Here give it to me.		

We might say that the social practice of handing has arrived in Example 15 at age one year, one month (13 months). B initiates handing by giving a book to R. R receives the book and says 'Thank you', and then pedagogizes with a question about further action. This is much like M's comment on using the crayon to draw or to give it to C which we saw in the early examples (3 and 4). Looking a bit teleologically at this example, this is the first instance in which B appears to use handing as a way of controlling the interaction including introducing her topic. Unfortunately, we are unable to interpret what she is 'saying'. This leads me to argue that the practice of engaging in topic control may well be integrated into the habitus well before there are any utterances of a phonological sophistication to indicate any actual topic.

Example 16 Age: 1:1.2

B	R	Context
[dayɨ] [dayu] [dayɪ] [dayʉ]	What's this? Thank you, Brenda. What are you saying to the doll? How come you say it so many times?	R brings hakata doll to B. B focuses gaze on doll in this sequence as if speaking to it.

Example 16 is a bit of an aside from the point of view of a study of the social practice of handing, as this is the first clear case of the practice of naming. I include it here, however, just for this reason. Earlier we have had examples of naming linked to handing as a kind of pedagogizing of handing, as in Examples 3 and 4 where M names the object. This example shows the pedagogical sequence first identified by Sinclair and Coulthard (1975) and also by Mehan (1983) of Question + Answer + Verification used so often in classroom discourse. Here R clearly takes this as performance on his behalf for making this clear contribution to his phonological study. It should be recalled that in Example 6 one month earlier this attempted sequence did not work.

Example 17 Age: 1:1.2

B	M	Context
[nayʉ]	Banana? Banana. What's this? ☺ You don't want? xxx No?	M brings and offers banana to B.

Handing, like gift exchanges at the more complex level of practice, is social practice because it is not perfectly automatic. It must be capable of failure and negation. In Examples 11 and 12 we saw that when the object was a cookie, B was apparently incapable of handing it to another person. Now a month later she is apparently capable of refusing to accept. Not only that, she is able to say 'no', or at least that is how M construes or glosses her utterance in Example 17. Perhaps we may now suggest that B's habitus in respect to handing is becoming somewhat more flexible than before.

Example 18 Age: 1:1.8

B	M	Context
ʌvʌ] [ki] [n]	Key. Yeah. Key. Mommy chodai. Thank you. Jingle. Jingle.	B has and shakes a set of keys. B hands to M who shakes keys.

Now a week later in Example 18 the linkage among handing, naming, and functional description seems quite smoothly integrated. B names the keys. She easily hands them to M who then comments on what first B was doing and then what M is doing *in imitation* of B. This latter point seems rather crucial in the overall progress of the development of the habitus. As in the very first examples where M took something said or done by B as a meaningful action, or in Example 10 where she has told B, 'Hear what you said? You said, "Chodai" ', she continues to reflect back to B her own construction of what B is doing.

Example 19 Age: 1:1.15

B	M	Context
[ə]	Mommy chodai. [ə] Charlotte liked ice too when she was about her age.	M asked B to hand her a piece of ice.

It is important to note, however, that there is never any mechanical and structural linkage among handing, naming, and functional instruction. That is, the linkage is not fixed or invariant. As Example 19 shows, handing is now a simple action which M can request of B without further complexities. Having said that, it should be noted, however, that there is always in these interactions with R and S (at least) M's reflection on B's actions. That is to say, we should never lose sight of the fact that these transcriptions represent throughout some degree of performance by M of the M–B relationship. In some cases (such as Example 24 below) this performance is foregrounded by all of the adult participants.

Example 20 Age: 1:1.22

B	M	S	Context
[abə] [ada] [ada] [adða'] [n] [ene]	 Hai.	She wants another one. Atha? Ada.	B drinking from cup, spills and/or empties it. M gives B more juice.

By Example 20 when B is now almost 14 months of age, that is, two months after we began this study, handing is fully integrated in B's habitus as a practice along with a verbal request. After spilling her juice she asks for another ('ada') which M simply gives her. As I have noted in my discussion of Example 10, 'Hai' is used by M as she hands an object to B. This may be situated squarely within what we might legitimately call 'Japanese' social practice in this case.

Example 21 Age: 1:1.29

B	M	R	Context
[næni] [nene] [ene]	 Oh, bottle.	 Here's your nene. O.K., here it is.	B asks for bottle.

Now a week later we can see in Example 21 that the routine handing of this routine object – B's juice bottle – can be accomplished jointly by M and R. In this we can see on the one hand that caregiving should not be thought of as restricted to any single caregiver, and on the other that R has been drawn into the caregiving circle of B's world over the past two months. We should further recall Example 1 in which even M is 'guessing' about B's utterance 'nene'. There are two months of development in this difference between 'nene' – 'Oh, bottle' and 'nene' – 'Want juice? Hm? Gave you milk. You want juice now, hm?'

Example 22 Age: 1:1.29

B	M	R	Context
[bæə] [bawə] [ba] [bauwə] [bauwa]	Ball? Oh, umhm. Hm? What'd you say? Ball. Hm. That's balloon.	 Hm?	 B points to picture of balloon in book.

Handing has been quite clearly constituted in B's habitus by 1:1.29; what is doubtful now is the pointing–naming–representation practice as we can see in Example 22. Here we can see in M the same degree of uncertainty about B's utterance (and therefore her social purpose in uttering). This constitutes a significant movement beyond handing, however, and is not just a question of phonology, though it is a phonological question as well. At 14 months, B's phonology was still rather in need of generous interpretation by a scaffolding caregiver as the five forms in this example suggest. What is important here is that this discursive practice of speaking about the world through nomination is being applied to representations of the world, not to the world itself. Two months earlier it was bottles of juice, dolls, crayons, and other such material objects about which B and M (and others) were 'talking'. Now we see the beginnings of talk about representations of objects including this picture of a balloon in a book. Of course we know but must always remember in speaking of these things that M and the rest of us do not say or prompt the child to say, 'This is a picture of a ball' or a balloon. We simply assert that the representation is the thing itself and leave it to the infant to work out the object–representation relationship.

Handing and discursive practice

Example 23 Age: 1:2.5

B	M	Context
[de']		B points to tea cup.
	Um? Tea. Yeah. Atsui, atsui.	
[de]	Um hm.	

Along with handing we have seen several linguistic accompaniments as well as linguistic silence. M's 'Atsui' (cf. Japanese 'It's hot') in reduplicated form might also be glossed, 'be careful'. Naming has been the most common, but we have also seen functional instruction ('Do X with Y'), interpersonal instruction ('Give X to Y'), and now in Example 23 we see behavioral caution ('Be careful with Y') coupled with the naming practice. This raises the question to which we will turn in the analysis below: What is the relationship between social practice and discursive practice? We have at least five discursive linkages possible (for the caregiver in relationship to the child – the child's repertoire is not as well elaborated, of course) as of 14 months of age:

- silence
- nomination
- functional directive
- interpersonal directive
- behavioral directive

If we are to take Chouliaraki and Fairclough (1999) seriously and say that each social practice has a discursive component, which of these should we take as 'the' discursive component which provides the key to this practice? To retreat into saying that all of them are the discursive component would be to posit a structural system as a rule-based system out of which these examples have been generated which, in my view, runs contrary to everything we have seen in these examples. And, of course, what do we do with silence as it could be either simple absence or systemic repression of utterance (van Leeuwen 1996)? If we allow silence to stand in as a 'discursive component' we have largely abandoned the project of developing a practice view of the habitus.

One further comment on Example 23 is the salience of the Japanese word 'atsui' ('hot'). Before this we have seen only 'chodai', 'hai', and 'nene' in these transcripts. Of course this can easily be explained by the presence of R and S who, while they both spoke Japanese – R's undergraduate degree was, in fact, in Japanese linguistics and S had studied Japanese as part of her graduate work – and were known by M to have this ability, had largely only used English in their social interactions both within the research sessions we are analyzing here and more broadly within the family social gatherings which were quite common. Of course, M's husband did not know or speak Japanese and so M's use of Japanese outside of the research sessions was necessarily rather limited within family situations. Nevertheless, in this example and in the next one, Japanese rises to prominence in the interaction between M and B. As I will argue below for Example 24, it is the pressure or urgency of the action – a warning about the possibility of being burned by the hot tea – which produces this code shift.

Example 24 Age: 1:2.5

B	M	R	Context
		Will she give you, give you if you say give me by name? Can you, see if she'll give you the wow-wow from these two. See if, ask her to give you the one that's the wow-wow.	R is using photographs of common objects in B's vocabulary as a two-photo discrimination test.
[ɨwə] [ɨwə]	Oh. O.K., Yuh. O.K. Which one is wow-wow? Wow-wow chodai. Motte kinasai wow-wow. Fang-Fang Mommy chodai. Which is Fang? Not that! Which is Fang? ☺	☺	

Example 24 continued

B	M	R	Context
[henle]	Yeah. Hai. Fang chodai. Mommy Fang chodai. Yes. Chodai. Oh, jozu jozu. Thank you. O.K. Baby. Dotchi ga baby. Baby chodai. Baby chodai. Oh. It's the one, the one, Baby. Thank you. O.K. Fang chodai. Dotchi ga Fang. nene. Yeah, nene. Fang-Fang chodai. One track minded. Huh? Is that what?	O.K. Tell her, tell her to give you the baby. Here. Give her baby. O.K. Um. Tell her to give you the dog. Yeah. She gives you – she's been giving you the new one. She give you the new one. The new one.	

Example 24 will require some background explanation. By 14 months B showed evidence of knowing a number of words and we were interested in the question suggested above in Example 22: To what extent would B be able to relate black and white photographic representations of objects to the words she used when pointing to or handing the objects themselves? In other words, we wanted to know if B could recognize a photo of common objects in her world.

Suzanne took photos (A5 size) of all of the objects for which we had had some evidence in the prior weeks that B could name them or would look at them if they were named by M. These included the ones here:

Wow-wow, Fang   the family's pet dog
baby   Brenda herself
nene   baby bottle

As the transcript shows, R suggested to M pairs to show to B to see if she could select the right one out of the pair. As one can see, B did not do very well in this task though she showed great interest in looking at the photos both then and later.

What is of greatest interest to us here is that this moved far beyond the sort of open-ended elicitation which we had used in prior interactions with B and M. It should also be noted that this session took place in R and S's apartment, not in B's home as all the previous sessions had done.

In this transcript we see an abundance of Japanese. While there is code mixing, mostly the central requests for handing are in Japanese: 'wow-wow chodai', 'Motte kinasai wow-wow', 'Fang-Fang Mommy chodai', 'Dotchi ga baby', 'Baby chodai', 'Dotchi ga Fang' and so forth.

As I have suggested above, here I would argue that it is the very formal test-like situation which has called forth the use of Japanese from M's habitus. In more open-ended situations we rarely heard her use Japanese with either of the children, whether in our research sessions or simply in doing things within the family around the house. B's performance in this test task is not particularly impressive and so it would be quite wrong to say that the use of Japanese as one further linguistic/discursive practice to be linked with handing is very effective. We can say, however, that for M there appears to be a strong linkage between Japanese and the severity or seriousness of the utterance, as we saw in Example 23 when she used 'atsui' to warn B that the tea was hot.

Example 25 Age: 1:2.19

B	M	R	Context
[duvə]	Give Mommy the money. Where's the money? Where?	Did she say, 'Don't know?'	B has found three pennies on the floor.
[ɨvæ]	Don't know? Where's the money? What did you do with the money?		
	Did you drop it?☺	Here. Here. ☺	
[dəce] [ɨvə' ə]	☺ Give money back.	Here.	
[ɨvəu]	Uh. 3, 3 pennies, see? Have one more?		
	Chodai. Chodai.		
[ɨwəu]	Uh hm.		
[dəwo]	Thank you.		
	One more.		

Example 25 continued

B	M	R	Context
[da'] [ɨwə'] [duo] [dowəu]	Thank you. One more.		

Example 25 shows that handing as a social practice was quite well constituted by the time B was 1:2.19 or 14½ months of age. Here it is used quite routinely by M to get B to hand pennies which B has found on the floor in R and S's apartment. In the original transcript it is clear that C cooperates in this collection of the pennies as well. One interesting wrinkle is that whereas in Example 24 we saw that M used Japanese in the test situation, here, just two weeks later, also in R and S's apartment, she has included 'give Mommy the money' and 'Give money back' in her repertoire.

Example 26 Age: 1:2.19

B	M	R	S	Context
[mgə] [dæpən]		What do you plan to do with those? Can I have one? Give one to me. Thank you. You're very stingy. You only gave me one.		B has some raisins. B gives a raisin to R.
	You say, 'Give me one.' ☺	I guess that's what I said. Give me two. Brenda, give me two.		
			She picked one up. She said, 'Give one.'	
	☺	Give me two. No, give me two, Brenda.		
			She doesn't know how to count to two.	

Example 26 continued

B	M	R	S	Context
		Give me two. Two.		B gives R another raisin.
		No, that's only one.		
[dəw]		Now I have two.		

I conclude this first segment of the data which I called BRENDA I in my original publication with Example 26. In addition to being able to say now that handing as a social practice is well established between B and M, we can see that it is also well established with R. So much so that we have moved on to other questions such as the number of the objects handed. Of course this begs the question of whether B has developed a social practice which can be called upon in interactions with relative strangers or, on the other hand, whether R has become more integrated within the inner circle of B's social world or nexus of practice through these weekly visits (and the other family occasions which have brought them together). Finally, the object itself – the raisin – has become somewhat neutralized. That is, B shows little difficulty in handing food in much the same way she handed pennies in the preceding example (25).

Summary of BRENDA I (12 months of age to 14½ months)

In this period what began as rough fragments of 'action' (which is not to say 'social action') is not fully constituted in B's habitus as the social practice of handing. At the beginning of this period we could not attest any separation of the object and the self. B could not walk. Her utterances were construed by M as meaningful in many cases but could not be related phonologically to recognizable adult utterances whether in Japanese or English. Now objects have been constituted as external to the self and they have been largely neutralized. That is, food or pennies are treated approximately equally. To some extent representations of objects are coming to be treated as equivalents of the objects as well, though as we have seen in Example 24, in a formal test of representation–object equivalence, B did not perform very well.

Handing is also to a considerable extent constituted reciprocally. That is to say, B hands to others at her own initiative or at the initiative of others, possibly with those who are at some social distance from her primary caregivers and family. Handing, to put it simply, works for B and for others who deal with B. Having said this, however, there is no evidence for what Bourdieu (1977, 1990) has called 'genesis amnesia'. That is to say, this practice of handing cannot yet be said to be naturalized by B and by her caregivers as they engage in frequent pedagogical rehearsal.

BRENDA II (1:7.2 to 1:8.21)

The data I will now consider were collected beginning five months after the set analyzed just above. At the beginning Brenda is 19 months old (1 year, 7 months, and 2 days) and as Example 27 clearly shows, she has developed considerably in the intervening five months. Much of what she says can now be fairly easily interpreted as 'saying', that is, her utterances are now largely taken as functional socially grounded utterances by her sister and by M, and much of what she says is also interpretable by R and S.

Example 27 Age: 1:7.2

B	C	R	S	Context
	You going to tape, right?			R and S setting up tape recorder.
[tʰɛɪ pɛi'] (tape)			Un huh.	
		What'd she say? Hm?	M. Tape.	
[tʰæɪ ptʰi] (tape)		What is that?		
[n] [n n]		Try hold it by her . . . more.	☺	
		What is that, Brenda?		
[n n gɔdə'] (n n corder)				B looks intently at tape recorder.
		Yeah, that's tape recorder.		
xx [njə']			What's this?	S holds out roll of scotch tape.
['ə'] [tʰoᵘš] (tape?)			What's this?	
[čoᵘč] (Scotch?)				
[tʰɛɪš] (tape?) [tʰɛɪš] (tape?)				
[tʰeitʰ] (tape)				

Now in Example 27 naming seems well established. There is no telling, of course, what B makes of the homophony of 'tape' in reference to recording tape and 'tape' in reference to cellophane tape. It is also unclear whether 'tape' in B's usage should be read as a nominalization ('This is a tape') or a functional/verbal form ('You are going to tape me'). C has just used 'tape' verbally. In any event, as in the earliest utterances of Examples 1 and 2, it is overinterpretive to read these distinctions into B's utterances. All that we can be sure about is that she is now using something more like words.

Example 28 Age: 1:7.2

B	R	S	context
[yutʰu] (you do/too)	You hear that?		B hands pen to R.
[tʰei' ɛi' pʰɪk] (tape)	Thank you.		B hands tape to R.
		Tape.	

In Example 28, now, we can see that some discursive element and handing are linked in B's habitus. That is, in the first case B does what we saw M doing in Examples 3 and 4, that is, she is handing a pen to R along with instructions about doing something with it. This is followed by the same sort of sequence with a cassette of tape. From a structural point of view this logical reversibility is now complete. That is, B can perform this social practice of handing with a discursive linkage much in the same way it was performed with her seven months earlier. From a Piagetian perspective, one would want to say that B has 'achieved' some sort of cognitive reversibility of the logic of this operation of object exchange. As Bourdieu (1977, 1990) has pointed out, it is only from this distant and objectivist analyst's vantage point that we can link what happened in February of 1972 with what has happened in September of the same year. We should be rather cautious about asserting a cognitive reversible logical structure in relating these rather distant concrete instances.

Mama shoe

Example 29 Age: 1:7.2

B	R	S	Context
[mami] (Mommy) [mami] (Mommy) [mami'] (Mommy) [ama'] (Mommy) [hengi'] (hankie?) [hengi'] (hankie?) [mami'] (Mommy) [maðə] (Mother)		Mama panty?	B looks in M's closet.

Example 29 continued

B	R	S	Context
[tʰi] (take?) [mama] (Mommy) [mama] (Mommy) [mama] (Mommy) [mam] (Mommy) [š] (shoe) [šɪ] (shoe) [š] (shoe) [šɪš] (shoe) [šu] (shoe) [šu'] (shoe) [šuš] (shoe) [šɪ] (shoe) [šɪ] (shoe) [šu'] (shoe)	xx	 Shoes.	B picks up several of M's shoes in sequence and brings to R.

With Example 29 we come to an exchange with which I have illustrated a good bit of my earlier understanding of the earliest development of linguistic structure (Scollon 1976, 1979). In that earlier research I focused my attention on the final 14 of B's utterances. I argued that prior studies of a one-year-old's language would have considered these to be unrelated single words, 'Mommy' and 'shoe'. These studies would have classified the child as being in the 'one-word' stage, and then would have gone on to argue that there was no cognitive capacity to relate two words in a syntactic construction which, in that generative-transformational line of analysis, was the 'true' beginning of language. I argued in the first place (as Ochs 1979 was also to argue) that one reason these appeared as unrelated was simply that they would not have been tape recorded but transcribed by an interested listener – often a parent – and the intermediate forms such as [š] and [šl] would have been considered to be nonsense sounds. Thus the 'meaningful' words would be separated by nonsense utterance and unrelated. I argued that we can rather easily interpret this sequence as 'saying' something like 'This is Mommy's shoe' given the clearer transcription of the whole sequence afforded by tape recording coupled with the contextual observation that B was picking up M's shoes and bringing them to R. Thus this 'Mommy's shoe' was, I argued, a meaningful construction of the type I coined as a 'vertical construction', that is, not closely linked within a single intonational phrase but nevertheless semantically and pragmatically functional as a constructed utterance.

In developing that earlier analysis what I did not do was construct for the reader how I felt I could make this interpretation. Now I am in a better position to argue that my interpretation is grounded in the preceding seven months of social interactions with B. This consists of three crucial elements: (1) the construction of the practice of handing since 12 months of age, (2) the linking of the practice of handing with the practice of naming – that is, the pedagogization of handing which we first saw in Examples 3 and 4 – and (3) my own induction into the social world, the nexus of practice, of B and her caregivers. That is, my analysis depended entirely on the prior construction not only in B's habitus but in my own of these two social practices – handing and naming – as well as their pedagogical linkage and through this development of homologous habitus the construction of a nexus of practice.

Example 30 Age: 1:7.2

B	M	R	S	Context
[mami'] (Mommy) [hyuš] (shoe) [šu] (shoe) [šu] (shoe) [šu] (shoe) [šu] (shoe) [e] [didi'] (Daddy)				B back to looking in M's closet.
[dedi] (Daddy) [dʸædi'] (Daddy) [dædi] (Daddy) [dedi] (Daddy) [dædi] (Daddy) [dedi] (Daddy) [dedi] (Daddy) [dedi] (Daddy)		Yeah.		B picks up several of M's shoes in sequence and brings to R.
[dædi] (Daddy) [dædi] (Daddy)		Is that his shoe? (to S) I guess she's not gonna say daddy's shoe or anything like that this week.		
[dæyɪgə] (?) [mama'] (Mommy) [mami] (Mommy) [mami] (Mommy)		Not together.	She said mommy's shoe.	
	Yes, that's for me. O.K. Thank you. Thank you.		☺	
xx			☺	
[ədititi] (Daddy) [dægi'] (Daddy)	Yes.			

Example 30 continued

B	M	R	S	Context
[dædi] (Daddy)	Yes. That's Daddy's shoes.	Don't take out all of your Mommy and Daddy's stuff.		B gets scissors from a drawer.
[kʰʌ'] (cut) [kʰʌ'] (cut) [kʰʌ'] (cut) [kʰʌ'] (cut) [kʰʌ'] (cut)	☺ Put them all back in. Oh, she opened the door. A – bunai, eh? Abunaibunai! Cut, yes, cut. Cut. Abunai, eh--		No, Charlotte opened it. Abunai.	

The degree of intentionality with which B is engaging in these linked practices of handing and naming can be seen now a few minutes later in Example 30. She is quite insistent; this is carried up to the point of R's saying, 'Don't take out all of your Mommy and Daddy's stuff' and M's saying, 'Put them all back in'. B then quickly switches to taking a pair of scissors out of a drawer. She is very actively engaged in grasping, bringing to R, and naming or talking about just about everything she can get her hands on.

To follow up on a theme suggested earlier, here M switches to Japanese to warn B of the danger of the scissors with 'abunai' ('dangerous'). Notice also S's adoption of this Japanese form in consort with M. In this case B uses 'cut' rather than a nominalization in this pedagogical practice. That is, she is discursively focusing on the function rather than the nominalization. Many examples of nominalization follow in the next several weeks where B says 'ball' when R is playing with a Mexican toy, B says 'pen' when R is writing in his notebook, B answers 'turtle' and then 'fish' when M says 'Tell Ron what swims'.

Example 31 Age: 1:7.16

B	M	R	Context
[f ʊ tʰ] [f ʊ tʸ] [f ʊ tʸ] [f ʊ tʸ]		Yeah. Your footʸ. I got your foot.	R grabs B's foot.
[f ʊ tʰ] [f ʊ ə] [f ʊ tʰ] [f ʊ t] [f ʊ tʸ]	Chodai. Mommy chodai. Thank you. Let me. Now it's mine.	Foot, foot, foot. ☺	M grabs B's foot.

Example 31 continued

B	M	R	Context
[nni] [brɛnda] [brɛnda] [brɛnda] [pɛn] [bɛnda]	No. Mine. That's mine.		

The distance we have come is clearly seen in Example 31. Whereas in Examples 11 and 12 we could just barely attest to the separation of object and self, here we see R and M playing at separating B's foot as an object within the handing social practice and also see B's clear and discursive resistance. First she clarifies that this is her foot and then that it is 'Brenda' and not alienable whether through grabbing or through handing within the 'Mommy chodai/thank you' set of linked practices. Thus here we see that she is not only able to deny receipt as she was in Example 17, here she is able to contest the separation of self and object when the object is part of the constituted self.

Example 32 Age: 1:7.16

B	S	Context
[i] [i] [i] [i] [ih] [i] [i] [i] [i] [i] [ih]	 'E' ? This is 'S'. 'S'. 'S'.	B hands felt 'S' to Suzie.

The resistance we saw just above is seen again here in Example 32 in B's refusal to be corrected by S. The object she has handed to S is the letter 'S' from a set of letters made of felt. B asserts that this is an 'E' eleven times in spite of S's correction in three cases. Whereas in prior examples B's intentionality was at best ambiguous, here it seems clear that she has an intention and, as in the case of bringing all of the shoes out of the closet, is very determined in her efforts to show us these things and say what she has to say about them.

Example 33 Age: 1:7.16

B	M	R	Context
[doh]	Donut. She figures you have yet. ☺	Thank you. ☺	B gives out pieces of doughnut. Sees that S is still chewing and takes the piece she was offering back.

More evidence of B's internalization of some sort of social analysis can be seen in Example 33 where B is, once again, handing out food. In this case it's doughnuts or pieces of doughnuts. As Bourdieu (1977:73) has pointed out, any exchange is not simply an action but also a strategic one with some anticipation of the receiver's likely response. As he has argued, we should not think of this as mechanistic strategizing or an intentional attempt to elicit a response, but rather we should note that as part of any social practice there is a dialogicality – a kind of practical inference – that takes into consideration not only the actor but those with whom the actor is engaged. Here B sees that S is chewing and takes back the piece she was offering. If we recall Example 11 where B was unable to hand over a cookie, then later when the object had become somewhat neutralized, we now see that B has gone beyond her own action in undertaking this handing to taking the receiver's actions into consideration.

Example 34 Age: 1:7.23

B	S	Context
		M and C are cooking, B is pretending to cook. B runs toward toy horse, stops at toy bear and feeds it pretend food.
[haši'] [hau]	Horsie. Oh, you gonna feed horsie.	
[biæ] [biə] [a] [bea] [beha'] [itʰi] [šupʰ] [šupʰ]	Eating. ☺	

I opened my analysis in Example 1 with B as a largely helpless infant whose needs were being looked after by M and other caregivers. Now seven months or so later, it is B herself who is engaging in the play practice of preparing food and looking after another – her toy horse and bear. The co-constructed 'bear + eating + soup' with the assistance of S's 'eating' shows just how much development of B's habitus in regards to the social practice of handing has taken place in these seven months.

Here one is reminded of Wittgenstein's comment: 'A child has much to learn before it can pretend' (1990:439). Here we have just seen how many concrete actions in specific social circumstances have gone into this practice of 'pretending to feed horsie' which are blurred and glossed over in saying something like the following: B has learned in the past seven months how to pretend to feed her horsie by imitating her mother feeding her.

The lexicalization of handing

Example 35 Age: 1:7.23

B	C	M	Context
[šɛ'] [šæ] [æ] [maintu] [maintʰə] [maintʰu] [wã']	You don't need your change.	Share? ☺ You want too? Why don't you give her one, she says, 'share' ?	C has a few coins. B holds out hand to C for C to give her money.
	No, she's gonna lose it.	No, I'll watch it for her so she won't lose it. O.K.?	
[dəpʰ] [dap] [dapʰ] [dapʰ] [dɛpʰ] [dæp] [dap] [dəp]	Give it to me!	Huh? Dop? Drop? Let her hold it for a while. She'll give it back to you, I'll make sure.	

Example 35 gives a good example of a new linkage of the social practice of handing with an original lexicalization of this practice. B wants the coins which C has. She gestures that she wants them to be given to her while saying, 'Share'. She further supports the expression of her intention with her 'Mine too' and 'Want'.

This lexicalization, 'share,' is common enough in the adult language, but as B uses it here there is no evidence that it has any comprehensive meaning. It is used quite specifically to mean 'You give that to me'. In this it is directly equivalent to M's frequent 'chodai' as we have noted frequently above. What is interesting here is that the lexical form 'share' has not been used by C or M in this meaning. That is, the form 'share' has been appropriated by B in a quite concrete, specific, and limited meaning which is tied directly to handing.

Example 36 Age: 1:8.0

B	R	Context
[tʰep] [tʰep] [tʰip] [tʰip]	 Thank you.	B brings tape recorder to R.

Example 36 is another case of B acting in a 'nurturing' capacity, though in this case it is not pretending as it was in Example 34. She is carrying the tape recorder to R which in itself is a rather strenuous feat. And again, there is an accompanying lexicalization of the action.

Example 37 Age: 1:8.14

B	M	Context
[redi] [rædi] [rædi] [redi] [redi] [redi] [šəm]	 Ready? All right, serve now. Some. Thank you. Oh, you had hair in this.	B and C are playing at baking cookies in the sandbox.

By 1 year 8½ months B carries on rather complex social interactions. In Example 37 she is playing at baking with C in a sandbox. She declares the cookies ready and when M suggests she serve them, she gives one to M while saying 'Some'. In my previous analysis (Scollon 1976) I described this all rather structurally as a symmetrical logical system in which 'share' meant 'You give to me' and 'some' meant 'I give to you'. I cannot, in fact, find an example in which both of these terms occur within a close enough timespan nor within a single exchange so that I might support this structural analysis. What my material will support is that every instance I have of 'share' is accompanied by B trying to get someone to hand something to her, while every instance of 'some' is accompanied by B handing or pretending to hand something to someone else or to one of her toy animals. From this I would now want to argue only that B has lexicalized the action <B hands to other> as 'some' and <other hands to B> as 'share'. She does not use either of these terms in reference to any other ego. That is, these terms are not to be confused with the quite generalized words in adult English which may be used independently of ego or of point of view. For B they remain at this time concretely linked in her habitus with these two, separate and not yet fully reversible acts of handing.

Example 38 Age: 1:8.21

B	S	Context
[šudži] [šuži] [šuži] [šuži] [šuži] [šuži] [šuži] [šuži]		B takes book to S.
	What, you think I'm gonna read your book for you? ☺	
		B gives book to S.
[giəuf] [giəv] [gɪv] [gɪv]		Give?

Having said in my discussion of the previous example that 'some' was used concretely in respect to the practice of B handing to another, now one week later in Example 38 we find 'give' in what appears to be the same function. Here I would want to exercise caution, however, as the examples I have of 'some' are all used in connection with food, real or pretend, whereas this 'give' is used with a book. Both the object and the 'intended' action are different. It is clear from the earlier construction of handing itself that B acted differently depending on whether the object was food or some other more neutral object. I see no reason to think that this specificity of practice is not continuing to be an active aspect of B's habitus.

'Hi', 'here': handing as summons

I have now come to the example with which I started in my earlier study. B has just turned two years of age. In this session, as I have written before (1976), she frequently handed me objects, sometimes quite insignificant ones, and then herself took the conversational floor. Among other things, this was the basis for the title of my book *Conversations with a one year old* as I argued there, and have now given further evidence here, that by the time she had reached two years of age, we had engaged in nearly a year of conversation. At first I was at a considerable distance from her as an outsider of that inner circle of immediate family. By this time not only had B experienced a full year of growth and development, I had also been brought further into the inner circle inhabited by her primary caregivers.

The session in which the data I used in this argument about handing begins is in Example 39 below.

Example 39 Age: 2:0.12

B	R	Context
Here.		B hands R tape recorder.
	What am I supposed to do with this? What is this for?	
In there.		B motions that tape recorder goes in R's briefcase.

In this example (39) B opens by saying 'Here' while handing the tape recorder to R. He asks what is, essentially, 'Why are you handing me this?' and B explains what amounts to 'Put it away'. As I have argued before, this shows not only that B has integrated handing as a social practice with various other discursive practices, that is, she successfully hands things, but she can *use* this social practice to do other things; one of the very important 'other things' she does through handing is to achieve topical dominance in conversation.

I will not elaborate on all of the seven 'Hi's' and twenty-two 'here's' which occurred within this one hour as that would now take us too far afield. For the present argument what I would like to conclude, not just from this example but from the sequence of thirty-nine examples, is that within one year B has moved from being an infant for whom it would be impossible to attest separation of self and object and for whom it would be impossible to say she could speak, to being a child who can engage in the complex social practices of conversation. I have tried to show how the practice of handing has been constituted in B's habitus over the period of 12 months through a long series of momentary and partial actions, in which at first some action of hers is construed by caregivers as handing but which a year later can be described as B intentionally handing something to another person – a common social practice.

I have also tried to argue that this social practice of handing is both linked to and independent of other discursive social practices. In this case the practice of handing is linked to the social practice of topic control through the call–answer–topic sequence (Schegloff 1972; Scollon 1976; Scollon and Scollon 1981, 1991, 1995). While arguing that this practice of handing is linked to the social practice of topic control, I do not want to argue that it is linked in any permanent, fixed, or structural way because we have also seen that handing is also linked to a variety of other discursive practices such as naming, interpersonal relationships, and the like.

In any event, what might be described in an objectivist view as a complex, logically reversible, structural system of exchange has nowhere emerged as a structural system. On the contrary, it has been assembled piece by piece out of concrete, non-reversible, and jointly constructed social actions. To the extent there is 'structure', the structure cannot be attributed to B's cognitive apparatus but must be attributed to the overall social interaction of the participating members of the particular event.

The ubiquity and ambiguity of 'practice'

One finds that concepts rise in value as academic currency from time to time. In the present wave of popularity of the term 'practice' it is striking for me to recall that when I entered Taft Junior High School in 1950, I passed under a phrase written in stone over the doorway of the school: 'Learn to do by doing – John Dewey'. As Mike Cole (1995) has recently reminded us, as early as 1938 Dewey had developed an understanding of practice which is remarkably similar to the position being outlined in some of the newer work being published over sixty years later. In what I write here I make frequent reference to Bourdieu's ideas about practice (1977, 1990), which I find stimulating and of considerable use in linking contemporary social theory rooted in the Frankfurt School as well as elsewhere, of course, with sociocultural theory, particularly that rooted in Vygotsky, Vološinov, and Bakhtin. I have flagged Dewey's work, however, as a reminder that currency may be accompanied by a kind of amnesia and that whatever use we wish to make of a term such as 'practice' in the present, it brings along its own history which lives right within our uses no matter how tightly we try to define them.[12]

As I would like to use the term, practice implies social practice; that is, I would like to set the idea of practice within a framework of the analysis of social life with a secondary interest in human psychology. Practice in this use is a count noun, as I have suggested above; that is, I would like to talk about multiple and many practices and these practices are relatively narrowly conceived. I take Cole's point that there is much ambiguity in the use of 'practice' and 'activity' and that on the whole the first term tends to signal the writer is grafted (S. Scollon 1999b) onto a line originating in modern thought in Marx, though it is important to note, again following Cole, that it is none other than Aristotle who is the root of the distinction between *theoria* (contemplation) and *praxis* (everyday actions). As an alternate, activity has been used as the unit of psychological and social analysis by psychologists in the sociocultural school following upon Vygotsky. Here I am using practice to mean social practice taken narrowly, and the particular practice I am studying closely is that of handing an object from one person to another.

This raises the immediate question of whether there are not different levels of practice, even when taken as a count noun. Do we want to return to Bourdieu's example with which I began and speak of a practice of gift exchange or a practice of giving out handbills in streets? The alternative I have proposed is that we see that level of analysis as the analysis of activity systems, Discourses (Gee, Hull and

Lankshear 1996), or as I propose in Chapter 5, nexus of practice, which is composed of linkages among more narrowly conceived practices of walking, of handing objects, and the like.

The analytical problem can be seen, for example, as Chouliaraki and Fairclough (1999) consider social practice central to their view of critical discourse analysis, though they do not focus much analytical attention on the concept so much as use it in developing further aspects of their theoretical framework. Practice for Chouliaraki and Fairclough is defined as 'habitualized ways, tied to particular times and places, in which people apply resources (material or symbolic) to act together in the world' (p. 21). As to the question of whether a practice is 'hardened into a relative permanency' (p. 22) or 'what is done in a particular time and place' (p. 21) they suggest that this ambiguity is useful because it places practice intermediate between structures and events.

I would argue against this 'usefulness' of the ambiguity, using Chouliaraki and Fairclough's own concern with developing a theory of critical discourse analysis. They assert that in practice 'people always generate representations of what they do as part of what they do' (p. 22), or 'Discourse is always a significant moment because all practices are, as we have said, reflexive – constructions of that practice constitute part of a practice' (p. 23), or again, 'all practices have an irreducible discursive aspect, not only in the sense that all practices involve use of language to some degree' (p. 26).

Of course Chouliaraki and Fairclough were not considering the infant practice of handing when they wrote this and it is perhaps unfair to make this extension of their work as a straw man to attack for convenience of the argument. In any event, in Chapter 5 I will return to reconstruct a position in which we can speak quite precisely about how discursive practice is linked to other practices within a nexus of practice. This position is entirely consistent with Chouliaraki and Fairclough's position and provides a more concrete understanding of how we can study the relationships between discourse and practice.

It is in the spirit of probing concepts through limiting examples, however, that I would like to argue that we cannot take their claim as it is stated in respect to the ontogenesis of the social practice of handing. As we have seen, handing from the inception in jointly constructed acts between the child and the caregiver up to the reasonably developed social practice of handing in the second year of life may or may not be accompanied by reflexive constructions of that practice. In some cases the caregivers do, indeed, comment on the practice of handing. On the other hand, in many cases the discursive practices which are linked to handing are not at all *about that practice*, and in further cases there is silence.

I believe that even in the case of this relatively simple and basic social practice of handing it is impossible to identify the unique discursive practice which is its reflexive element. It does not seem that the complexity of the linkages of discursive practice to social practice can be resolved by simply blurring the focus on the concrete level I have chosen to analyze here. It seems that it is exactly this level of concrete analysis we need to address if we wish to achieve a closer understanding of the linkage of discourse and practice.

It is possibly arguable that practice, if considered as those hardened relative permanencies, might sometimes have a reflexive, discursive element, but it is very doubtful to me that if practice is taken also as meaning what happens in a 'particular time and place' that anyone would assert that all times and all places always have a reflexive, discursive element. In other words, it seems clear that either we have to take practice as meaning some very broad, 'relatively hardened permanency *which includes a discursive element*' or we have to place into abeyance the assertion that all practices always have a discursive and reflexive element.

From the few examples Chouliaraki and Fairclough actually mention – examples such as 'sheep farming' and 'teaching philosophy' (p. 26) – we can infer that for them a social practice is a much larger entity than the entity I have in mind here and which I have elaborated in detail at the one-year-old level of habitus. If the idea of practice is not central to a theoretical position, I would imagine that such a level of generality would be acceptable, but I would want to argue that to be useful, practice has to be central and to be central it has to be quite tightly defined and rather narrowed in scope. Such large analytical entities as 'sheep farming' would, for me, be more usefully terminologized and theorized as Discourses in Gee's definition: 'ways of talking, listening, reading, writing, acting, interacting, believing, valuing, and using tools and objects, in particular settings and at specific times, so as to display or to recognize a particular social identity' (Gee, Hull and Lankshear 1996:10), or as activity systems (Cole 1995), and understood to consist, as I have suggested above, of many practices and networks of linkages among practices, or as I shall argue in Chapter 5, as nexus of practice. There would be little doubt that such Discourses or nexus of practice would contain reflexive, discursive practices as part of that network of linked practices, but as my data suggest, it is a significant problem of analysis to discover the nature of those linkages rather than to simply assert that they exist and then rest back to study just the discursive practices as the key which will unlock social life.

Calhoun (1995), in summarizing Bourdieu's notion of practice, writes that

> It is necessary that a theory of practice give a good account of the limits of awareness which are involved in lived experience, including both misrecognition and nonrecognition, as well as show the kind of genuine knowledge which is involved, often nondiscursively, in practice.
>
> (Calhoun 1995:145–6)

This comment of Calhoun's provides a useful reminder of the 'poor logic' (Bourdieu 1977) nature of practices. Crucial to Bourdieu's concept is that practice is based in time. That is, there is an irreversibility in social practice. Agents act in real time, uniquely, and their actions cannot be undone, they can only be responded to. There is in this conception much of Bakhtin's (1981) notion of non-repeatability and dialogicality. As I have suggested in note 7, this is much like Lashley's argument that formal logical structures such as the alphabet, although they are formal structures, are nevertheless learned as serial behaviors and in practice we have little access to the formal structure. That is, we can recite the alphabet or sing a tune forward but must basically relearn the structure in the other direction to perform it that way.

For my purposes this is crucial in coming to understand social practice. As the material I have presented above argues, it seems most useful to speak of a single, unique action as a 'mediated action' based in the Vygotskian sociocultural psychology of mediated action of James Wertsch (1998), and to use the term 'social practice' to speak of such actions when they are instances or tokens of a chain of such actions which are taken to have a history. This is quite close to Bourdieu's (1977:78) suggestion that a practice is an action with a history, or Nishida's (1958) action-intuition which is based in the historical-body.

For my purposes, then, the narrowest unit of analysis – to be defined elsewhere – is the mediated action: that is, an action taken in real time as a unique and irreversible moment. To the extent that more than a single mediated action is taken to have a history, it is a social practice. That is, to the extent that the mediated action is a token of a type, an instance of a practice, we can speak of a social practice taking place. I believe making this distinction will help resolve the ambiguity left by Bourdieu and by Chouliaraki and Fairclough in their shifting definition of practice as both 'hardened into relative permanency' and as occurring in a particular 'time and place'. Crucial aspects of this concept of practice are these:

- a practice is defined narrowly; I have used handing an object from one person to another as my central example.
- a practice operates by a 'poor logic' ; that is, there is no assumption that it is in any way understood or commented upon by agents.
- a practice is grounded in mammalian, biological reality.
- a practice embeds not just actions but beliefs, values, and emotions.

Practice and habitus

In his *Outline of a theory of practice* Bourdieu (1977) introduced the idea of the habitus, which he defined there as

> systems of durable, transposable *dispositions*, structured structures predisposed to function as structuring structures.
>
> (Bourdieu 1977:72)

A bit later in the same chapter he defined the habitus as

> the durably installed generative principle of regulated improvisations [which] produces practices which tend to reproduce the regularities immanent in the objective conditions of the production of their generative principle.
>
> (Bourdieu 1977:78)

These definitions have been carried over virtually unchanged and word for word to his later revision (1990) and so I will not concern myself with making a reconciliation between other differences in these two texts of Bourdieu.

While phrases such as that about 'structured structures predisposed to function as structuring structures' are rather off-putting in a definition, the idea of the habitus itself as used throughout that work seems an important concept for the material location of the social world in the cumulative historical experience of the agent. Of course, it would be to indulge in a form of scholarly amnesia to neglect to recall comments such as that of Bateson (1972 – originally written in 1942) which points to the same notion:

> Perhaps the best documented generalization in the field of psychology is that, at any given moment, the behavioral characteristics of any mammal, and especially of man, depend upon the previous experience and behavior of that individual.
>
> (Bateson 1972:89)

Nishida, writing a bit before Bateson, wrote:

> The body is no longer [conceived as] a mere biological body, but a historical one.
>
> (Nishida 1958:196)

Or in another place:

> All our actions originate as action-intuition; they originate through a mirroring of the world by individuals.
>
> (Nishida 1958:217)

And:

> The concrete personality is essentially 'historical-bodily'. Society originates essentially as a historical production from the formed towards the forming.
>
> (Nishida 1958:229)

There seems little alternative when one comes down to it: structure in a material analysis can exist only in the somatic substance (including perceptions, memories, thoughts, musculature, and nervous system) of the individual human agent or in the extra-somatic substances of our world – our buildings, furniture, cityscapes, texts, and tools as well as, of course, other organisms not insignificantly including other humans. The contribution Bourdieu has made, then, is not in the invention of a concept so much as in reminding us that social theory must ultimately ground itself in the concrete realities of the physical and material world. The term he has proposed for this is habitus and it is, in my view, a good term as long as we proceed with two cautions. First, we should not let the concept slip between the material and the ideal or immaterial as Bourdieu allows it to do by sometimes referring to the habitus of a group, class, or, most often, a field. Second, we need to remind ourselves of the ultimate fuzziness of the boundary of the biological organism.

To take up the first issue, Bourdieu makes it clear when he introduces the concept of habitus that he is writing of the aggregated experience, conscious and unconscious, of the 'agent' – he is quite rightly evasive of terms such as 'person', 'human', 'individual', and any others which might very strongly signal 'volunteer-ism' or excessive autonomy in individual action. Nevertheless, when he writes of the 'cognitive and motivating structures making up the habitus' (p. 78) or of the law 'laid down in each agent by his earliest upbringing' it is clear he is speaking of the biological individual. Unfortunately, he then immediately idealizes this notion (p. 81) by arguing that because people are 'members of the same group or, in a differentiated society, the same class' they are 'endowed with an objective meaning that is at once unitary and systematic'.

I would argue that it is of considerable importance to decide whether or not person X and person Y have *identical* habitus or *the same* habitus. To say X and Y have *identical* habitus because X and Y have had the same history of action is to say that the habitus is, in fact, objective and located in the materiality of the human organism. To say that X and Y have *the same* undifferentiated and 'object-ive' habitus is to say that what is not in fact material, some ideal substance, is shared across two different material objects. To me this makes nonsense of the entire enterprise which is to do away with idealism in its objectivist and structural-ist forms. Further, it requires us to believe that it is possible for two human individuals to, in fact, have the same history, the same sequence of objective experiences, and to have taken the same actions. I would argue that there is simply no need for this obfuscation, and that it is quite sufficient to argue that two agents who have sufficiently overlapping habitus can be considered members of the same nexus of practice (or Discourse or activity system). Having said this, it is important to note that in his revision (1990) Bourdieu seeks to clarify the distinction between habitus (that of a person) and 'homologous habitus', that is, the like habitus[13] that 'underlie the unity of the life-style of a group or a class' (p. 55).

Of course this is a problematical solution. The first problem which the somatic interpretation of habitus raises is the problem of being a great deal more specific about the actual, concrete, historical objective conditions within which each sep-arate agent aggregates his or her habitus. The second problem is to theorize how two different habitus come to have sufficiently like amounts or types of social practices and linkages such that they might be recognizable as 'the same' prac-tices. Finally, it raises the question of how the many complexities of networks of practices and their linkages and of incommensurabilities of practice within the habitus are to be understood.

It is the purpose of this book to propose, first, that even though this is a complex enterprise, it is not theoretically impossible to do, and second, that it is our responsibility to put forward a coherent theory of practice that will take into consideration the complexities of the earliest accomplishment of social practice by infants.

Before going on to take up the question of how generally we can interpret the analysis I have given above, there remains the second question alluded to above of the fuzziness of the boundary between the human organism and the environment. To insist on the organismic, mammalian materiality of the habitus is not to return willy-nilly to the individualism and volunteerism Bourdieu and others are at pains to escape. It is rather to ground our theory in an ontology of the biological organism as organism-in-interaction with an environment.

To return for a moment to Bateson's (1972) often cited example of the blind man and the stick, by which he argues that 'the mind' is constituted in cycles of interactions with an environment:

> Obviously there are lots of message pathways outside the skin, and these and the messages which they carry must be included as part of the mental system whenever they are relevant.
>
> (Bateson 1972:458)

To illustrate this he first gives the example of a man cutting a tree with an axe, in which we must take into consideration not just the action of the man (nervous system, musculature, etc.) but also his perception including retinal images of the notch he is making in the tree and the axe itself as part of the perceptual system by which the actions are taken. He then goes on to ask:

> What about 'me' ? Suppose I am a blind man, and I use a stick. I go tap, tap, tap. Where do *I* start? Is my mental system bounded at the handle of the stick? Is it bounded by my skin? Does it start halfway up the stick? Does it start at the tip of the stick?
>
> (Bateson 1972:458)

On the same theme, Piaget has written (1969 [1929]):

> According to all the evidence it is impossible in any biological reaction whatsoever to separate the organism from its environment. The intellectual adaptation and the motor adaptation from which the former is derived are no exception to this rule. Reality is a complex system of exchanges and complementary currents, the first determined by the assimilation of things to the organism and the second by the adaptation of the organism to the facts of the environment. . . . There is thus in the beginning neither self nor external world but a *continuum*. The social factors also tend to the same result; from its earliest activities the baby is brought up in a social atmosphere.
>
> (Piaget 1969[1929]:235–6)

The position, then, that I want to take is that as I use it, habitus refers to the aggregate, cumulative, historical experience of the historical-biological individual which consists of a very large number of social practices, their linkages, and their systematic incommensurabilities as well. Social practices in this meaning are narrowly defined as actions with a history. That is, while a first instance – as we have seen with the case of an infant handing a crayon to her mother – we would not want to call a token of the type 'social practice', over a period of a year or so the child comes to have a habitus which includes the history of many occasions (actions) of handing which comes to constitute a structure which is a social practice. That is, she can exchange objects with people with whom she has not had the concrete experience before. This notion of habitus is no less grounded in socio-cultural historical objective reality, but it is concretized in the actual experience of the infant, not an idealized representation of the actions of a class. It is an additional theoretical problem to develop the argument which I will address in Chapter 5 that under some circumstances these social practices come to be located in social groupings such as class, ethnicity, and culture.

Other children: ontogenesis or ontogeneses?

Now it is necessary to clarify the nature of the claims I am making in this analysis. I have argued that one child, B, has, in the course of a year, come to develop a habitus which consists in part in the aggregation of actions which we can now call the social practice of handing. At what level can we develop a generalization from this and to what can this generalization apply?

The claim I am making is this: a social practice (any social practice) as I have defined it develops in the habitus of the person through the process I have described in detail for this one practice. In a sense this is a negative claim positioned against an objectivist, cognitivist, and structuralist view of social practice. That is, it is a claim about what a social practice is not. I am claiming that a social practice does not enter the habitus full-blown as a reversible, logical structure of reciprocal operations. While we can ultimately come to describe such a system through the observation of multiple instances of handing in the same person or across persons, I argue that for the individual, the practice is the aggregation, over a considerable period of time, of a history of concrete, specific acts of handing. Each of these acts is different from each other; each may be carried out with different participants; each may involve different objects; each has its own constraints on the act of handing; and each act may be different from the others in the linkages made with other social and discursive practices. What we refer to more abstractly as the social practice of handing is none other than this history and some small degree of 'predictability' for the social actor which arises from the momentum produced by this history.

Thus I make no claim at all of any regular developmental sequence that would hold from child to child. There is no reason to argue that handing a cookie successfully would occur before or after handing a crayon even though, as we have seen, B at one time was rather reluctant to hand a cookie but not a crayon. There is no reason to argue that handing an object and saying 'thank you' should occur before or after handing an object and saying its name. All of these specifics would arise quite accidentally in the course of the concrete, specific life of a particular child.

I am also rejecting the possible suggestion that all or any other child/caregiver groups would undertake these particular actions of constructing the practice of handing in this particular way. To develop this point I will make reference to the parallel body of work I did with our own daughter, Rachel, two years after the original project with B. I also include in my understanding of this process data which I collected on a one-year-old girl at Arctic Village, Alaska, and incidental data from other one-year-olds with whom I collected data but which I will not systematically develop here.

To begin with, as we saw in Example 13 above, Rachel at age 0:8.23 was engaged in social interactions which had to some extent carried with them the history of our interactions with B two years earlier. That is to say, B's actions and our own habitus which had developed in interaction with B, was concretely part of the interaction with Rachel. In that example we saw that S used 'chodai' in linkage with trying to get Rachel to hand an object to her. This is just one of the many historical influences of these interactions with B that became part of our own habitus.[14] Thus in the first place, no small part of Rachel's linguistic environment, if I can depart from a rigorous use of terms for a moment, was the research we did with B two years earlier. Rachel's handing practice is constructed to some extent upon portions of B's history through the habitus of her parents/researchers. I would argue that, far from being methodological corruption, this is, in fact, the nature of social life, and that any theory of practice and of social structure must take into account this cumulative, historical structuring of social interaction.

At the same time, this example shows another side of historical practice. In the interactions between B and M it would be legitimate to consider M's use of 'chodai' for 'please give that to me' a 'Japanese' word. That is, we can argue reasonably that M, as a native-born Japanese speaker, is speaking to her own daughter in Japanese. When S speaks to Rachel saying 'chodai', this can hardly be thought of as occurring 'in Japanese'. It would be much more to the point to call this 'M–B' language as that is where S learned it, and the history which is being brought to Example 13 is in no way *Japanese* history, it is *M–B* history, now nearly entirely separated from any location in national-historical culture.

To put this in terms of Wertsch's (1998) mediated action, the mediational means (the word 'chodai') carries with it a historical location in the Japanese language. When M uses it, because that location is linked to M's very complex competence with other mediational means in that network of mediational means (the Japanese language) as well as with the social practices of a particular community of practice (including other Japanese speakers), the mediational means brings to the situation of asking B to hand her something much of that linguistic and cultural history. Within those situations – our taping once a week and making transcriptions – we have altered the mediational means to a considerable extent. This has been done largely by unlinking it from the host of associated links with other Japanese language. For example, M says, 'Motte kinasai Wow-wow', in Example 24, as a more complex paradigmatic choice in place of 'chodai'. This paradigmatic choice is not within S's habitus and thus we know we would not find[15] in Example 13 that S would say 'Motte kinasai'. That is, 'chodai' should be paradigmatically patterned with 'some' and 'share' which were B's rather distinctive utterances at the time we did the original research, and it is *that* M–B 'language' from which S is appropriating 'chodai', not 'the' Japanese language.

In a second way we can see that Rachel's habitus for the practice of handing was constituted of many rather different specific actions. In Example 40 just below, we see R is attempting to 'play catch' with Rachel.

Example 40 Age: 0:11.30

Rachel	R	S	Context
[kʻɛʃ·ɛʻ]	Here, catch. Catch. ☺ Yeah, you caught it. Throw it now. Thank you.	☺	R tossing 'ball' (of yarn) to Rachel. Rachel 'throws' ball by handing to R.

It is possible that Rachel was a bit younger than B when she 'arrived' at the Piagetian Stage of the Tertiary Circular Reaction. I would not want to engage here in an argument either for or against Piaget's ideas about these cognitive stages and am only using them as reference points. It seems clear enough that at some point an infant does not easily separate the self from objects and that at some later point she does. It does not seem significant for my purposes to establish just at what point this happens nor to argue comparatively that such a development happens before or after another one. What does seem important in the analysis of B's development of the social practice of handing is that there is abundant evidence that this was happening socially *at the same time* as it was happening 'cognitively'. That is, there is simply no means of arguing that the social development or the cognitive development have happened independently. B was taken as handing objects somewhat before she could be attested to have reached Piaget's Tertiary Circular Reaction.

Here in Example 40 we can see R trying to engage Rachel in a game of catch. The game of catch is predicated upon throwing (or dropping), which is the classical analytical action upon which separation of objects and self can be attested. While Rachel showed some ability to capture an object thrown to her, this is not sufficient evidence for the separation of self and object. On the other hand we see that Rachel does not throw the ball but moves to R and pushes the ball at him. As with B two years earlier, this act of 'handing' is taken by R as partial completion of the social interaction and, as with B, R says 'Thank you'. We should note that this is appropriate only if it is handing that has occurred, not throwing. That is, what I would like to suggest is that in Rachel's case we see the same presumption of a meaningful action on the part of the child which is construed by the adult as handing. It is an action which even the adult began as characterizing differently, as throwing, but then he repositions it as handing when that is what, in fact, is accomplished jointly between the two of them.

I would not want to make more of this example than it deserves. I include it here to suggest that the collection of experiences which come to constitute the habitus for the social practice of handing do not have to be the same in any way for the social practice to be constructed. What is important is the interaction between the child's actions and the construal of those actions on the part of others, in these cases the primary caregivers.

One final example illustrates how closely tied are the actions of the caregivers and those of the child in constructing the child's (and the adults'!) habitus.

Example 41 Age: 0:11.30

Rachel	R	S	Context
	Hey, you wanna play catch? Hey, you wanna play catch? Oh, I was gonna see if she could find the ball by herself. I can't do my experiments.	☺ ☺ ☺ Nope, Mommy's sabotaging Daddy's experiments.	S reaches to get the ball for Rachel at the same time that Rachel turns to reach for the ball.

In Example 41 R is trying to discover two things: (1) would Rachel be able to recognize the appropriate action suggested by 'play catch' – she had said 'catch' a few minutes earlier, and (2) would she respond to an indirect request to hand something to him? As we see, this attempt was 'sabotaged' by S's reaching for the ball and handing it to Rachel. Throughout my transcripts are examples like this one in which the child is assisted in interpreting the indirect or presupposed or even direct request of someone else. Thus it is not just that the adult construes the child's act as something which fits within some more regularly formulated social practice – in many cases others present lend a hand in constructing the action itself, not just the discursive construal of the action.

One further point needs to be made here concerning an overall difference between the interactions between B and M and the ones we have recorded between Rachel and R or S, that is ourselves. Here in Example 41, we see that R has asked 'You wanna play catch?' He does not say 'Where's the ball?' or 'Daddy chodai' or 'Give me the ball'. That is, the nominalization is not directly used with Rachel, it is presupposed. In the same way the expected action is presupposed. While it would take another study which would focus specifically on this question, my re-examination of these data indicate that in the interactions between B and

M there was a much higher degree of explicitness, nominalization, pointing, and direct requests for actions than there were in interactions between Rachel and R and S. In the latter case there were presupposed actions and indirect mentions. For my purposes here I only want to argue that while both B and Rachel have come to adulthood as people who can relatively successfully hand objects to others and even to each other, they did not in any way have identical social interactions with primary caregivers.

If I were to summarize the differences between B and Rachel in a few words, I would say that to begin with, from very early in her life caregiving between B and M included much handing as B was fed by bottle whereas Rachel was breastfed for nearly seventeen months, that is, until she was well beyond having developed the tertiary circular reaction. A second difference I have observed in the data I have is that even as late as the beginning of the second year, Rachel was very often the object of handing herself. B was carried by M very frequently, but not nearly so often transferred between M and F (B's father) or other adults. I do not have the data to be able to analyze beyond these rather casual observations what differences in habitus this might have produced in the two children. What I do want to note here, however, is that the most fundamental of social interactions, those of caregiving between the infant and her mother and father, were noticeably different between these two children.

In addition to these differences are at least two others that must be remembered. First, B was a second child and Rachel was a first child. While in this analysis I have largely ignored the older sister, C, she was present and participating in virtually all of the interactions we observed with B, both those we have tape recorded and those we observed as members of the family. She often made interesting contributions to the construction of social practices in B's repertoire. These varied from contributory to obstructive. Rachel had no such 'other' against which to construct her own habitus.

Second, as I have suggested above, naming in linkage with handing was much rarer with Rachel than it was with B. As I have argued, B had come in the second year of life to use handing as a central means of topic control. I have no cases of Rachel using this same handing/naming/topic control linkage of social practices.

The point I would like to draw from this brief digression into the development of the habitus of another child is simply that my data argue for two conclusions: (1) a social practice is aggregated in the habitus through a unique and historical chain of actions, and (2) that unique and historical chain results, nevertheless, in the production of common or homologous habitus. Put in a few words, B is different from Rachel; but B and Rachel can successfully hand things to each other. B and Rachel came to the social practice differently but the social practice constituted through these different pathways is nevertheless a homologous social practice.

Class, social group, culture

This argument leaves us with the obvious question of whether we want to or can say anything about class, social group, culture, or any of the other social structures above the level of the immediate family and caregivers. I would answer this by saying that certainly we can and should, though I must face the argument that I have not done so yet. This will be taken up again in Chapter 5 when I address the idea of the nexus of practice. I can mitigate my position to some extent by two arguments: (1) social class is somewhat more difficult to 'see' in these very immediate, concrete, caregiving social interactions at the infant level, and (2) we have, in fact, 'seen' social class in operation throughout these examples without commenting upon it until now. Furthermore, we have here an invisible cultural voice in a body of data which I was unable to collect as part of my original data.

Class

The transcripts I have studied are full of objects to be handed. These objects include crayons, papers, books, food, tape recorders and many others. B's home was, in fact, an abundant source of materials with which to learn the practice of handing. As members of a family placed solidly within the American middle class, B and M (as well as the researchers) not only had available all these resources for handing, but also could take for granted the process of academic research into a child's language. *A fortiori* our own home was one in which academic research into a child's language was the dominant family theme when Rachel was born (she was born within a few weeks of when I defended my dissertation on B). It would be disingenuous in the extreme to suggest that what I have described here was independent of or free from class associations.

The position I would like to take here is that on the one hand this research was conducted within a class-constructed environment of social interactions which have as their primary relevant aspects here (1) the abundant presence of material objects including books, crayons, and other pedagogical materials, and (2) a positive valuation on academic research into the cognitive development of members of their own class. On the other hand, I would like to argue that the social practice of handing which has become part of the habitus of B and of Rachel *is not* limited to actions taken with other members of this class. That is to say, I would argue, though I realize I have not demonstrated it here, that B or Rachel can successfully hand objects to people who are not members of their social class. To put this in a few words, the social practice of handing, while aggregated in the habitus of a member of a particular class, is nevertheless homologous with that practice in members of other social classes. I regret that I do not (yet) have the research or the data to establish how the social practice of handing is constituted in members of other groups or classes so that we can begin to see how handing is linked to other class-based practices in the overall production of class (and other social group) habitus.

Culture

This brings us to the question of culture. There are two questions to be dealt with here. The first of them has been suggested above when we examined M's use of the term 'chodai' followed by S's use of 'chodai'. In the first case I argued that 'chodai' in M's use was a case of the use of a Japanese discursive practice. Said more simply, she was speaking a Japanese word as a Japanese mother to her child. In the second case, however, when S was using 'chodai' she was using a B–M word in speaking to her own child. One might say this more simply by saying she was speaking a family word as a family member to her child. That is to say, S had to some extent replaced or stripped the 'Japanese' language history and used a B–M interaction history as the social location of that term. Here we see that 'culture' cannot be constructed out of the use of any particular social or discursive practice but must be construed within its particular, historical sequence and nexus of practice (Chapter 5). For S, 'chodai' is what B and M say; for M 'chodai' is what Japanese mothers (and no doubt others) say.

So the first question of culture to be dealt with is this: how, when, and under what circumstances can we say a social practice is a 'cultural' social practice? I would argue that in the B–M case, a cultural argument can be made to some small extent. B is in a minor way becoming a Japanese child. In Rachel's case she is not becoming a Japanese child; she is becoming a child of researchers in child language who studied B. The socialization in the first case is to Japanese language and culture, in the second case to academic research. The question we need to develop a research agenda to answer is: what are the conditions in which we can rightfully consider social practice to be cultural social practice?

The second cultural question is much more difficult: how do we conduct the ethnographic research necessary to study the first question when, as I have suggested, the study of children's language is itself embedded in social class and culture? It is no accident that the data I have available are from these particular children. In the summer of 1972 we went to Arctic Village, Alaska. Our purpose in going was to locate a child with whom we could conduct a study to parallel the study of B's language development but who was learning a language other than English. We found a child there who was almost exactly the right age for such a study. But what we also found was that it was nearly impossible to construct the circumstances through which we could make tape recordings of her speech. In two months we were only able to contrive to be in this child's presence for about one hour. We did manage to record that hour, but it was clear that the family and the community regarded it as quite inappropriate for strangers such as ourselves to make tape recordings of a young child. Some years later an Athabaskan woman from the adjoining Koyukon language community told us that it was 'something like child abuse' to closely pay attention to what children say. That is, the research I have described here is in at least one community considered unconscionable behavior in respect to children.

I would like to conclude three things from these considerations: (1) first, we should consider social practice to always be grounded in the practices of particular social, cultural, and class groups (nexus of practice); (2) second, we should not assume that social practices do not operate successfully across the boundaries of these social groups just because the habitus is produced within a particular group; and (3) we must also consider it highly problematical to draw conclusions on 'human' (i.e. universal human) behavior on the basis of analyses made within groups whose social practice supports those analyses.

Commensurability of practice: contradictions in the habitus

If what I have argued here is right, then we must consider the habitus to be a complex network of social practices. These practices must inevitably be of different 'strengths', that is, some will be new practices at the earliest stages of aggregation and others will be ones consisting of many, many actions over a long period of time. Among these practices will be those which are very narrowly construed within a group as tightly constrained as a mother–child pair or, perhaps, a family or other group of intimates. Other practices will be the basis for actions taking place with members of other groups and with complete strangers – social practices which cross many lines of class, culture, or ethnicity. Among and between these practices will be linkages of practices which are idiosyncratic, linkages which serve as badges of membership in nexus or communities of practice, and linkages to which little or no meaning can be ascribed. Put another way, the habitus must be considered a complex network of both commensurable and incommensurable practices which produce fissures of contradictions for every person.

Calhoun (1995) has argued that rather than consider the habitus of members of the same class (or other social group) to be the same or homologous (Bourdieu 1990), we must look much more closely into the question of incommensurable practice (Kuhn 1962) out of which the boundaries of groups are ultimately produced.

Incommensurable practices are of several kinds which would include at least the following problems:

Simultaneity. One cannot do two things at once. One cannot play basketball and football at the same time. In the broad sense of practice, then, the practices of these two sports are incommensurable. There is, of course, no restriction on sequencing. One might play one game in the morning and the other in the evening (though see *materiality* below). More narrowly conceived, one cannot take a jump shot and do a layup at the same time. When the Sergeant Major handed Hong Kong's Governor Patten the flag, they could not accomplish the handing and the saluting in the same move, and the two participants in this act became momentarily confused about which practice they were engaged in. At a more mundane level, one cannot give way both to the left and to the right. Pedestrians who give way by moving to the right when approaching others who give way by moving to the left ultimately find themselves in each other's way when they are, in fact, intending to pass without further notice.

Materiality/physicality. Some practices alter the physical or material structure of the persons involved. A game of football in the morning might well exhaust the player or leave bruises and muscle strains which would be incompatible with a game of basketball in the afternoon. The hand positions and muscle structures which are developed for playing the classical guitar are to some extent incompatible with playing the violin. The extended fingernails needed for flamenco guitar click on the ivory keys of the piano and are thus incompatible with at least classical piano performance. Any social practice which produces, over time, an alteration in the physical, muscle, or nervous structure of the human body will clearly become incommensurable with any other social practices requiring a different physical, muscle, or nervous structure. The Japanese practice of sitting cross-legged at a low table for meals is inscribed on the body of elderly Japanese in a way that makes this an unremarkable action. A visiting American businessman who has not sat this way since his youth is physically incapacitated in his attempt to show respect by joining his counterpart at Japanese-style meals. To join this universe of practice is not only a cognitive or conceptual matter but one of intense, difficult, and perhaps ultimately impossible physical training. While we are aware of these materialities of practice in reference to sport, I would argue that there is likely to be some degree of this physicality involved in any social practice.

Structure. Color terms provide a clear example of incommensurability of practice based in some formal or semiotic system of representation. As Berlin and Kay (1969) have argued, the Chinese term *qing* represents a point on the color spectrum exactly intermediate between English *blue* and *green*. Thus *qing*, and *blue*, or *green* cannot be used in unmodified translation of each other. As a kind of social practice, translation between Chinese and English can never be managed as a simple matter of conceptual equivalents. Languages, of course, are enormous complexes of such incommensurabilities. Wierzbicka (1985, 1991, 1993, 1994a, 1994b, 1998) has explored a very wide range of such lexico-semantic incommensurabilities across world languages.

Ontology. What I have phrased just above as a structural question might also be thought of as an ontological issue. As Calhoun's (1995) example illustrates, in Chinese and Western medical systems, not only is there a difference in treatments and technologies, the very object of analysis and treatment – the human body – is ontologically produced as a different reality. Closer to the home of this study, I would argue following Piaget that what occurs in the first year or so of life of a child is the ontological reconstruction of the world beginning with an undifferentiated self and moving into a self which is separable and differentiated from objects which are themselves constructed ontologically as having an existence independent of the knowing self. One criticism of Piagetian psychological process, of course, is that his research and writing constructs a distinctively Western ontology. It has been argued by other psychologists (Allinson 1989; Bond 1986, 1996; Hsu 1953, 1983, 1985) that the self constructed within Chinese society is based in a fundamentally different ontology. This leaves open for further examination, then, the question of whether an infant handing an object to her mother in China is engaged in the same action, the same social practice, as an infant and her Swiss mother.

Complementarity. Some social practices are not incommensurable in any of the ways mentioned above, but are linked, at least within some social groups, in a complementary way such that one practice only occurs when some other practice does not. Thus conversation is complementarily linked to silence in courtrooms, religious services, public lectures, and other formal social events. Having a chat with the person sitting next to me does not make it physically impossible for the teacher to deliver the lecture, for the priest to give a sermon, or for the judge to inform the jury of their responsibilities, but such a chat is proscribed as an incommensurable practice in such settings. This sort of linkage is, of course, very 'cultural' in its definition. I would argue that, in fact, much of what we think of as distinctive of particular social groups consists not in the practices themselves but in the network of complementary linkages among them.

There is another set of complementary practices which Bateson (1972) discussed as producing complementary schismogenesis. That is, more of practice X is responded to with more of Y. The case discussed by ourselves (Scollon and Scollon 1981) is when the conversational practice of rapid turn exchange is brought into play by the habitus of one speaker in a group and slower turn exchange is brought into play by one or more others. The result of this complementarity in practice produces increasing amounts of talk in the 'faster' participants and increasing amounts of silence in the 'slower' ones.

Commensurable practices are the basis for much of the production of group, class, or categorical habitus. Our understanding of commensurable practices must include at least the following several types:

Unlinked. Some social practices have no relationships among them, such as eating with chopsticks (or knife, fork, and spoon) and driving a car. One might say that eating with any hand-held utensils is incommensurate with driving but the specific (and cultural) practices are simply irrelevant to each other. Practices for handing objects are not linked to practices for television watching in most cases, though, of course, one might find linkages between handing and the social disposition of the remote controller. Ang (1996), for example, has noted that favored viewing position as well as disposition of the controller are ceded most often to men. The key here is that many practices are in most cases just irrelevant to each other because they very rarely occur at the same time or as aspects in the production of the same actions.

Linked, but disruptive. A practice may be linked to another practice, but in such a way that one disrupts the other and the social trick of accomplishing the action is overcoming this disruptive link. One thinks of sports and other cultural phenomena such as classical musical performances as being based in disruptive linkages.

Running around a track is much easier if there are no hurdles placed in the way. It is easier to answer questions about one's research when that questioning practice is linked to the practice of having a conversation over a cup of coffee than when it is linked to the practices of formal examinations around university conference tables. In Examples 11 and 12 we saw that it was difficult at first for B to link handing practice to eating practice.

Linked but not integrated. Some practices are linked but not as an integrated network or nexus of practice. Driving a car is linked very often with practices for reading commercial road signs. They very often happen together as part of the same act but one can quite safely and practically manage a car without giving over attention to billboards. In some cases it might be argued that there is a disruptive linkage, as in Hong Kong when for many years it was prohibited to post flashing or moving lights for any purposes but traffic regulation. This linkage is not made in Tokyo where street corners in some cases are blizzards of flashing lights among which traffic signals are hard put to compete for the driver's attention.

Linked and integrated. Some practices are not only commensurate and not only linked, but one practice has important consequences for another practice. As we have argued elsewhere (Scollon and Scollon 1981, 1991, 1995), practices for turn exchange (such as longer or shorter pauses between turns) are linked to quite separable practices for topic introductions (early or later in the social interaction) so that if some participant in a conversation *both* takes shorter turn exchange pauses *and* practices early introduction of topics, it would be virtually impossible for him or her to discover a topic which another participant, who is different on both of these practices, wishes to introduce.

Such linked and integrated practices are, I would argue, much of the stuff of class, group, or categorical membership. That is, one might find one of these practices as a homologous practice across very different groups – New Yorkers and Tokyoites are often said to turn over turns very rapidly – but topic introduction in some cases is very deductive (early introduction) for New Yorkers and inductive (topic introduction follows extended face work) for Tokyoites. Thus it is the linkage of turn exchange to topic introduction which produces the experience of cultural difference, not the practices for turn exchange which are quite homologous.

Discourse, practice, and habitus

In concluding I would like simply to reiterate my central argument. It is of considerable importance to the project of a critical analysis of practice, discourse, and habitus to analyze concrete cases of specific practices. Here I have argued that this project is made difficult at best and perhaps impossible if we focus our attention on too general a notion of practice, as it is ultimately impossible to falsify the claim that every practice has a reflexive or discursive element. If our concern is with understanding practice our focus must attend rather carefully to the construction of practice in the habitus. While it is not the only way to achieve this attention, the study of the ontogenesis of a single practice – handing in this case – is a useful site in which to examine the slow aggregation of habitus in social actions.

As a limiting case, the ontogenesis of the social practice of handing an object from one person to another has shown that, while we can see the construction of the habitus for this practice evolving over the course of a year, it is very difficult to maintain that there is any unique or necessary linkage between this social practice and the discursive practices which have accompanied the separate actions of handing. We have seen that the social practice of handing is pedagogized as a site upon which to construct the naming of objects, it is sequentialized or dialogical-ized, that is, the discursive practice focuses on how this act fits into a sequence of acts – 'give me X + handing + thank you', it is exploited for conversational interactional control, and in some cases it is played out without any discursive element at all.

The argument I hope to have made here is that we cannot take at face value the claim that every practice has a reflexive discursive element (Chouliaraki and Fairclough 1999) if we take the word 'practice' at this material, concrete, specific (count noun) level of analysis. At the same time it is clear that discursive practice is very closely linked to many of the acts in which the social practice of handing is constituted. My purpose in this argument is not to undermine the project of critical discourse analysis and its focus on discursive practice. On the contrary, it is to suggest a theoretical and methodological basis for moving the project forward through the longitudinal and ethnographic study of the constitution of social practice in the habitus of specific social actors. This is the task which I will take up in the following chapter.

NOTES

1   Sandy Silberstein has pointed out that birds feed their young by placing food directly into their mouths, which is a useful reminder of the sub-mammalian stratum of such transfers.
2   In using Gumperz's term 'inference' I do not mean to suggest that these inferences are conscious, rational, or logical processes of drawing meaning from analyzed action but rather to insist that conscious and rational process cannot operate meaningfully at this level because of the ongoing flow in real time. I would prefer to use the term 'practical inference' to emphasize the unconscious nature of this 'inferential' process.
3   Wertsch (1998) uses the term 'mediated action' for this moment and I have adopted his usage (Scollon 1998).
4   Ages of the child throughout are given as 'years:months.days', thus 2:0.12 indicates two years and 12 days of age.
5   Elsewhere (Scollon and Scollon 1981, 1991, 1995) we have argued that this practice must be localized with at least a 'North American' social domain, as other practices can be attested for Northern Athabaskans and for Chinese in Taiwan and, in some cases, Hong Kong.
6   The author is husband of Brenda's cousin, Suzanne Scollon. Both of us were present as active participants in all of the situations which I recorded for analysis, as was the mother and the older sister (Charlotte) of Brenda.

7 We might also recall Karl Lashley's argument about serial behavior made many years ago. While the logical (ordinal) structure of such series as the alphabet or a song are such that 'b' always follows 'a', 'p' is always two letters after 'n' and 'n' always two before 'p', nevertheless when asked to say what letter follows 'j' we can say 'k' a great deal more easily than we can say that 'i' immediately precedes 'j'. That is, our knowledge of these serial orders reflects our learning of them in a particular order more than our logical knowledge of their internal structuring.

8 I hesitate to introduce 'cultural' factors except where they are directly and obviously relevant, but it will be useful for the reader to know that Brenda's mother was born in Japan and is a naturalized US citizen. Her father was born in Hawaii of Chinese parents. The father's father was born in the Zhongshan area of China.

9 But please see the discussion of Example 13 below where the 'Japanese' status of this utterance is more fully examined.

10 This study was undertaken beginning 4 April 1974, at birth, and paralleled this study of Brenda for the first year and a half of life. Most of the materials collected and prepared have not been reported before this. Some of that research found its way into our comparative study at Fort Chipewyan (Scollon and Scollon 1981).

11 We can ignore the chance utterance 'read the book' which seems much of a piece with B's 'chodai' in Example 10, that is, it is impossible to assert that she has 'said' this phrase and, in fact, neither of her parents heard this at the time as having said anything at all. The transcript given here is based on a relistening made in 1999, 25 years after the fact, and should not be taken overly seriously.

12 I have already noted in Chapter 1 that my own thinking about practice was first based in the Buddhist philosophical writings of Nishida (1958).

13 I take *habitus* to be both the singular and the plural form as is the case with *nexus*.

14 Twenty-five years later, long after B and her family have forgotten them, we continue to jokingly use 'some' and 'share' within our own family to mean 'Here, I'm giving you this' and 'Would you give me that?' respectively.

15 I am aware of the impossibility in practice theory of making the statement 'we would not find', as this implies knowledge not only of actual practice but of some generative schema for that practice which is specifically denied in a rigorous practice theory account. Nevertheless, it would be bulky in all such cases to say something closer to the truth, which would be: 'Having a large homologous habitus with S and knowing that in no circumstances over either the seven years prior to this act or the twenty-some years since has she ever said this, I am confident that she would not have said it.'

3 On the ontogenesis of a social actor

From object to agency in baby talk

From dogs to gift exchanges again

Yesterday on the way through the park where I often see people exercising their dogs, I overheard this moment of conversation:

('sing-song' intonation) Give it to me, give it to me, give it to me.
(dog drops ball; intonation even more extremely accentuated) Good girl; good girl.

Yesterday when I bought a cup of coffee I participated in this conversation:

Cashier: That'll be two-twenty five.
RS: Here, that should do it.
Cashier: Thanks.

In both cases we have the exchange of an object. I have argued in Chapter 2 that it is difficult to construct the first case as a social practice in the narrow sense in which I want to use the term. Perhaps not even Bourdieu would want to argue that exchanges between people and their dogs are in themselves social practices even though I am sure he, and we, would want to situate the activity of playing with animals in the park within some domain of social practice. Goffman, like Bourdieu, would no doubt also want to see this talk to the dog as socially occasioned action, much as he argued that our response cries when tripping over a crack in the sidewalk while walking along in a public walkway are social talk (Goffman 1981).

The question, of course, is: what sort of talk is this? On the one hand I would be happy to accede to the common pet owner's notion that her dog can understand her. Bateson (1972) has argued cogently that there is a mammalian substratum of communication underlying our more referential or ideational utterances. But one would not want to attribute to the dog anything like a lexical knowledge of the words used ('give', 'it', 'to', 'me', 'good', 'girl') nor knowledge of any sort of lexico-grammatical ability to produce them as utterances nor even interpret them as constructions. At best we would want to grant Bateson's phatic level of mammalian communication in this exchange. And so the question remains: what sort of talk is this? Why the particular pronoun and level of politeness? Why 'Give it to me' and not 'Drop that fool ball' but sung with the same sweet mammalian voice?

Because we ask such questions in paying attention to the pet owner and her dog, we should not forget to also ask them when we're attending to the purchase of a cup of coffee. Why do we not expect to see the exchange:

Cashier: That'll be two-twenty five.
RS: Here, that should do it.
Cashier: Good boy, good boy.

The answer, as it has been often spelled out in several places (Sinclair and Coulthard 1975; Mehan 1983; Scollon and Scollon 1995), is that these situations are different genres of discourse and therefore provide different generic 'slots' to be filled. Such an answer, however, while appearing to be an answer, has had to make recourse to an objectivist schema of genres, slots, typical forms and formulas which it might be difficult to make square with actual practice. If one is comparing this 'dog talk' to the service encounter (Merritt 1976a, 1976b, 1978) one can objectivize two distinctive genres and the rules for the provision of utterances within each one. But if one begins to move further afield to include classroom exchanges, there is little to distinguish the 'handing' that occurs between the dog and the pet owner from the pedagogical questioning that takes place in the elementary classroom. Do we argue here for two distinct but very similar genres – classroom talk and dog talk? And if so, how do we account for my main interest here – baby talk – or the talk of nurses to patients and the rest of what amounts to an unbounded continuum of forms?

I have argued at some length in Chapter 2 that the action of handing in each case arises out of the person's habitus as a unique social action within a particular set of concrete circumstances. Ontogenetically one comes to talk about handing as a social practice when one sees a sufficient history of the practice across a reasonably wide variety of circumstances. In the early instances of the handing done by a child, I have argued that this cannot be thought to be purposive action on the part of the child at all but, instead, I have argued, as have others (Lyra 1999), that the action is construed by caregivers as a social action. In the examples I have given over the course of the second year of life, what we have seen is that in the beginning the child makes movements which are taken as actions, construed as actions, and therefore in some crucial social sense must be thought of as actions. Later on, however, what we see is that the child becomes a much more active agent in this process of acting/construing so that by the time she has reached two years of age, the construal of caregivers is much better described as negotiation between the child and the caregivers. It is, perhaps, this agentive resistance[1] which is our warrant in saying that the social practice has been aggregated in the child's habitus.

But what of the talk? I have argued, to some extent against the position taken by Chouliaraki and Fairclough (1999), that there is no clear link between the linguistic accompaniments of these acts of handing and the acts themselves. In Chapter 2 I found at least five different discursive accompaniments, though there would certainly be more with further data:

silence
nomination
functional directive
interpersonal directive
behavioral directive

In some cases I found the linguistic focus was on the action (behavioral directive): 'Here, take this.' In others it was upon the object (nomination):'This is a pen.' There was a focus on the expected outcome (functional directive): 'You could use this.' And in still other cases the focus was upon the relationship (interpersonal directive): 'Could I ask you to hold this for me?' And in yet other cases there was no discursive practice linked to handing at all (silence).

If we conceive of a social practice in the narrow sense in which we can say that handing is a social practice, it is very hard to evaluate Chouliaraki and Fairclough's claim that 'all practices have an irreducible discursive aspect, not only in the sense that all practices involve use of language to some degree' (1999:26), or that 'people always generate representations of what they do as part of what they do' (1999:22). I cannot determine any irreducible discursive aspect of the act of handing, either in the case of infants or in the case of adults. An act is not a practice, of course, even within the narrow definition I am developing here. We might want to rephrase what I have said here as having found that there is no unique or fixed functional linguistic/discursive accompaniment to any of the acts of handing I have analyzed and so the question remains: is there any discursive practice that is associated in some irreducible way with the *practice* of handing (as opposed to the separate actions)?

To examine this question I will return to the specific cases of handing which we have already examined to see if there is, not in the specific acts of handing but in the practice overall, any 'representation of what they do as part of what they do'. I will argue that even though I have not found any unique and therefore 'irreducible' discursive practice which is linked to the practice of handing, there is a lot of talk. I will then argue that what much of this talk is about is the discursive representation of the social actor. That is, what I will argue is that the discursive practice which accompanies handing is not focused upon the handing itself as a social practice but, rather, both the handing and the talk – the discursive practice – are focused upon the discursive construction of persons as social actors. In the beginning of life, talk which positions the infant as an object in the world is notably mixed with talk which ascribes social agency to the infant even when there is little behavioral possibility of this agency. By the second year of life, I will argue, the talk has moved predominantly into the domain of acceding agency to the child by others and by the child's increasing assertion of social agency.

The limiting case

I want to open this discussion with the limiting case of an infant who is just in her third day of life. This child, our own daughter Rachel, was being visited by her grandmother (GM) and her eleven-year-old auntie, Suzanne's younger sister. The transcription below requires important elaboration because it fails to capture a very wide range of 'sing-song' intonation, lightened or thickened voice qualities, and rapid tempo changes including speaking both much faster and much slower than usual. Other features of 'baby talk' are more clearly indicated, such as grammatical reductions, lexical forms, repetitions, vocatives, summonses, and the rest. These will be taken up in turn below.

Example 42 Age: 0:0.3

Rachel	S	R	GM (grandmother)	Auntie	Comments
(crying or fussing throughout)		What's the date? 6th? April 6th?			S is holding Rachel
	Oh yeah.				
		What? 2 days old?			
	Yeah.				
		What time?			
	Ten to twelve.				
		Ten to twelve.	Hungry . . . Oh. Hungry. E::yes. I know. Oh. Ye:::s.		
	It's not time to be hungry. One o' clock is your feeding time. ☺				
			No. Hungry now! Hungry now.		
				Whyn't you open your eyes? Oh, she got nice eyes.	
	Yeah.		Ye:::s. Oh, what dey doing to you, hah Rachel?		
	Don't worry.				
			Sure:::		

Example 42 continued

Rachel	S	R	GM (grandmother)	Auntie	Comments
(sneeze)			Say, Hi Auntie. Hi, Auntie. Very pretty. She got double eyelids. Double eyelids. And she's fat. Oh, gesundheit, gesundheit. Ooh.	Look at her eyes ain't dey pretty [pʷɪdi]	

The set of discursive practices often called 'baby talk' form a complex set of linguistic features ranging from prosodic and other paralinguistic overlays on the linguistic form to register characteristics of the forms themselves. If we begin with just what we can find in this example, we see first of all the contrasting case. This stretch of conversation begins with R and S ignoring the infant Rachel. Their first conversational sequence, in which they fix the date and time of the recording for the sake of labelling the tape, sets a kind of baseline for their normal speech, intonation, and interaction style. It is notable that this occurs within the general conversation in which the infant is fussing, whining, and crying a bit and GM and Auntie are saying a variety of things to the infant and to each other. That is, this opening sequence might be labelled *without baby talk* (WI). That is, it is speech that does not take the presence of the infant or, in fact, the others, into account in its formulation. This is said as an aside of this *with* of two people (Goffman 1981), on record for the tape, but off record within the conversation then in progress.

Several of GM's utterances are the common stuff of baby talk. She speaks *to* Rachel in a cooing, sing-song voice. The first word, 'hungry', is long and drawn out. This sequence is said very slowly, about perhaps one-fourth GM's normal rate of speech. Pitch is highly variable. One could represent these pitches both much higher than normal and much lower than normal, as follows:

```
Hungry.        hungry. E              I    ow.        Y

                        e              kno             e
.................................e...........................s
        Oh,                     yes,        Oh.        s.
```

These same features are used again in her other utterances, such as the response to Rachel's sneeze just below as well. Furthermore, there is phonological alteration as in 'What dey doing to you', which might be thought of as deriving from GM's Hawaiian English Creole speech, but a few minutes later in another case of speaking to the infant, GM says 'what's the matter?' with a highly distinctive phonological form:

[hᵂɔčəmʸætʕə]

And, of course, there are grammatical 'simplifications' in other stretches of this conversation, such as:

Oh, Gramma rock-a-bye baby. Gramma rock-a-bye baby. Gramma know.

This sort of babytalk might be labelled *to baby talk* (TO). It is said with the gaze fixed on the eyes of the infant and expresses sympathy for the state of discomfort being attributed in this TO to the infant, including the pronoun 'you' in 'What dey doing to you, hah, Rachel?' and elsewhere.

Another aspect of baby talk in general is the very high use I have found in my data of kin terms and vocatives. This 'hah, Rachel?' or 'say, Hi Auntie' just below is perhaps difficult to quantify, but in this study I found in this very early speech to the infant a strikingly high amount of the use of kin terms for self and other reference. This is much like M's frequent handing request, 'Mommy chodai'. Later when B (and Rachel) are older we find that 'Give it to me' has begun to appear in these interpersonal requests, but at these earliest stages of social interaction there seems to be a major concern with identifying the participants by kin relationship and by name. We have only to imagine the chair of a business meeting saying to her secretary, 'Bobby. Bobby. Give the minutes to the Chair now please', to realize the extreme distinctiveness of these vocatives and self-labelings within baby talk.

Speaking without regard to the infant (WI) and to the infant (TO) do not exhaust the possibilities of baby talk, however. Far from it. S's utterance begins as TO, as indicated by the pronoun 'your' as well as a light, soft, breathy voice quality. Furthermore, this is said extremely rapidly – much faster than S's normal speech or her speech in the 'baseline' WI just above. But then without any change in these baby-talk characteristics she responds sequentially to GM's 'No. Hungry now!' not as in GM's speech as *for baby talk* (FO) but as what I could call *around baby talk* (AR). What I mean to capture here is that GM has shifted from an alignment as an adult speaking baby talk to the infant (TO) to speaking on her behalf in response to her mother's insistence that it isn't time for her to eat. This 'No, hungry now' is spoken to S *for Rachel*. While it is still baby talk (i.e., lightened 'baby' stage voice) is it uttered with infant firmness. S's response does not dispute GM's claim nor does she reassert her own insistence that it is not time; she agrees, but by staying within the intonational and paralinguistic register she is speaking neither for herself (WI) nor to the infant (TO) nor for the infant (FO), which leads me to argue that here, as in many other cases, we find the register used in the presence of the infant, speaking from the voicing of an adult, to another adult. I call this *around baby talk* (AR).

Switches in alignment or changes in footing (Goffman 1981), if you like, occur rather frequently and quickly in this conversation. GM switches within utterance as in:

> (FO) No. Hungry now! Hungry now. (TO) Yes. Oh, what dey doing to you, hah Rachel? Sure. Say, 'Hi Auntie'. (FO) Hi Auntie.

She opens this 'turn' – and it is very difficult to establish turns here as there are multiple participants responding to each other and often from differently established footings – speaking *for* the infant. She switches back to speaking *to* Rachel but then the 'repeated' phrase, 'Hi Auntie', is said with the second one nearly an octave above the first which is already high in GM's vocal register. That is, she first says *to* Rachel what she should say and then says it *for* her to the Auntie (GM's daughter).

This is followed by an important alignment from the point of view of positioning, utterances *about the baby* (AB). Unlike the opening utterances of R and S which are said in a baseline adult vocal register, these utterances *about the baby* place the infant into the third person as an object – often a simple material object. At the same time, however, these utterances are framed within the baby-talk register with the characteristic sing-song intonation, altered and softer voice qualities, and other features we have noted. Here GM notes,

> Very pretty. She got double eyelids. Double eyelids, and she's fat.

This is said while continuing to gaze at the infant, not at another adult interlocutor, additionally signalling a baby-talk utterance but the infant is positioned with the third person pronoun, 'she', and the observations are of the physical characteristics of the child now being discussed as an object. Note that this is a conversational response to Auntie's,

> Look at her eyes, *ain't dey pretty* [pʷɪdi].

The second half of this utterance exemplifies yet another alignment which I've called *like baby talk* (LI). This utterance remains in the same stance of speaking to another person about the infant but the phonological shift to [pʷɪdi] signals 'baby talk' for an eleven-year-old. It is heard as regressive; this is the sort of thing where an adult in another situation might say, 'Don't talk like a baby'. Here, in speech about an infant, it is taken as an entirely appropriate conversational alignment.

Some months later when Rachel was perhaps 2 months old I was carrying her in my arms in an electronics store where I was buying cassette tapes to, of course, record more of the same. As the cashier – a middle-aged woman – and I made the transaction about the tapes we had the following conversation:

Cashier:	That'll be (the amount of money).
Me:	O.K. (handing her money).
Cashier (baby talk):	Where's Mommy?
Me (baby talk):	Mommy's at home.
Cashier:	Here's your change.
Me:	Thank you.

Many such conversations occur throughout my recorded materials as well as in other unrecorded situations such as this one. I see the footing set up here as *through baby talk* (TH). That is, the two participants are speaking to each other with the presence of the infant to mediate what might otherwise be impossible or difficult utterances. At the time this occurred it was, especially in Hawaii, where this took place, very unusual for such a young child to be cared for by a male. It is possible that a further consideration was that the child displayed clearly 'Asian' physical characteristics and so it could possibly be questioned whether or not I was, in fact, her father. The hidden dialogue (Bakhtin 1984 [1929]) might be paraphrased as:

| *Cashier:* | Where is this child's mother; who are you and why are you caring for the child? |
| *Me:* | I'm the father; her mother's at home. And everything is O.K. with this relationship. |

Of course I do not wish to read anything into what is a brief, highly ephemeral social interaction without further evidence. I present this just as an illustration of the quite frequent alignment in which two persons choose to shift into a baby-talk register even when the baby present cannot be imagined to be a party to the conversation. In this case the cashier's ostensible TO alignment and my ostensible FO alignment seem to me better characterized as both being speaking through the baby (TH). Of course, this is the alignment frequently seen in the park when two people caring for their dogs strike up a conversation with each other by speaking through their pets.

My analysis of these complex alignments is based on an array of linguistic and paralinguistic features of the utterances, most of which I have illustrated above. To summarize, these include:

Intonation: Sing-song intonation
Pitch: Higher or lower than baseline; often alternating
Rate of speech: Faster or slower than baseline; often alternating
Voice quality: Soft, breathy, light, whispery, mock or stage sternness
Grammatical reductions: Copula deletion, simple verb forms, absence of tense marking
Phonological shifts: Palatalization, [d] for [ð] ('dey' for 'they')
Lexical: Kin terms – Gramma, Auntie, Mommy
Lexical: Baby terms – potty, nene
Lexical: Vocatives – Rachel, Brenda

Repetition: 'Hol' Gramma's han, Hol' Gramma's han, Hol' Gramma's han'
Summons: 'Hey', 'Hi'.

Of course there is no fixed linkage among any of these particular features and any of the specific alignments I have outlined. One constructs the alignment through an interaction between these contextualization cues (Gumperz 1977) and other conventional semiotic resources for producing conversational alignments such as eye gaze, body position, pronominal reference, and conversational rhythm and sequencing. Based in these contextualized alignments we can see that there are at least the following footings which can be taken up through baby talk:

WI   Talk that is irrelevant to the baby – marked by 'baseline' linguistic features. In a sense all talk is this, but it is only an alignment when it occurs as the marked exception within a conversation centering on the presence of an infant.

TO   Talk to the baby – marked primarily by gaze, body orientation, pronouns, and empathy for the infant's position.

FO   Talk on behalf of the baby, speaking *for* the baby – marked by taking up the point of view of the infant and speaking as if the utterance is addressed to another present participant (including the speaker her/himself).

LI   Talk like the baby – marked by speaking about the baby but with regressive baby-talk features.

AB   Talk about the baby – marked by third person descriptive statements made about the baby or her behavior.

AR   Talk around the baby – marked by using some feature of baby talk but in conversational sequences with other participants.

TH   Talk through the baby – talk between other participants which is marked as being either TO or FO the baby. That is, the baby is a foil to mediate a conversation between other participants.

While I have outlined just these seven alignments which might be taken, I do not mean to suggest that this completes a taxonomic description of some baby-talk register. In the first place there are yet other, though perhaps less frequent, alignments such as what I have labeled 'PL' for playing with the baby talk. These are nonsense utterances made to no apparent purpose other than playing. One tapers off quickly into trying to decide if imitating the baby is worth considering as another separate alignment or not, and a host of other largely fruitless determinations.

What I hope to argue here is just the fairly simple point that across my data of two children, Brenda and Rachel, over a considerable amount of tape recordings and transcriptions, and confirmed against dozens and dozens of others, I have found a very complex set of alignments and positionings taken up by adults and others in the presence of the child and in interaction with her. For each of the seven alignments I have sketched out here with just two illustrative examples I have many hundreds of examples, and while it is obvious that in some cases classification might be difficult, these types represent fairly distinctive alignments that are taken up by the social world into which an infant is brought at birth.

What I would like to argue based on these alignments is that there are really two extreme positions taken up in this baby talk. The first of them occurs in the WI, AB, and FO alignments. In these the infant is positioned as either not existing – in WI the talk occurs as if the infant is not there at all – as existing as a sensitive but entirely non-agentive object (AB), or as simply a puppet or marionette to be animated and ventriloquated by another speaker (FO). As we will see in the discussion of the Brenda material, I should make it clear that while in the example I have given above (Example 42), the talk in the WI alignment was about the time and date, it might well have been about Rachel as well. In these three alignments, the infant is positioned as an object in the world to be ignored, to be talked about, or to support the talk of others, but not as a speaking/acting agent herself in any way.

At the other extreme the position taken up is that the baby is, in fact, a social actor to be spoken to and who might be expected to give a response in answer (TO). Speaking around the baby (AR) also at least allows this as a possibility as the speech, while directed to another participant and not to the baby, is signalled through contextualizing cues to be spoken taking her into consideration as a participant. In AR the infant is positioned as a third person participant in the social interaction. Similarly, speaking like a baby (LI) might be said to represent the infant as a social participant or at least a potential participant in the interaction.

Finally, speaking through the baby (TH) sets up a paradoxical position for the infant social actor as in this case the baby may be positioned by one speaker as a social actor (TO) ('Where's Mommy?') but as a puppet to be ventriloquated by the other (FO) ('Mommy's at home'). Of course, it's possible for both to take up TO alignments as in this hypothetical conversation:

Cashier: Where's Mommy?
Me: Tell her Mommy's at home.

It seems much less likely, however, and I do not have any cases which come to hand of both speakers taking up a FO alignment to produce the TH alignment as in:

Cashier: *I wonder where Mommy is?
Me: Mommy's at home.

I believe this is because in any event baby talk is staged as conversation within the well-established turn exchange practices between and among participants. Such a 'conversation' would run up against the difficulty of a single participant, the infant, being staged here as being concerned about Mommy, enacting multiple roles and footings within a two-utterance sequence.

What we see here in the limiting case of the infant in her third day of life is that there is a social world which is working through a rather complex set of discursive practices to produce her in a variety of ambivalent and even paradoxical roles. She is from moment to moment an object to be viewed, a sensitive but incompetent participant in a conversation, a mediating foil for others to carry on their social actions, and a full-fledged conversational interactant. Note in this latter case the direct response to her sneeze as a full social 'utterance' when GM says 'Gesundheit'.

From the first days of infancy, indeed the first moments as I have observed with my own two children, there is a highly complex absorption of the infant into the discursive needs and plays and positionings of the social world into which she is born. The child is at once a social actor and a physical object, a mediator of social relationships, and a puppet to be ventriloquated. The shifts in these positionings may move rapidly, even within the bounding intonation contours of an utterance. It is this kaleidoscopic chiaroscuro of social alignments and positions which is the discursive world of the infant, and in what now follows I will examine the cases of handing which we have already studied to see how this complex set of discursive practices is deployed by Brenda's social world to ultimately come to produce her as a specific kind of social actor – a hander.

The discursive practices of handing

Before returning to an analysis of the Examples of Chapter 2 in which we plotted the course of the development of handing as a social practice it is important to make clear what my intentions are here, what is included and particularly what is not. Because I wanted to limit my analysis to one quite specific social practice – handing – I have excluded the bulk of the data I have on the development of B's language over the course of the second year of life. As I have said before, that development itself has been treated at length elsewhere (Scollon 1976) and need not be replicated here. Here my goal is much more limited in that what I would like to try to characterize are the discursive practices or the discursive practice which is associated with the social practice of handing. I leave open for the moment whether we should speak of this as practices in the plural (a count noun, and there are many), as a single practice (a count noun, and there is one), or as practice (a mass noun, and this discourse should be left unconcretized as a countable, enumerable, and concrete entity). Of course the reader will be aware of my interest in avoiding the third of these possibilities as I have argued in Chapter 2.

As I have noted in my analysis of handing in Chapter 2, I found at least five discursive accompaniments to the practice of handing:

silence
nomination
functional directive
interpersonal directive
behavioral directive

I have included silence as a discursive accompaniment as later cases are quite marked in that handing occurs without anything being said. It might almost be thought part of the evidence that the practice of handing has been constituted in the habitus, that it occurs without anybody saying anything about it. In any event, I found in my earlier analysis that there was no unique linkage between any one of these and any particular act of handing. That is, as a discursive action, nomination is not uniquely linked to handing, nor are any of the others.

As I have given ample examples of these discursive actions, I will not focus on them in my analysis here more than to say that nominations, functional directives, interpersonal directives or responses, and behavioral directives all occur in these data as TO baby talk. Obviously, this is true almost by definition, but in what follows I will elide over the specific pragmatic nature of these TO utterances so that I can focus upon the broader question I wish to address here: how is the discourse which surrounds the child in these cases of handing constructed so as to produce the child as a social actor who is not only capable of handing but who, in fact, acts as a hander?

Of course, as I have said, there is much that I am not treating here. I will not be able to address the question of how B becomes a social actor in respect to other social practices such as pointing, nomination, requesting food and attention, playing at cooking, and all the rest of the social practices for which I have abundant evidence in my materials. Here I will focus concretely on B as a hander – a child who begins as an infant who cannot be argued to have constituted the separation of self and object and ends a year later as a child who can and does agentively use the act of handing to accomplish social purposes such as establishing relationships, initiating conversational topics, and the like.

BRENDA I (12 months of age to 14½ months)

The discussion in Example 42 above was based on transcripts made of a neonate just in her third day of life. I argued that there was a rich chiaroscuro of positionings and alignments of which I classified seven stances taken by caregivers to the infant. Brenda (B) at the time I take up this study is one year of age. In contrast to Rachel, B is now an active child though she does not yet walk. As I have argued, it is also not yet possible to attest the Piagetian stage of the separation of self and object, nor of object permanence. The majority of B's utterances are not intelligible to the researchers nor to the mother who claims that she says 'just a few things'. As I noted in my earlier analysis of Example 1, much of what M says seems directed at working out what B is trying to say. (Examples will not be repeated here as they are available in Chapter 2.)

In Example 1 we see a complex sequence of utterances from the point of view of the alignments taken up in baby talk. The first utterance is TO. That is, M is speaking to B. This is marked by her gaze and orientation to B, a lighter voice quality, repetition, the second person pronoun, and the frequent 'hms' to elicit a response. Note that B's first utterance is the 'word' 'nene'. This is considered by M to be one of B's 'words' which is a bit empty of specific meaning as it seems to mean that B wants her bottle. In any event, even though B is saying it, M's attempts to elicit a meaning fail.

This is followed by an utterance that I didn't classify in my earlier analysis, which here I'll call 'echoing' (EC) as it is an echoing of the child's utterance. As I have argued in my first study of these data (Scollon 1976), this could be broadly paraphrased as: 'I have heard that sound you just made as the word "apple", is that what you intended?' I may be justified in considering this more than just TO as in some cases it is only the echoing of the child and perhaps the intonation that indicates to whom the utterance is made.

In many cases, of course, EC is combined with TO or FO as later in Example 1. Here M says: 'You want Momma, yeah?' That is, she speaks in place of the child but with the twist that she does so with the second person pronoun. In the earlier cases I analyzed, FO was spoken as a kind of ventriloquation on behalf of the child. Here that ventriloquation is subsumed to the pronominal shift but nevertheless M's utterance explicitly articulates what M believes B is saying and then checks with B ('yeah?') to see if B will confirm this construal.

This shifting among TO, EC, and FO positions M in relationship to B very much in the same way the client-centered therapist positions her/himself in relationship to the client (Rogers 1951). I would not want to exaggerate this comparison to Rogerian, humanistic psychology beyond saying that as we see here and see in many other examples, M frequently engages in this echoic responding to B's utterances with the same apparent intention the therapist has, which is to simply say: 'This is what I hear in what you are saying; is it your intention to be heard in this way?'

Thus reflective or echoic response is the consummate act of explicit discursive construal, and so it is interesting from the point of view of the discursive construction of the social actor that it occurs so frequently in these interactions between the primary caregiver and the child, and it occurs well before we can attest that the child can, in fact, interpret M's utterances. B is constructed in the parlance of humanistic psychology as an 'honest communicator'. In the parlance of pragmatics, M is imputing to B adherence to the Gricean maxims, foremost among which is the assumption that one is saying something meaningful. Put another way around, M is positioning B as an active, intelligent, discursive agent who is capable of saying what she intends and, as the client-centered therapist does, positions herself as a capable but non-valuing listener who is providing a social service of explicit intersubjectivity as a sounding board for B's agentive self-construction.

Example 2 provides yet another new type of baby talk, what we could call *appeasing baby talk* (AP). It might also be thought of as distracting talk as well because in this case the purpose is to call the child's attention away from her crying or her fall and to orient her attention where M wishes it to be directed. The string of vocables are nonsensical, said rapidly and with considerable force and do have the effect of catching B's attention. Once B's attention is caught, M shifts to TO with an affirmative 'O.K.'. While it isn't clear what this is intended to mean, it seems to be a discourse marker (Schiffrin 1987) to signal the end of one state of talk/action and the start of the next.

From the point of view of the production of B as a social actor, it seems clear that this process involves not only the production and legitimation of the actions that are approved of within the community, but also it involves the sanctioning of those actions which are not acceptable. The question to be resolved for caregivers is how to bring about these sanctions. Here we see that M is using the strategy of refocusing the child's attention. From this point of view, we can see the discourse marker 'O.K.' as an explict marking of the boundary when B begins to give her attention to M. That is, it is at this point that B becomes a social actor who can be addressed as TO.

While we should not attribute much to R's WI, 'Look how fast she stops', we shall see that on the whole he engages in much more WI talk in B's presence than does M. This might be interpreted as indicating that he is an outsider yet at this early stage of the process of the research – we are still in the first week of recording and although he is related to B and they visit the family perhaps every second week ordinarily, he is unaccustomed to social interactions with young children, whereas B is M's second child.

The third example calls our attention to a frequent action sequence between B and M. It begins with an action of B's, in this case holding up the crayon. M first speaks TO B. As we have said, she pedagogizes this action of B's as an opportunity to teach her colors and actions. From the point of view we developed earlier, this is a case of nominalization and both functional and behavioral directives. It is functional to the extent that M is saying 'You draw with that', and behavioral to the extent she is saying 'Now I want you to draw'; and obviously we cannot determine which of these should be favored in our interpretation.

M begins this little interaction by first taking B to be a competent, agentive, but novice social actor – somebody who can answer the question: 'What color is that?' But then we see the characteristic and paradoxical shifting we saw with Rachel when M immediately shifts to speaking *for* B in saying (FO): 'Green.' We see further shifting in M's assessment of B's agentive competence when she first says 'Draw now' as a straightforward directive and follows this with the query, 'Draw?' Whether or not this means 'did you understand that I just said to draw?' we cannot determine, but what is important to note in this brief example is the shifting positioning of the child. In a brief sequence of four utterances she is positioned as an agent, a ventriloquized puppet, again as an agent, and then her agency or at least her understanding is queried.

Shortly after the sequence in Example 3, in Example 4 B repeats the action of holding out a crayon to her mother. First we should note the TO in which M is issuing directives to B to perform for the visiting researchers: 'say' and 'give' are explicit; 'name' and 'talk' are implicit. We can see in these that M is responding to our actions in making these recordings by trying to prompt or elicit these discursive actions from her child. When she says 'Yeah, this is yellow', she is responding to B's holding out the crayon and imputes to B some success in her action, though it is not clear whether the 'yeah' is intended to approve of her handing or to suggest even further that she might know something about its color. In any event, M construes this as a successful social action – handing – by saying 'Thank you'.

While I have not paid close attention in my analysis to the work of the other child, Example 4 indicates what is quite common: C ratifies very little social interaction with B at any level during these early recording sessions. Even as a four-year-old, she uses WI to seek to set up exchanges with M, R, and S which will exclude B from the social interaction. I say 'ratifies' because, in fact, both children were coloring together when this strip of talk took place. In most of the recording sessions both children were, in fact, acting together in playing, coloring, making sand cookies, and other child activities. C's talk, however, is highly competitive for our attention to B and she uses this WI positioning frequently, apparently to seek to exclude B from the dyadic interactions she has with others.

In this case, however, we see that C accedes to M's construction of B as a social actor and plays the happy recipient of the required action – giving a crayon to Charlotte. She accepts it without thanks but cooperates in requesting another one to extend the game of handing another turn and to position B as an agentive social actor.

In Chapter 2 I described Example 5 as an act of 'pure' handing. From the point of view of the ontogenesis of the social actor, it shows B and M enacting a straightforward exchange. From a discursive point of view, M construes it as entirely unremarkable, speaks TO B and, almost as she might for an adult, says 'Thank you'. There is in the repetition, perhaps, some of the baby-talk register as well as in the lighter voice quality she uses in speaking to B. As I will argue later, the representation of B as a social actor is keyed to B's own discursive actions. This exchange begins with B's utterance which might well be construed as a baby form of 'crayon'. This is the reciprocating action that seems crucial over the year in jointly producing unmarked instances of handing. It is what I have suggested we might call agentive resistance (to the social construal being done by caregivers); that is, when B produces herself as a competent agent, the response is in kind and ratifies this implicit claim of agency for her.

What we should remember, however, is that at the time of Example 5, B is still just slightly over one year of age (1:0.9) and this agency is at best very partial. We do not see such clear and regular social actions until many months later. What we are seeing here is not so much B's agency as the construal of B's actions as that sort of social action.

While Example 5 illustrates that an action can occur which is construed as a straightforward social action quite early in the history of the child–mother inter-actions, Example 6 shows a much more characteristic example of how complex the interactions often are. We see here that M provides links among the partici-pants. R's opening utterance is directed to M (WI) to which M responds in kind but then moves in her next utterance to speak TO B directly. One might think of this as translating R's question or at least his topic for the child. B responds to the mother by looking directly at the doll and saying [da^w], which the mother ratifies for B, and then she holds the positioning of B as a social interactant with the AB baby-talk register (lighter voice than in WI just above) while speaking to R. When B repeats her utterance, M returns to speak to B (TO).

In Example 7 M again takes on the Rogerian stance of reflecting her interpretation of B's utterance back to B. First she speaks TO B and then engages in a bit of nonsensical talk (AP). It is difficult to determine the stance of the repeated utterance of 'up' – are these to be heard as 'You want to come up' or 'I am picking you up' or 'I want up' – but we see quickly that the stance is the mix of TO/FO. That is, M is speaking TO B in order to interpret FO her when she says 'You want to open it but'. Again, it is important to note in these examples the kaleidoscopic movement of positions M is producing. She does not clearly contrast WI and TO, speech to R and speech to B. In speaking to R she includes B through the mitigated voice quality of AB; in speaking to B she reflects an external perception of B's actions through her own FO.

Example 8 was included in my analysis of handing to show that mixed into the same events in which handing between B and others was being constructed were these actions of handing among the adults. I reference it here again to show that in and around the talk to B and the talk about B are many cases of this WI talk which simply ignores her presence. It will be salutary to remember that the data we are examining have been selected specifically to show interactions in which B is involved, and that there are also many such contrapuntal interactions within the same situations in which the children are not involved.

By contrast with M, in Example 9 R and S show much less interest in or ability to use the more mitigated or intermediate forms of talk to B. Here there is a clear demarcation between R's TO and his WI which is reciprocated by S. Further, it should be noted that R's TO carries many fewer of the characteristic features of baby talk than M's.

Having said that, R and S use a register that is considerably less inclusive of B than M, in Example 10, when B is trying to capture S's juice glass. S's question 'How can I write?' shows enough adaptation to B to be thought of as AR rather than WI. R's speech remains clearly WI here, however. M positions herself and B much more closely together through the shifting between TO and AR. That is, when M does speak to R and to S ('she said, "chodai"') she stays very much within the same pitch register and voice quality she is using to speak to B. On the whole it is her lexico-grammatical structure which shows the shift by speaking of B in the third person and in her explanation of the meaning of 'chodai' for R and S that moves this utterance into alignment toward R and S rather than B.

Here again we see the Rogerian reflection of B's utterance but now carried to an extreme that perhaps Rogers himself might never use. M not only tells B what she's said, she suggests that even B hasn't heard it. B is positioned here as being equally outside of and in observation of B with M's 'Hear what you said?' This should be compared with Example 40 where R, in 'playing catch' with Rachel, says 'Yeah, you caught it'. While the positioning is difficult to capture here, it seems the child is *simultaneously* being positioned as a sentient, rational, intentional, and speaking/listening social actor through the explicit structure of the message – 'Look, this is what's going on here' – and at the same time being positioned as a third-person, objectivized, and minimally competent organism – 'Look at what *she* just did'. These two positions are commingled within a single utterance structure

– 'Look at what you have just done; even you yourself couldn't possibly have noticed or known.'

Example 11 gives several further instances of R's fairly clear demarcation of WI and TO, of S's more intermediate positioning of B through the use of AB, and M's much higher level of flexibility in providing a reflexive positioning of B as simultaneously within and outside of the social interactions which are taking place around her. We see this in R's TO being spoken with very little modification from his baseline WI style, but S's AB with some baby-talk features.

In Example 12 R and S make an attempt to adopt M's 'chodai', but as we have noted before, it fails as a case of handing at least in part because the object is a cookie. This is notable only because it shows the beginning of R's accommodation to the discursive practices of M and B. This accommodation, as has been noted before, carries over into the habitus of R and S in the care for their own child, Rachel, two years later, as Example 13 shows.

The extent to which M discursively constructs B's position is seen quite clearly in Example 14. The surprise utterance 'Oiyo!' cannot easily be placed. It might be considered M's own utterance of surprise when the orange is dropped on the floor in the handing between B and M. But we might also think of this as M engaging in FO baby talk as she frequently uttered these response cries (Goffman 1981) when B would fall or drop something, and they are frequently said with features of the baby-talk register.

Even further argument for M's alignment with B as a conscious and explicit reflection of B's intentions is seen in her 'gone'. As I have argued in Chapter 2, B has reached the stage of the tertiary circular reaction and we can see M's tracking on B's gaze as she looks back at the floor after she has picked up the object and transferred it back to M. I hear this 'gone' as saying on B's behalf something like: 'I dropped the orange and picked it up and now I see both that it is in M's hand and that it is no longer on the floor where I last saw it.'

In Examples 15 and 16 we see R and S again constructing relatively clear and distinctive positions for B as either in the social interaction (TO) or not in it as an object of observation (WI). That is, these two participants position B as a social actor not much more narrowly and definitively than does M. A further note which can be made here is that the categories of linguistic accompaniment to handing which I observed earlier are predicated virtually entirely on talk produced within this TO category. That is, nomination, social interaction, function, and behavior are constructed within speech marked as directly TO the child.

We are beginning to see two things here:

1   such speech directly TO the child is more characteristic of the outsiders than of the primary caregiver (M), and
2   a focus on these bits of discourse to the extent of excluding the speech around, about, for, on behalf of, or echoing the child would miss much of the significant discursive work that is going into the production of the child as a social actor, a hander.

I have commented in my discussion of Example 5 that B showed a bit of what I called 'agentive resistance'. In that case I believe it could be argued that even that agentive resistance, that is, even B's apparently spontaneous social action, was construed to be that by M. In Example 17, however, it seems we have come closer to some evidence for B's agency and it shows itself in her denial – again still apparent – of M's construal of her intentions. M speaks TO B but also reflects back to her what M sees as her refusal of the offered banana. When B answers with [nayʉ], M reflects this back (EC) as 'no'? Here we can see that M is taking herself as being positioned by B's utterance.

Examples 18 and 19 provide two further examples of the Rogerian reflective mix M produces by echoing B's utterances. Then in Examples 20 and 21 we see that both S and R are beginning to adopt a similar strategy in speaking to B. That is to say, now two months into the process, while B is showing some development, for our purposes here, it is the development of R and S that may be most interesting. They are bringing into their habitus M's discursive practices of constructing B to herself as both a social actor (TO) and as a social object to be echoed or commented upon.

In Examples 22 and 23 we see nothing really new but it is worth a comment that these utterances, which are more closely linked to handing as such and which construct the act of handing perhaps as much as the actor – the hander – are becoming more frequent in M's speech to B. We noted in Examples 15 and 16 that R and S maintained a fairly clear distinction between TO and WI. We then noted that by a few weeks later they were beginning to 'learn' M's manner of interacting with B. Now we need to note in preparation for Example 24 that M is also shifting toward a clearer focus on B as a social actor. Her speech to and around her is less ambiguous than it was earlier.

Most striking about Example 24 is that now, at age 1:2.5 and in this 'testing' situation in which M and B are looking at photos at the request of R, the intermediate and ambiguous forms of baby talk have disappeared. M quite clearly marks her speech as either to R (WI) or to B (TO). There is no AR, AB, FO, or any of the other forms we have seen. Here, in the situation that we have already argued she perceives as a kind of testing situation, M marks out her speech to R as not for B's consumption and vice versa. That is, she produces B as an independent and responsible social actor.

In Examples 25 and 26 two weeks later (at age 1:2.19) there is no perception of a testing situation but we see that M speaks to B as if she were a responsible agent. Of course, in the first case the objects of concern are a few pennies and M is taking it seriously that B 'return' them to her. We have already seen that B has come along to the point of being able to hand food to another without difficulty. What is important for our analysis of the discursive construction of B as a social actor is that the agentive resistance or agency that B is beginning to show is being reciprocated by the adults in her company by these constructions of B as a responsible social actor.

Summary of BRENDA I (12 months of age to 14½ months)

The historical development of B's habitus as a social actor begins in my data at one year of age at which age we have seen that her actions are construed as social actions, even where there is little evidence of volition or agency on B's part. What is most noticeable is the kaleidoscopic array of inclusions and exclusions (van Leeuwen 1996) which are achieved, particularly by M but increasingly by R and S. From moment to moment, even within an utterance, B is constructed by others first as a fully agentive social actor, then as an object for observation. Sometimes, as in Example 10, she is even simultaneously constructed as a social actor and as an object to be observed. Over the period we have just analyzed we see a steady progression toward a clearer construction of agency for B by M, R, and S as evidenced in clearer distinctions between WI and TO talk. B is treated either as somebody who is included as an interlocutor or who is talked about, but there are fewer cases where she is talked TO while being spoken about, and almost no cases now where she is spoken for (FO), through (TH), about (AB), or around (AR) in the sense of modifying the speaker's utterance with features of baby talk in the vicinity of B. She has gone in these two months or so from largely not being involved as an agent to being granted the modified but full agency of what Lave and Wenger (1991) have called a legitimate peripheral participant.

BRENDA II (1:7.2 to 1:8.21)

When we return to look at the material from five months later when B is 1:7.2 years of age we see that now B has clearly established herself as a social actor. She is now a person who acts and speaks and is treated as such by M, her sister, and by R and S. A glance through Examples 27 through 30 shows B is now simply engaged in conversations though, of course, these are rather minimal in terms of the content of the actual utterance. The argument I made in my earlier analysis of these materials (Scollon 1976) was that the first step in the development of the more complex constructions of the so-called two-word stage of language development was for the child to become engaged in discursive social interactions with other speakers of the language. This is why I called that work 'Conversations with a One Year Old'. There I argued that this was the first task of a child's language development.

Here I am looking more closely at how that 'conversation' has come into being. In the material of BRENDA I we saw that at first B was constructed rather ambiguously as sometimes in and sometimes out of the social interaction. Even so, the discursive work of the participants in those situations was accomplished through rather complex alignments on B's side, even often when speaking to other adults. At the same time, many of B's own fledgling utterances were reflected back to her and construed for her through a quasi-Rogerian 'honest listener' discursive strategy.

Now in these first examples of BRENDA II we see that others are taking B as a conversational participant, that is, they have moved from a work of construction to presupposing social agency. Note, for example, M's warning about the scissors in Example 30. This 'abunai' ('dangerous') is uttered as a stern warning in a low voice register which no longer carries much of the baby-talk contextualizing features. This is no longer the earlier functional/behavioral pedagogizing; it is a clear warning of the danger.

The clear agentive status of B as reflected by M is seen in Example 31 where B and M actually begin to argue over the ownership (or at least possession) of B's foot. M says it is hers; B says it belongs to 'Brenda'; M counters, 'No. Mine'. This is the agentive resistance which at first in Example 5 we saw was constructed *for* B by M but now is clearly being produced in resistance to M by B.

Again in Example 32 we see B's developing agency in her argument with S over the felt letter 'S'. B claims it is the letter 'E'; S counterclaims that it is 'S' and the argument goes on. No longer are we seeing a helpless infant making noises which adults are construing as meaning this or that. However wrong she may be from S's point of view, B is holding her own as a social actor in this transaction.

The interest of Example 33 is in M's WI 'She figures you have yet'. This is a clear case of M now taking B as a relatively 'normal' social actor who is either marked as a participant or not. She is speaking about B now much in the way R and S were at the start of these weekly encounters.

B herself begins to engage in the practices we have seen when in Example 34 she pretends to feed the toy bear, or so she might be construed as doing. She says 'Bear, eating, soup', much in the same way that M once said TO/AB her, 'she said, "chodai"', and 'Hear what you said? You said, "Chodai"'. Of course we could never determine B's intentions here, or whether she is speaking *to someone* about what the bear is taken as doing or *to the bear* about what it is doing itself. What we should note is that there is little here to separate the child's discourses about her toys and her pretended actions and the adult's discourses about the child herself and her imputed and construed actions. I have already quoted Wittgenstein as saying, 'A child has much to learn before it can pretend' (1990:439). Now I would like to suggest that a child must often be pretended to act before she can act. These pretend actions of the child can be seen to originate in a habitus constituted in part by the child's own previous location as a site of such social imagination.

Examples 35 and 36, in which B lexicalizes handing of objects to her in the first case as 'share' and to R in the second case as a nominalization ('tape'), show more of her ability now to assert her agency as a social actor. She now links discursive practice to social practice apparently to seek a strengthening of the directive force of her request or action. These are further examples of B taking on discursive practices as agent for which she was an earlier recipient.

The concluding examples from B show her now able to quite fully reciprocate the act of handing and its linkage with the discursive practices I noted above. In Example 36 I have noted that she nominalized the 'tape' she was handing. In Example 37 she lexicalizes the interpersonal transaction with 'some' as she does with 'Suzie' and with 'give' in Example 38. In Example 39, as I have argued before, B integrates handing into the discursive practice of topic control.

The discursive practices of handing

My concern in this analysis has been to ask whether or not we can speak meaningfully about a discursive practice which is 'an irreducible discursive aspect' (Chouliaraki and Fairclough 1999:26) of the social practice of handing and to test whether or not it is fair to say that 'people always generate representations of what they do as part of what they do' (1999:22). Now that we have looked carefully at the ontogenesis of the practice of handing, and now that we have looked at much of the language associated with this practice in the case of one child, I believe we can draw two general conclusions:

1   The study of discursive practice, like the study of practice itself, cannot be based in isolated and historically decontextualized utterances and actions, texts and events; and

2   The discursive practice which is seen in the longer historical view is focused less upon the practice itself and more upon the production or representation of the agents of that practice as social actors.

In what follows I will summarize the arguments which I believe lead to these conclusions.

I believe we have seen that there is from birth and at least up to two years of age a historical progression from a highly complex and kaleidoscopic play of alignments of the infant as an object and as a social actor for whom many of the roles are acted out by interactional accomplices. This chiaroscuro of inclusions and exclusions (van Leeuwen 1996), of objectivization and of subjectivization which is sometimes simultaneously construed by caregivers, culminates in this data around about two years of age in a relatively clear distinction between agency (TO with relatively minimal baby-talk adjustments) within a social encounter and exclusion as being a currently non-ratified participant (WI). At this age B is still treated as an object about which the participants talk in addition to these socially active roles. We have also seen that this progression is cogged into the increased display by B of what I called agentive resistance, that is, by active agency within the social interactions. To the extent caregivers come to perceive B as an active social agent, they withdraw their explicit construals of her actions and of her person and shift toward treating her as a participant with whom they negotiate their mutually constructed positions.

Concerning the discursive practices which accompany handing I believe we can make two useful observations. The first is that the five types (if we include silence) of linguistic accompaniments I observed in studying handing as such are located within the framing of B as a participant in the social interaction, what I have called the TO baby-talk register. That is, B and others discursively engage in nomination ('crayon'), functional directives ('draw'), interpersonal responses ('thank you'), and behavioral directives ('give it to C' or 'Mommy chodai') when they are marking their speech as directly to each other. It must again be borne in mind that at the earliest stages of this directive and labeling discourse, there is little evidence on the part of the child that she is either capable of understanding what is said or, if understood, carrying out these requirements.

Perhaps more important than this observation is the observation that such fairly closely linked discursive practice emerges out of a much more complex mix of discursive practice focused on the production of the infant as a social actor. The concern might be better said to be about the actor as social actor in general than about either the social practice of handing or about that particular act of handing in that particular moment. This conclusion might be strengthened by noting that B herself has no sooner aggregated handing within her habitus than she begins to exploit it as a means of controlling discursive practice, that is, for controlling topics in social interactions. To put this another way, it might be better to say that the social practice of handing is used to control discursive practice than to say there is a discursive practice which is in some way causative of the social practice of handing.

In the analysis of the B material we found a particular stance taken by M, much like that taken by R in relationship to Rachel, which was captured by such coding as EC (echoing) and the FO/AB/TO mix. I suggested that we could think of this as being much like the stance or alignment taken by the Rogerian psychologist in client-centered therapy in which the strategy of the therapist is to reflect back as an external friendly and honest listener what she/he hears the client to be saying. These cases suggest that the caregiver is making a Rogerian discursive construal of the child's utterance which is sometimes complete with a suggested answer or response to that utterance.

In this light it is interesting that this stance or alignment, which is quite frequent around the first year of life, particularly in its echoic form, drops off rather quickly once B has begun to display active (and genuine) agency on her own. As an aside we might note in contrast how it would be interpreted in an adult–adult conversation for one of the adults to engage in such echoic or *speaking for* responses:

I'm afraid I can't agree with you on that.
Look, you just said, 'I can't agree with you on that'.

Such metalinguistic frame jumps violate the Gricean maxims and must be accounted for. I would argue that this is because of the inherent objectivization of the other which is occurring that is in direct and paradoxical conflict with the subjectivization of the other as an interlocutor. That is, on the one hand this is not said to a third party ('He just said . . .') which would amount to a full objectivization of the other. At the same time, it is disclaiming the speaker's assumed agency in knowing exactly what he has just said. In any event this paradoxical, one might say schizophrenic, alignment, which is quite common at the moment in life when the child is herself making at least ambiguous if not paradoxically 'advanced' utterances, drops off as the interpretation of those utterances becomes less problematically resolved as representing social agency.

As B has moved from being minimally able to engage in social interactions to discursively and agentively producing herself as a social actor, this move has been paralleled by a progressive reduction in these Rogerian reflections and construals of her actions and of her discourse. There is only one situation in which there was an important difference in the framing of the event; in Example 24, R arranged a discrimination test using photographs of common objects in B's world. In this case we saw a shift toward the rather severe discursive practice of making a clear distinction between WI and TO by M. That is to say, M took it as incumbent upon herself not to engage in the complex set of scaffolding practices which were common in her interactions with B at that time. As we saw before, this narrowed range of discursive practices for the inclusion or exclusion of B as a social actor were linked as well to the somewhat unusual use of Japanese ('Wow-wow chodai. Motte kinasai wow-wow').

We should consider this particular example relevant to two points of discussion. In the first place there is a general developmental sequence found for phonology, more complex 'syntactic' constructions, and for lexical items (Scollon 1976) in which an 'advanced' form appears as if out of nowhere. That is, one has not heard it before, it strikes even M as remarkable ('She said, "chodai"'), and it does not recur for some time again until the form emerges from the child's habitus in more reduced forms which then seem to undergo a slow development toward the more competent adult forms.

We might be able to argue as well that from the point of view of the construction of the child as a social actor, the caregiver as well may extend or withdraw her degree of support or construal for the child as a social actor. There are, thus, two ways in which more 'advanced' social actions might occur. In the first case a child might spontaneously produce one of these erratic forms, a form found far from its source in the habitus (perhaps through imitation or simply through accident), but it might be taken by caregivers as actively produced by the child and therefore responded to in kind. On the other hand, the caregiver might seek to produce such erratic forms by a reverse causation, by using the appropriate responses for utterances and actions much beyond the productive capacity of the child at that particular age. The case of Example 10 appears to be one in which the erratic is produced by B, and the case of Example 24 is the opposite where M speaks to B in a way which will not become characteristic of their interactions for another few months.

The second point which we should notice about this testing in Example 24 is that M is engaged in more than the production of B as a social actor in general or as a daughter/cousin in a family situation. She is actively working to produce B as a test performer. This is attested by her withdrawal of her more common scaffolding in the more open-ended research/observation sessions we had conducted. While it is somewhat incidental to the point I am trying to develop here, it would be an important extension of this work to examine across different social situations how discursive practice was called upon in the construction of children as social actors.

Somewhat more generally I would like to argue that while I am not concerned here with what sort of a social person is being constructed, this is far from a trivial or obvious question. My central concern is with explicating the discursive mechanisms which have accompanied the social practice of handing in this one case. I have to some extent relied upon, though I have not presented much evidence from, a parallel study of our own daughter. To provide a glimpse, however, of what sort of differences might be encountered when research moves further afield, we can look at Example 43 below which involves another child in a very different family.

Example 43 Age: 1:0 (approximately)

J	M	R	Context
[?ɛ?]	Ah No, no; throw it away. Thow it away. Thow it away. Thow it away. Slap your hand. Thow it away.	What's that?	J picks up a piece of trash from the floor. (grunts) Makes as if to eat.

If we compare Example 43 to Example 10 where B was almost exactly the same age as J, we see a rather different construction put on the type of social interaction. Whereas here M tells J to throw this away and threatens to slap her hand, M tells B in Example 10: 'Chodai. Mommy throw that.' That is to say, in the one case the child is taken to be an actor who can throw away an object; in the second case she is taken to be an actor who can hand an object to her mother. The first case is accomplished with a directive accompanied by a threat; in the second it is accomplished with the directive and a tone of TO baby talk inclusion. I would not want to make more of this than my data can support and so should only comment that the sort of social actors that are being produced here could be argued to be different. But from the point of view of my argument, the discursive process is the same. That is, each mother is using a strategy of discursive construal of the child's action as action and imputing to the child a degree of social agency which it is unlikely that the child is able to perform at that age.

We might also note the studies done by Miller's group (Hengst and Miller 1999; Miller et al. 1990, 1992, 1997). In these studies they have shown how different uses of personal narratives, both those told by a child and those told about a child, are important discursive means by which the social agent is constructed in early life. Thus they have argued, for example, that Chinese (Taiwan) children are produced as moral/ethical agents, white American children as truthful describers of events, and African-American children as performers through their stories and the responses of their caregivers to those stories. Here I am not focusing my attention on the sociocultural differences argued for in Miller's studies, though I am certain that that point of view could also begin to be constructed within my data. While I cannot do more than speculate, I believe there is significance to the fact that the Miller group's analyses begin at about two and one-half years of age whereas my studies have ended just before that. By the time their work begins, I would argue that the first social constructive work as a social actor is largely completed.

While I would never want to argue that the social construction of the social actor in these earliest stages is non-ideological, for the purposes of my task of analyzing the linkages between discursive practice and social practice, I have set aside these equally important issues. I have included these examples here as a flag to remind the reader that I do not wish to draw any inferences about what sort of social actor B is becoming or about the social group into which she is being inducted. This is not to say, however, that these questions are irrelevant to the project of the discursive analysis of practice, but just that I have not taken them on in this more narrowed focus on the discursive means by which discursive practice is linked to social practice. I will sketch out how such an analysis would be made in Chapter 5 when I examine the idea of the nexus of practice.

In summary, then, I would like to argue that in the first place a social practice such as handing is a linked, historically constituted chain of specific and concrete actions which takes place in real time. As such it is always provisional, unfinished, and unfinalized in its consolidation in the habitus. That is, as Bourdieu has argued (1977, 1990), while the habitus is a disposition to act in practiced ways, the concreteness and uniqueness of each separate situation means that each act in the aggregated chain of actions that constitute a practice is original, new, and indeterminate. It is what the participants make of it, to put it in a few words, but the participants can only make of it what this history in habitus will allow. As a kind of practice or a subset of practice, discursive practices such as those we have just seen which are linked to the social practice of handing are also provisional, unfinished, and unfinalized and form in the habitus a disposition to act in particular ways, but produce concrete and unique utterances which, like the actions of all practice, are only what the participants make of them and nothing more.

From this I draw the conclusion that we can learn relatively little about discursive practice from the direct and exclusive study of discursive acts (texts), and less about the linkage between discursive acts and other social acts from single, decontextualized, or isolated instances. On the other hand, I would like to argue that we can learn a great deal about social practice and discursive practice by seeing them in light of the historical sequences within which they participate. And notice that I am not saying that we must see discourse or social practice in light of 'history' in some large but non-concrete sense. What I mean to say is that we can learn much from studying the very specific and concrete set of actions which form the linked chain from earlier to later in the habitus of social actors, or as Nishida (1958) puts it, in the historical-bodily sources of action-intuition.

One final point on the relationship between B's utterances as utterances and her ratified status as a social actor. In my first study of these data, I observed, as I have mentioned here, that she came to use handing along with the lexical terms 'Hi' and 'Here' as a means of gaining topical control of the conversation (Scollon

1976). An observation I made then, but was unable to ground in a practice understanding of her habitus, was that the phonological quality of her utterances at two years of age was directly related to her status as a ratified social actor.

> There is a special condition, however, that shows up when Brenda is excluded as a possible participant. Brenda's speech becomes quite unintelligible. As an example of this was a stretch of wholly unintelligible speech while her mother was speaking Japanese on the phone. No one else was able to gain access to Brenda during this time and yet she continued to speak. Another example of this occurred when Brenda and I were interacting. I spoke several sentences in an aside to Suzanne and during this time Brenda said several things which were quite unintelligible. These lapses suggest that Brenda considers herself to be in interaction with a receiver but is also aware of the uselessness of speaking clearly to a receiver who is not really interacting. In every case, when the interruption ends, Brenda immediately returns to speaking clearly.
>
> (Scollon 1976:128)

At the time of writing this, I believe it would be fair to say I was working within a model of cognitive processing and intentionality of utterance to a great extent. In viewing these same data now, I would prefer to say that it is simply impossible to attribute greater or lesser intentionality to the actions of the child. What we can say is that when B, at two years of age, is jointly constructed as a participant in the social interaction – through her agency ('Hi', 'Here') and through interlocutor ratification of that agency – she produces utterances as social actions within that constructed agency. When that agency fails, there is simply no basis in the habitus for the production of social actions; as she did as an infant, she may make sounds but there is no social entity to construct these sounds as utterances. I believe in this we can see the workings of what Vygotsky has spoken of as the internalization of the social. At two years of age, B has become a relatively competent social actor *when jointly constructed as that* by others but has yet to achieve an internalized *historical self* (Nishida 1958) which can ratify and sustain this social construct.

Individual, person, and self

Harris (1989) makes a useful distinction among three aspects of human experience. She distinguishes

biological: the *individual*
sociological: the *person*
psychological: the *self*

When I write of the human playing with the dog, it is as (biological) individuals that we see them exchanging the ball. That is, we see them within a biological and mammalian analysis. If we go on to speak of this person engaging in a social activity, we have moved to a sociological or historical analysis. We might further want to talk about the construction of the human self as a particular kind of person – a pet owner or dog lover – and do so within a psychological perspective.

Within this framework we can see that the child is discursively positioned by others rather frequently among these analytical frames from earliest infancy. At one moment when we are speaking about the child – 'Look, she got double eyelids' – we see her as the biological individual, an objectivized entity. 'Say "Hi" to Auntie', on the other hand, squarely places the child within a framework of kinship relationships and social obligations to speak, and in this moment the utterance positions the child as a social person within the interaction. Still further and, I should add, concurrent with this sociological positioning, is often a psychological positioning as when the mother speaks to the child to determine psychological states ('Hungry?' or 'You want juice?').

A child comes to learn the social practices of her community as part of her habitus as she grows into the community. But at the same time we can say that the child becomes a member of the community only insofar as members of that community deal with her, and speak to her and about her in ways that attribute to her the identity of a competent social actor. As I have tried to argue here, in the ontogenesis of the social actor these processes of being *taken as* a social actor are crucial in coming to being able to undertake social actions.

NOTE

1   The term 'agentive resistance' was developed out of discussions with Philip Levine, whom I wish to thank.

4 Objects as mediational means

The crayon appropriates a child

Coffee and small change

When I buy my morning coffee I engage in a sequence of practices. I could begin, somewhat arbitrarily, with one which has to do with standing in line or queuing. As that practice sequences into the next one, I end up in position to engage in the practice of making an order.[1] In the shop where I usually get my coffee I then have to do a version of the waiting practice which is particular to that place. That is, I move away from the position where I made the order to the position where a loose queue has formed to receive the orders. As the drinks never arrive in the sequence in which the orders were placed, this entails having a looser queue, examination of the particular items as they arrive, and verbal exchanges with the people who have prepared the drinks. Concurrent with my waiting are the practices of the people who are preparing the orders. This is followed by picking up the drink and making whatever further adjustments are needed, and the sequence culminates in various practices for drinking the coffee, either at tables in the vicinity or elsewhere, either with company and conversation or alone with something to read. I have argued that to advance a theory of practice it is useful to see my morning coffee as such a collection of rather specific and narrowly defined practices rather than try to speak more generally about all this as 'the practice of having a cup of coffee in the morning'.

In Chapters 2 and 3 I have been focusing my attention on the social practice of handing in order to further narrow the scope of my investigations. When I buy my coffee, handing takes place twice. In the first case I hand over the money to pay for my coffee. In the second case I pick up my coffee from a small shelf on which the server has placed it. The first is handing of the hand-to-hand variety where the object goes directly from person to person; the second is handing of the place-and-pick up variety where the handing makes use of an intermediate physical space. In both cases the handing is material in that in both cases objects are transferred from person to person.

Overall this sequence of practices – queuing, ordering/paying, waiting/preparing, delivering, and consuming – makes use of a number of material objects by which these practices are grounded. Most central to these practices are the money exchanged in the first case and the cup of coffee which is given to me in the second case. Other material objects, however, are equally crucial. The place-and-pick up form of delivery makes use of the narrow counter space. The coffee makes use of the cup – something which may be negotiated as my cup or their paper cup, for instance. The cashier makes use of a cash register. The preparer makes use of the espresso parts of an elaborate apparatus for making coffee of different kinds. Perhaps more peripheral to these practices, but not to be dismissed, are the physical arrangements of counters and tables, made so that a queue may form in front of the cash register, and the disposition of the milk, sugar, napkins, and other objects for self-service in the area where the order is delivered.

Now I have engaged in an inversion of significance. I have spoken here as if money and coffee and the rest of this physical apparatus exist so that I may daily indulge in the practice of handing. My analytical purposes – to talk about hand-ing as a social practice – have led me to phrase my interest here as an interest in how small change and coffee are exchanged so that handing can take place. This is, of course, the inverse of our common sense about what is going on every morning when I get my coffee. I do not say 'Let's go do some handing', any more than I might say 'Let's have a conversation', and this latter point shows up the problem which I will try to address in this chapter through a study of the objects and other mediational means by which a young child comes to be able to under-take social actions.

When I want to have a conversation I am likely to say 'Let's have a cup of coffee', whether or not it is ultimately coffee we have. The social practices of having a conversation are the goal here; exchanging money for the coffee is entirely instrumental in achieving that goal. Looked at more narrowly, if I say the goal is to buy a cup of coffee, then we can see that the social practices of handing are entirely instrumental in achieving that goal. Conversely, if I were working on the business plan for a coffee shop and I wanted to increase sales I might say 'Let's get people to have conversations here', and the sales of coffee, the queuing and pick up, and the distribution of the tables and chairs and other decorations would all be instrumental in producing conversations. The conversational practices themselves would be instrumental in producing economic exchanges. From such a point of view it is crucial to the financial prosperity of the shop that my handing of the small change proceed smoothly, that I have the right sort of change (not, say, Austrian Schillings or Hungarian Forints in Washington, DC), that I know what sort of drinks are available and on sale and their prices (menus), how to queue, and the rest.

There is an inevitable question of point of view which must be taken up in the analysis of social practice if we want to analyze the exchanges I participate in each morning as I buy my cup of coffee. From my point of view as the consumer, I look to the coffee shop (and to the entire world-wide coffee industry upon which their work is predicated) to maintain a smooth flow of beans and a steady price in places that I regard as comfortable. My part in this process is to arrive, queue, order, hand over my change, wait, pick up my drink, and enjoy it within the stimulating environment of an intellectual conversation. The financial planner cares little, we presume, about the quality of the conversation I have. It is his or her goal to produce customers. The cashier and the person who prepares and delivers the coffee will also have rather different goals along the lines of having and maintaining employment, and they care little for my conversation on the one hand or, most likely, only incidentally for the planner's concern with producing customers. But, of course, all of our purposes can be achieved only to the extent there is some general cooperative arrangement by which we agree to trade the achievement of our goals for their instrumentalization as means for some other participant's goals.

Political economists and other theorists deal in these matters. In handing over the coins by which I pay the price of my coffee, I pay for the spaces we enjoy – the chairs and tables, the ambience – for our conversation. Correspondingly, the recipients earn money for their school fees or other activities. It is a blinding simplification to say that I have bought a cup of coffee. Embedded in the handing of the coins and the delivery of the cup of coffee is the purchase of space and time as well as a beverage, the use rights of objects as well as their servicing through cleaning between customers, and the subjection of my own purposes to their instrumentalization by a global economy of coffee production and financial exchange. From such a point of view, the social practice of handing which I am seeking to understand here, particularly ontogenetically in the life of an infant, seems far removed from sociopolitical questions of the global economy. When the question is the purchase of a cup of coffee in a coffee shop, it is not difficult to see that those coins and this coffee, these tables and chairs, and this ambience are necessarily cogged into and are carriers of such a sociopolitical reality, even if we do not pay attention to that interdependency in our daily cup and conversation which may wander through topics from tonight's dinner to the actions of a two-year-old twenty-five years ago.

When the focus of attention for analytical purposes is, in fact, that same infant of twenty-five years ago and the objects are crayons, an orange, a rice paddle and pot, a few pennies, or a cookie, the ambience is the infant's home, and the actions are the handing of these objects between B and her mother, it is much more difficult to see the linkages among multiple purposes and goals on the one hand and the linkages between those actions and the sociocultural world outside of this rather sheltered environment. What I will argue here is that, in fact, the study of how these mediational means arise ontogenetically is crucial to our understanding of mediational means in all cases.

To make this argument I will first make reference again to the work of Wertsch (1998) in which social actions are theorized as being mediated by mediational means (or cultural tools which, as I have said, he uses as interchangeable terms). Within this mediated action theory, Wertsch argues that these mediational means embed sociocultural and sociopolitical history. This history is embedded in such a way that mediational means both constrain and enable the actions which are taken through the use of these tools. I will then develop an examination of the properties which Wertsch posits for mediational means, which we will need when we come to the analysis of handing between the child and her mother.

Then I will return to the instances of handing we have already analyzed to see what objects and other mediational means are called upon to accomplish those actions. From this I will argue that, in general, mediational means predate the user; that is, they arrive in the life of the person as 'givens'. In making this argument I will show that we must make a distinction between the concept of appropriation and the concept of use. 'Appropriation' is most fruitfully used to speak of the development of a mediational means over time within the habitus as an aspect of practice. By contrast 'use' calls upon the unique, irreversible, and concrete object as used in real-time action. This distinction implies, then, that we maintain a distinction between mediational means and object, the first of these referring ultimately to a class of objects and the disposition for their use within the habitus, and the second referring to the concrete objects with which a specific act is performed.

My argument will close with taking up two problems which arise in this analysis. The first of these is that of the relations between practice and mediational means. As in many cases mediational means arise as codifications and materializations of practice, I prefer to speak of this process as the technologization of practice. The reverse process also occurs in which a mediational means exerts pressure upon social practice toward rigidity, objectivization, and standardization.

The final problem, which can really only be suggested here, is the place of semiotic mediational means or cultural tools within a theory of mediated action. It is common enough to refer to language and other symbol systems as mediational means or cultural tools, but here I will examine whether or not this is simply a metaphorical extension of the idea of a cultural tool or if there is, in fact, a theoretically grounded means of incorporating language and other semiotic systems within a theory of mediated discourse.

Cultural amplifiers and cultural tools/mediational means: the New Literacy Studies

The notion of a cultural amplifier was first proposed by Bruner (1966) to capture the idea that the actions of the psychological individual[2] are amplified by cultural means much in the same way that a physical tool may amplify the physical capacity of the biological individual. A stick extends my reach; a hammer extends my strength. A cultural amplifier such as literacy, in this analysis, extends my memory. There is much that is attractive about the idea of a cultural amplifier and many scholars have taken up this idea over the years since Bruner first proposed it, including Cole (Cole and Bruner 1971).

Taking the occasion of a collection of articles in honor of Bruner, Cole and Griffin (1980), however, began a re-examination of the idea of amplification. Their critique was based in two sources. The first of these was Cole's own apprenticeship with the Soviet psychologist Alexander Luria, as part of which he came into engagement with the psychological work of Lev Vygotsky. The other source was inherent in the problems with the metaphor of amplification itself in regards to not only psychological but biological phenomena as well. The point made by Cole and Griffin is simply that tools, whether material or cultural, not only amplify our actions, they also reduce or constrain them in other ways. Furthermore, the tools themselves are not neutral or purely objective but they, in fact, engage in a transformation of our most fundamental psychological and physical characteristics.

To elaborate on this point a bit, we can see that while a stick may amplify my reach, at the same time it reduces my touch. I can knock a mango out of a tree with a stick when perhaps I could not reach it with my hand, but with the stick I cannot feel whether or not it is soft and ripe. That is, Cole and Griffin argue, there is no amplification of some dimension without a cost which is brought about through the narrowing of the range of sensation or other physical involvement.

Taking this argument to the next point with the same example, if I use a stick to 'pick' fruit, and if I do this regularly, my muscle structure begins to change through the exercise with the stick. That is, the habitual use of this tool, like the use of the hammer for the carpenter or the Schneider guitar for the classical guitarist, brings about amplifications and reductions not only in the moment of use but overall in the physical and psychological structure of the user. That is, in the terminology we have been developing, the use of a tool in a series of actions brings about changes in the habitus (Bourdieu 1977, 1990) or the historical-body (Nishida 1958) of the user.

Cole and Griffin go on to examine less physical, more cultural 'amplifiers' taking the case of literacy as an illustrative example. They examine the new and rapidly growing literature on the question of whether or not literacy is a simple amplifier of memory and other cognitive skills or if it should, in fact, be thought of as in some way transformative of psychological and social process. It would take me far afield to develop this particular discussion which in more recent times has come to be called the New Literacy Studies (Gee 1990, 1996; Gee, Hull and Lankshear 1996; Street 1984, 1995; Barton and Hamilton 1998). Early arguments were developed which focused primarily on the psychological transformations which literacy was said to produce (Goody and Watt 1963; Goody 1977, 1987; Havelock 1986; Ong 1982). In these so-called 'great divide theories' of literacy as Gee (1990) and Street (1984) have labeled them, it was argued that literate societies and the people in them have fundamentally different psychological and social structures than oral societies and the people in them. In response to the argument that no society is, in fact, uniform, so that a 'literate society' has nevertheless significant aspects of 'orality', Ong (1982) argued that literacy, as a cultural form, was thoroughgoingly replacive. That is, once literacy had entered a society, he argued, that society could never return to its earlier forms of communication and while some members of the society might remain illiterate, in Ong's view they would always be in an inferior and subordinate position to those in the society who had attained the higher cognitive processing structures of literacy.

Ong goes on at some length to describe the specific qualities such a literate society/personality has that are absent in the non-literate society/person. These qualities are essentialized as positive psychological traits of the person and

cognitive values such as logical and comparative thinking, the ability to decon-
textualize and objectify experience, and constitutes what we have argued
elsewhere are basically value characteristics of what we call the Utilitarian
Discourse System (Scollon and Scollon 1995). It is important to note that these
'great divide' theorists view these qualities as primarily positive and essential
psychological characteristics, wrought in the human psyche by literacy which is
often seen more as a matter of human character and values than as a set of skills
or practices. These values are taken to be the fountainhead of the characteristics
of the societies in which these people take their leading cognitive roles.

Three studies in the late 1970s set themselves up in opposition to this essentialist view of literacy: the work of Scribner and Cole (1981) on the relationships
among school-based literacy, Quranic or religious-based literacy, and vernacular
Vai literacy in an African community within a cross-cultural psychological
research framework; Heath's (1983) ethnographic study of literate practice in an
East Coast American rural piedmont community; and our own ethnographic
studies of literate and oral practice of Northern Athabaskans in Canada and
Alaska (Scollon and Scollon 1979, 1981). More recent studies in this framework
have been published in conference collections (Cook-Gumperz 1986; Keller-
Cohen 1993), and Barton and Hamilton (1998) have carried forward this project
into the present in a social-practice-based study of literacy in a British working-
class community.

While researchers within the New Literacy Studies group are not entirely in
agreement with each other, the central argument of this practice-based analysis
of literacy has made use of the concept of the cultural tool or mediational means,
though in some cases this is developed explicitly by the researchers and in other
cases it is not. Literacy in these practice theories of literacy is understood neither
as an essential set of psychological characteristics and values nor as a simple
matter of neutral cognitive skills in encoding and decoding texts. Literacy has
been seen as a set of social practices which stand in ideological relationship
among themselves. This ideological view of literacy, as Street prefers to call it,
argues that the characteristics which distinguish the literate from the non-literate
on the one hand do produce rather significant differences in habitus. Put another
way around, becoming literate produces a complex habitus of literate practices
which may or may not be incommensurate with the practices of non-literacy, but
what is crucial is that struggles produced by the contradictions between these are
sociopolitical struggles, not simply cognitive differences. If to some extent one
social practice of a certain kind of literacy is the production and use of decontextualized text, the valorization of this practice is an ideological and political
issue, not an objectivist and simple cognitive issue.

As a cultural tool or mediational means, literacy is viewed, within practice
theories of literacy, as a complex of social practices – there are always multiple
literacies, not some unitary phenomenon – something that is aggregated over a
long period of time within the habitus of individuals, complexly related to society,
embedded in various technologies, and positioned within the contestations of
power within a society. From this point of view, literacy is not seen as a simple

cultural amplifier which increases the user's memory, processing skills, and cognitive capacity. Nor is it seen as the essential and defining characteristic of the person who is literate. It is seen as a mediational means which (1) is acquired over time through an interaction between the habitus of the person and his or her actions in society, (2) affords or enables certain actions such as memory over time, but also (3) constrains or reduces other actions or capacities. As Plato feared, literacy may increase our ability to keep records and thus increase memory over time but at the same time, by producing a reliance on external records, it may well decrease our own personal memory in habitus.

Wertsch's mediated action theory

James Wertsch (for which I will use his 1998 book as the present definitive statement) has been the theorist who has most comprehensively elaborated the Lurian/Vygotskian school of Soviet/Russian psychology for the English language reader. Wertsch has continued to use the Vygotskian notion of psychological tools, which he phrases as mediational means or cultural tools, to capture one of the ways in which sociocultural and historical process enters into the actions of the person in society and, ultimately through internalization, into the intramental, psychological structures of the person. While not making direct reference to the practice theory of Bourdieu and others, Wertsch constructs a psychological model of the person which is, in my view, much like the habitus of Bourdieu or the historical-body of Nishida.

Wertsch puts forward the mediated action as the unit of analysis for much the same reasons that Bourdieu puts forward the idea of practice, that is, to cut the Gordian knot of the individual–society antinomy. This is Wertsch's move to finesse the now perennial debates about whether it is most useful to conceive of the human individual as the core building block out of which all else is fashioned – groups, classes, societies, cultures – or the society (group, class, culture) as the primary entity from which the behavior of individuals may be derived. Wertsch argues that both the human individual and the society are categorical entities, neither of which has concrete, material primacy. In preference to this, he posits the mediated action – the human agent acting with or through the mediational means (cultural tool) – as the most productive unit of sociocultural analysis.

In taking this position, Wertsch locates himself as a sociocultural practice theorist, though he himself does not develop the idea of practice to any great extent. The bulk of his work focuses on the mediated action. To some extent there is an ambiguity in his writing about the mediated action–mediational means dialectic in which he seems sometimes to be focused more upon the actions and at other times more on the mediational means. As I shall argue below, this is a direct outcome of the need to make a distinction in respect to mediational means which parallels the distinction I am trying to argue for here between the social practice and the social act, that is between the extended, historical process of aggregation in the habitus and the immediate, irreversible, one-time-only real-time action.

There is, of course, a second problem we will need to address and that is the considerable ambiguity entailed as a result of a shifting scope for the concept of a mediational means. Literacy theorists, for example, have considered literacy to be a cultural tool or mediational means. But so is a typewriter or word processor, and, as we shall see with B, so is a magnetized letter 'X' to be stuck on a refrigerator door. For Vygotsky 'the word' is a prime example of his psychological tool. For Wertsch (and his colleagues) the historical narrative of the Soviet control of Estonia is a cultural tool (Tulviste and Wertsch 1994; Tulviste 1994; Wertsch 1997) as is the underground, unofficial counter-narrative told by Estonians wishing to be independent. But in developing much of his argument about cultural tools or mediational means, Wertsch uses the pole of a pole vaulter. That is to say, as Wertsch has developed the concept of the mediational means, and consequently the concept of the mediated action, there is an ambiguity of scope and an ambiguity of concreteness or specificity – some mediational means are physical objects, such as the pole, and other mediational means are highly semiotized, psychological objects, such as the official history of the Soviet Union. As I will argue below, the concept of the mediational means is one of great utility in a practice theory of social action, but it will take some work to tease out and seek to resolve some of the inherent contradictions.

The characteristics of mediational means

As a way to clarify his conceptualization of the cultural tool (mediational means), Wertsch outlines ten characteristics of all mediational means, though to be sure some of these are more salient in some mediational means than in others. For my purposes I prefer to rephrase these ten characteristics Wertsch gives as just four and to add a fifth one not treated by Wertsch. The five characteristics I will focus upon are these:

> *Dialectical*: There is a dialectic between the external (material) aspects of the mediational means as an object in the world and the internal (psychological) structures of the person as one who has (or is) a habitus for using the mediational means. This dialectic ranges from nearly totally external, objective existence in the case of the novice user of the mediational means to nearly totally internal, psychological existence in the case of the expert. Different mediational means may be themselves positioned differently along this dialectical cline; the multiplication tables are largely psychological, the coffee I buy at the counter is largely external and objective.
>
> *Historical*: A mediational means is simultaneously linked to a history in the world as an economic, political, social, and cultural entity – coffee is part of a world-wide political economy – and to a history for each person who has appropriated it. This might be my first cup of coffee or it might be something I have daily at this time. Because mediational means embed a history both in society and in the habitus of a person, mediational means inevitably embed the power and authority structures of society.

Partial: The mediational means never fits the action exactly. Only some of the characteristics may be called upon in any specific action. Thus a mediational means affords some actions but this lack of exact fit to concrete actions means the mediational means also limits and focuses that action. Thus the mediational means is transformative of actions that are taken, by both doing and saying more and less than is intended by the users.

Connective: A mediational means connects or links both multiple purposes and multiple participants. The coins I hand the cashier are to purchase a cup of coffee; the coins the cashier receives summate in a daily tally out of which he/she is paid. Same coins, different purpose for the two participants in this action. The coins may also link my own multiple goals – buying coffee, having a conversation, supporting a student-run coffee shop.

Classificatory and representational (not concrete): Mediational means are classes of objects or representations of objects, not the objects themselves. It is not the same cup of coffee I buy each day and not the same coins I hand across the counter. Each day I exchange tokens of the type, coins, and purchase a token of the type, coffee. It is the representation in dialectic with that object which is constituted in my habitus as a mediational means, not the specific tokens which I use in each separate, specific, and concrete action. This accounts, of course, for the partiality of the mediational means. The mediational means is a class of objects suited to a class of actions constituted within a practice which is located within a habitus.

Through these five characteristics (at least) a mediational means embeds a socio-cultural, sociopolitical history and brings that history to the social action. While there is something very attractive about the concept of the mediational means, there are ambiguities and contradictions that need to be resolved. As I have suggested above, the concept has wavered between very large entities, literacy or languages, and very small ones, the word; it has been used to encompass what are most easily thought of as material objects, coins, a cup of coffee, a pole vaulter's pole – but with the understanding that these always have a psychological or internal aspect – and also to encompass what are most easily thought of as psychological processes or schemata such as histories, genres, and multiplication tables. In the analysis which follows I will try to begin a clarification of some of these questions by focusing closely upon a very few and very simple mediational means. These are the objects that are handed between B and her mother or the objects that are used by them in the actions we have already had occasion to study. It is my hope that by taking this strategy of fixing my analysis to the mediational means within actions and a practice that is now quite well defined, we can begin to sort out the dimensions of the concept of mediational means.

The mediational means of a one-year-old

I must begin by reiterating that there is a possible problem of inverting our priorities here. If my goal overall were to analyze the theoretical basis of the concept of the mediational means, it would perhaps have been most practical to fix upon one or a few mediational means and follow their ontogenesis through the second year of this child's life. Had I done that, I might have been able to develop a clearer idea of the mediational means but I would have lost the perspective I have been able to gain on the social practice because a single mediational means would be used across a panoply of practices that would be difficult to analyze within a book-length treatment. The result might well have been the current rather indefinite and ambiguous understanding of practice that exists in the field.

In contrast to this, I have preferred to fix upon a single social practice – handing – and to keep that as my constant frame of reference as I then look at the discursive processes by which a child is produced as a particular sort of actor, a hander. Now within that perspective I want to consider the mediational means which were appropriated by this child and by her caregivers as they have accomplished this construction of the social practice of handing and the person of the hander. To do this we will necessarily miss much that is important about mediational means. We will also have to engage in a certain amount of speculation or reconstructive history to come to see these mediational means as genuinely sociocultural and historical objects. I hope that the concreteness that I gain by this strategy will offset the necessary incompleteness of my treatment of mediational means.

Whose action, whose mediational means?

The first problem we have to face up to is that we cannot argue in any convincing way that B, at the age of 1:0.2 when we began these studies, is a competent social actor. As I have argued before this, when we begin at the earliest age here, B cannot be said to have come to a separation of the self and objects at all. There is little basis for attributing agency to her and so, when she falls over and cries, as she did in Example 2, and M brings her a pot, a spoon, and a rice paddle, how do we come to speak of these objects as mediational means and in what mediated action?

In the case of Example 2 the action seems clear enough. B is crying as a result of her fall and M is seeking to distract or placate her. What do these objects – pot, spoon, and rice paddle – bring to the situation? Why did M choose them? How do they do their work as mediators of M's action?

M told us outside of the recording situation that these objects do, in fact, have a short history with M and B. B likes to play with them, presumably because of the noise they make. On other occasions M has given them to B to play with, perhaps also in such a situation when M wanted to distract B from some other action. Thus, here when she wants to quiet the crying and to distract B, M brings out the noise-makers she has called upon before. The qualities that make them suitable as tools to mediate this action are that they make noise, are very durable (within B's use of them), are easily available close-by in the kitchen, and B already has a practiced use of them. That is to say, M can use these as objects to mediate her action of quieting B in part because B has begun a practice of playing with them. They are a mediational means for M's practice of quieting her child *because they already are* a mediational means for B's practice of play. The pot, spoon, and rice paddle stand as a fulcrum between these two actions. They are a kind of hinge which connects two actions, M's and B's.

These objects also have a broader history and this is in two senses. In the first sense, they have a history in the kitchen in this home. They are, after all, cooking and eating utensils. This history predates B's presence in the household. In the second sense, they have a history in the world that predates M's use and knowledge of them. I have no data to substantiate this history for M and for their household, but we may suppose that at some point these utensils were bought by them. They are quite likely to remember just how and when they came into their possession, and it is fair to assume that they bought them out of some perceived need. That is, at some earlier point in the history of this set of mediational means – perhaps separately for each of the pot, spoon, and rice paddle – M or her husband appropriated it through purchase to mediate actions in the kitchen. That history will have as part of its structure the price, the quality of the store, and the perceived positioning of them as consumer goods.

One of these mediational means, the rice paddle, carries with it a sociocultural history. While it does not in itself define this family as a rice-eating family, it is a mediational means widely associated with the practice of cooking and eating rice in the family. Taken together with an electric rice cooker and other such utensils and appliances it materially embodies and reproduces a social structure. As a semiotic structure it displays much about culinary and dietary practice in this household. This history and social structure are presented to B as given in this minuscule action of using the rice paddle to placate her when she is angry. She takes the rice paddle and plays. We have no evidence to attest that at this age she is able to cognitively or practically separate herself from these objects. To that small extent we can say that B, in her infant mind, already *is* the rice paddle, and the spoon, and the pot to the extent she has internalized them as mediational means in play. Of course it remains for her to incorporate more of these means and practices into her habitus. Our point here is that even in this very brief moment B is becoming a rice paddle user; there is a dialectic between the external object and her internalization of its use.

These mediational means are also clearly partial. In Example 2 both for M and for B these mediational means are being used in their 'spin-off' functions. We will want to return to this question later. Here we should notice that the appropriation of these utensils for play in earlier cases or for distraction in this case makes use of just some portion of what Halliday (1975, 1978, 1985) might call the meaning potential of the utensils, and it is not at all the normative or expected meaning; it is a spin-off use that makes use of the qualities of noise-making and durability of the utensils in the hands of a child.

A final point should be suggested before moving on to some early actions taken by B. In the data I have, this one action – handing B a pot, spoon, and rice paddle – I cannot say whether in previous cases M used exactly the same pot, the same spoon, and the same rice paddle. She would have in the kitchen several exemplars of each of these classes of objects. Thus this example is not directly illustrative of the categorical nature of mediational means. We can suppose, however, that the action taken by M might just as easily have been accomplished with a different rice paddle (or a different spoon or, perhaps, a different pot). In the dialectic between the psychological and the material, the internal and the external, the mediational means which is entering into B's habitus is the rice paddle as a type or class of objects, even if in the first instances it may be a class of a single member.

The crayon acquires a child

When she was 9 days into her second year, B held up three different crayons within a few minutes of each other as she and her sister played at drawing (Examples 3, 4, and 5). As we have argued, she cannot be said to have known what this object was nor, actually, to what extent it was separable from herself. It would be very difficult to call this a mediated action taken by B although it is a movement or a behavior, which was animated by B, not by anybody else. While it is very much at the outer margins of social action, M nevertheless produces it as a social act through her actions and through what she says, but in each case it is constructed somewhat differently, as we have seen.

In the first case (3) M construes this move as an opportunity to teach a bit of color terminology, 'Green'. She embeds this terminologization within a question and answer sequence which she animates entirely herself: 'What color is that? Green', and goes on to elaborate the function of this object as a mediational means, to draw. That is to say, from the point of view of mediational means, M appropriates this crayon, not as a crayon, but as a visual aid for her pedagogical instruction. We cannot say whether or not B hears or understands this in this instance. What we can say is that the crayon, through the work of M, has moved a minute step further into the habitus of B. In this sense we can say, as we suggested with the rice paddle, that the crayon has begun its acquisition of a child user.

The second instance (4) is much like the first, though in this case M positions the action within the expectations of R and S (as well as her own) that B will say something. Here, rather than constructing B's action as being in need of nomination, however, M constructs it as handing, as a bit of social interaction, and asks B to hand it to C. The crayon in this case is appropriated by M as a mediational means for accomplishing social interaction, not drawing. The nominalization is embedded within this action as a presupposition.

The third case (5) shows that B herself is taking on a bit of the constructed agency as she says 'crayon', or can be construed as saying that without too much exaggeration, though at this stage the word is an eccentric, not a normal utterance. M takes the crayon from B and thus constructs this as a normal instance of handing and nominalization.

Like the rice paddle, the crayons have multiple histories. I will set aside the history of crayons in general except to note that they might well embed a personal history for the adults in this and other such social interactions with infants. I have heard a mother in a shop rejecting a box of crayons by saying: 'No, I'm looking for the kind I had when I was a kid.' It is often the case that objects of play or other common household objects are passed from generation to generation, either as the actual objects or, in this case, the class or category of objects which are thought to be the same as those one had as a child. In this case, however, as M was a child in wartime Japan, the crayons with which her daughters are playing may well be an innovation within the universe of practice of that family.

There are two crucial histories in the appropriation of the crayon. The first of these lies outside of the data we have examined here but for which we have abundant somewhat more casual observations. B and C frequently played together at a low table with paper and crayons. This activity went on from before we began these recordings and continued on well into and beyond the period of our research. In these play sessions the crayons were appropriated by B quite naturally and without comment through practice. It is interesting to note that her older sister, C, at four commented from time to time when B was just one that 'she doesn't know how to play', or 'she can't say'. That is, B was said by C to be outside the circle of practice in many cases. C's motive in saying these things, of course, was easily interpreted as trying to correct our misguided research focus. It is clear that C felt we should be observing her as she was considerably more competent than B in so many ways.

The other, more local history is this little sequence of three examples (3, 4, and 5). There were many other instances before this, of course, and many to follow, but what we see here is that each appropriation of the crayon by M or by B is different from the others in some way. As Lyra (1999) points out, this highlights the importance of understanding the non-uniformity of practice in the experience of the child on the one hand, and on the other hand it points to the necessity of coming to our interpretations of specific acts within the historical sequence of which they form one link. As I have suggested above, each particular act connects or links multiple practices – handing, nominalization, interpersonal socialization – and conversely, no act can be seen as pure or as uniquely located in just one social practice.

Likewise then, we cannot argue that the mediational means by which those acts are performed are uniquely fit to specific actions or practices. What is a crayon to draw with in one point of view is a colored object to teach colors with in another; what is an object to demonstrate interpersonal politeness with in one point of view is a way to get the attention of M from another. There is in each of these acts an intersection of the purposes (including the non-purposiveness of the infant) of multiple actors, of the social practices being instantiated, and the appropriation of the mediational means. These mediational means are simultaneously appropriated by different actors within their separate habitus in different ways and instantiate for them different histories of practice within their habitus. The cultural tool, here the crayon, cannot be conceived as an object with anything like permanent or object characteristics that are the same for all participants or within each of the separate practices. The object, the crayon, may have certain objective characteristics – its malleability as something to be appropriated relies considerably upon these characteristics – nevertheless, as mediational means it can only be constructed within a specific practice which is virtually always linked to another practice with the tool as the hinge or mediation between practices and between the habitus of the participants.

In any event, in these cases the crayon is acquiring the child as a user through use in mediated actions which are NOT the normative ones for the use of crayons. That is, here we are not seeing the appropriation *in use* or *in the practice of drawing*, but we are seeing it *within its use in a different practice*; in this case they are the practices of nomination ('yellow crayon'), terminologization ('green'), and interpersonal interaction ('thank you', 'give it to Charlotte'). These practices are occurring concurrently with the appropriation of these crayons in practice, as throughout this session and at many other times the two children played together at drawing without this intervention on the part of M (and R and S with their research agenda).

In this we can see that the crayon as a mediational means is appropriated by B through practice (with C for example and possibly her own activities) but at the same time the crayon is being used by M within other, pedagogizing, social practices to bring B into a universe of practice in which these crayons are named, their colors can be read off in response to interrogation, and when one gives or receives them, the utterance 'thank you' is an expected accompaniment.

Instrumental and inherent use value

These examples we have now looked at have all shown the partial aspect of mediational means in that the pot, spoon, rice paddle, and the crayons, as we have seen them here, are not being used in the first place to cook a meal nor in the second to draw. It has been what we might think of as secondary characteristics of the objects as objects that have been exploited in constructing them as mediational means, not for cooking or drawing, but for appeasing a crying child or for the pedagogical interests of the mother hoping to display her child's abilities for the researcher.

From this we can suppose that virtually any mediational means might be exploited in any particular action either for some inherent, normative characteristics – cooking or drawing – or for more peripheral characteristics of those objects – noise-making, color, as a neutral object to construct the social interaction of handing, or for all objects in the child's world, as objects to be named.

While I do not know, I believe it is likely that when M brings candy to B in Example 7, it is just to exploit her interest in it as food in order to elicit somewhat higher levels of interaction than she was able to achieve with other objects. In this case there was not much to see that is worth comment, but in Examples 10 and 11 we saw much higher levels of agency in B. In Example 10 she works very hard to grasp R's taco and then S's juice. In Example 11 we saw that B was unable to actually separate herself from the cookie which she was attempting to hand to R.

By the period of BRENDA II, that is five or six months later, B had demonstrated herself to be a competent hander of objects around her social world. Not only does she do this regularly and frequently, by this time she has come to use objects for their incidental characteristics as mediational means as often as for their inherent characteristics as objects in use. We have noted, first, in BRENDA I that she was able to hand a green magnetized letter 'X' (Example 9), a book (Example 15), a set of keys (Example 18), and pennies (Example 25). Now she hands R a pen and a cassette tape (Example 28), and shoes (Example 29). After this it is a felt letter 'S' (Example 32), the entire tape recorder (Examples 36 and 39), and a book (Example 38). By these later examples we can see that B is engaged in active social action with intention. She is able to threaten and cajole. At (1:8.0) Brenda produced the monologic series of utterances below, which pretty much describes the project as well as shows how B's interest had become vested in its continuation:

tape
tape
word
word
word
word
word
paper
paper
paper
paper
paper
pen
pen
tape
tape

A few weeks later (at 1:8.21) she raises her foot over the tape recorder and says: 'Tape. Step.' Two months after that (1:10) we had a further discussion about the research project which, because by this time B's phonology could be reasonably written orthographically, can be conveniently summarized as:

B: Tape 'corder
R: Yeah
B: Use it
     Use it
R: Use it for what?
B: Talk

'corder talk

Brenda talk

Example 30, however, presents an interesting reversal. What we have seen, in fact, is that most of the mediational means handed to M and R (or S) by B are used in some instrumental purpose which is rather removed from any inherent function. B has not cooked rice, cannot spell any words, does not know how to open a house door nor operate the ignition in a car, does not know the value of money, nor how to write with a pen, nor what a cassette tape is, and she cannot wear her mother's or father's shoes. None of these objects are used in any inherent function. In fact what we might want to argue is that it is not the inherent functioning of mediational means that B has incorporated into her habitus at first at all, but rather what she has incorporated is M's pedagogical work of taking almost anything at hand and talking about it as an object to be named or located as a possession ('Mommy's shoe').

We might argue that the progression in the development of these objects in her world as mediational means has been toward overriding the inherent functionality of the objects as food (primary) or in other uses as clothing or for drawing, and coming to be able to use them for their peripheral characteristics as objects to name, to hand, to describe the colors of, and the rest of the pedagogical panoply of non-functional instrumentalities. In Example 30, however, we see that M in some cases picks up the opposite theme, the theme of real-world activity and functionality. When B picks up the scissors and says 'Cut, cut, cut, cut, cut', much as M has said earlier of the crayon 'draw', M rushes in to warn that this object is dangerous and should be put away immediately.

From these examples what I would want to argue is that the history of a mediational means in the habitus is one of the aggregation of the mediational means as a class of objects which includes the pluralization of function that comes with now using the tool for one characteristic and again using it for another characteristic. Now it is an object to be named, later an object with which you draw. This inherent plurality of function of objects is incorporated into the habitus of the mediational means so that one of two things may happen. In the first place virtually any mediational means may be used for a wide variety of functions outside of their inherent or normative use. In the second place other objects with those same functions may be substituted within any particular action *as that mediational means*. The result is the fundamental multifunctionality and polysemy of any mediational means which can be instantiated with a rather wide range of material objects in any particular instance of social action.

The objects Brenda uses

In the transcripts we have examined to arrive at our understanding of the ontogenesis of handing we have seen about fifty objects in use within four general groups: (1) handleable objects, (2) food, (3) ambient objects, and 4) represented objects. This is a loose grouping as I have included objects that were actually handed as well as objects which were proposed to be handed, such as a banana, but rejected by B. Furthermore, I have included such things as the TV which was simply mentioned by M as being where she then had to put things to keep them out of the grasp of B. Specifically, the objects which appear in these transcripts are:

1   *Handleable objects* (20)
    pot
    spoon
    rice paddle
    ball
    crayon
    magnetized letter
    candy box
    napkin
    book
    doll (when carried to B)
    keys
    pennies
    scotch tape
    pen
    recording tape
    shoes
    scissors
    foot (Brenda's foot: not quite successfully handed)
    coins
    tape recorder (later when B carries it)

2   *Food objects (also handleable)* (14)
    juice
    milk
    apple
    orange
    gau (Chinese glutinous rice cake)
    taco
    cookie
    tea (when handled)
    coffee
    pancake
    banana
    ice
    bottle
    raisins

3   *Ambient objects (or objects of deixis)* (14)
     doll (hakata doll)
     painting (boat): also represented object
     refrigerator
     cat (fortune cat)
     horse (toy rocking horse)
     TV
     table
     floor
     room
     tea (when pointed to)
     tape recorder (earlier when B refers to it)
     closet
     hanger
     briefcase

4   *Represented objects* (5)
     balloon
     baby (photo of B)
     Wow-wow/Fang (B's family's pet dog)
     pretend food
     sandbox cookie

Perhaps it is obvious that objects in the first category (handleable objects) are the most abundant and those in the fourth category (represented objects) are, perhaps, the most interesting. If we put categories (1) and (2) together because they are, in fact, objects which were central to the production of the social agency of the hander, there are about 35 of these which certainly make up the bulk of our examples. Nevertheless, bulk is never necessarily quality, and to some extent it is the mediational means which fall into the ambient and represented object categories which ultimately provide the substance for our understanding of the development of the mediational means in which we have a major interest, the semiotic mediational means.

Ambient objects as mediational means

On the whole I have tried to restrict the focus of this project to the ontogenesis of the social practice of handing as a way to limit the scope and thereby increase the sharpness of my focus. As I have said, because of this sharpened focus I have narrowed the range of mediational means for which I have the data to study at all carefully. Because of this narrowed range, then, we see that the bulk of the mediational means which have come to our attention consists of handleable objects, including food such as cookies, milk and juice bottles, and fruit.

Example 44 Age: 1:0.2

B	C	M	R	S	Context
[ne:ne:]		What's that over there? What's that, hm? What's that, hm? [e::] What's that, hm? You're not sick? Nene? Hm?			M pointing to hakata doll.
[ka:]		That's a hakata doll.			B looks at doll, M points to painting.
[ne:ne:]	I know how to run xxx.	Yeah. Doll. What's that? That's a boat.		She's got one thing on her mind.	
[æ:pʰ]		☺ Want juice? Hm? Gave you milk. You want juice now, hm? Apple? You want apple? Hm? [məman]? Yeah? ☺ You want Momma, yeah? Hm?			
[nɛnnɛn]		No?			
[nne:]					

An object that began its life in my data as an object of decoration in Examples 44 and 6, the hakata doll, became more transactionally active in Example 16 a month or so later. In the first case M uses it within the pointing or nomination practice: 'What's that over there?' which results in B looking at the doll on the cabinet. In the second case M asks, 'Where's the hakata doll?' and B looks directly at it. A month later, R brings the doll to B asking, 'What's this?' and B answers 'doll' (4 repetitions):

[dayɨ]
[dayu]
[dayɨ]
[dayʉ]

A hakata doll is a traditional Japanese doll – a work of art that often decorates the homes of Japanese families as well as those of many others around the world. As a decorative object it could be thought of as part of what Eco (1995) has called 'anonymous design'. I would want to include in such decorative objects and anonymous design virtually all the material arrangements of the spaces within which we take action. This would include the floor plan, furniture, wall hangings, doorways, and the rest within our homes and the streets, architecture, and the rest of the world we move through in living. As mediational means these objects, including represented objects to which we will return shortly, may be appropriated for use in a rather direct way, as in this case where R picks up a loose piece of the background and brings it to B. More often they are appropriated, as the hakata doll was in the first two examples, simply by having attention called to them, as in the pedagogical pointing of M with B ('What's that over there?'), or as in getting directions for oneself by looking at a street sign, or as in locating a shop of a particular brand name on a shopping trip. Even more removed from direct appropriation, but not at all insignificant, is the use we make of ambience as mediational means – the layout and design of tables and lighting, for example, in a restaurant of a particular kind to set the mood for a conversation.

The dialectic between internal and external, psychological and material, is quite attenuated. The only action required of B or made by her is recognition at first and later naming. Perhaps she might never come to appropriate this hakata doll in any more material sense nor internalize psychologically any greater understanding of it as a cultural or historical object. Nevertheless, I would argue that the doll, like the painting of the boat and many other objects about the house, as well as the house itself, are mediational means which may be appropriated by B and by M for the actions taken within those spaces.

In another perspective, when R actually removes the hakata doll from its display position and carries it to B, he has materially dislodged this ambient mediational means to use it as a connective or hinge among three practices, the pedagogical practices of pointing and naming to the pedagogical practices of handing and naming. In dislodging and therefore decontextualizing the hakata doll, R makes this linkage or hinging among practices rather concrete in a way that we then see B pick up and do in Examples 29 and 30 when she begins to pull shoes out of her parents' closet to bring to R and to name them ('Mommy's shoe').

There are two points I would like to draw from this use of ambient (or deictic) objects which it would be useful to study further with other data:

1   Ambient objects may function as mediational means through the merest acts of signaling, pointing, noticing, and appreciating for their general ambience. While the terms 'appropriate' and 'use' may feel rather strong for these actions, and the word 'action' also feels rather strong for 'notice' and 'appreciate', I would argue that these ambient objects are no less mediational means than the material objects we have seen B hand to others or has handed to her.

2   Because ambient objects are normatively appropriated in such peripheral ways, when an ambient object is focally appropriated as when R brings the

hakata doll to B, or when the carpenter constructs the counter upon which I will receive the cup of coffee I have bought, when a teacher analyzes the characteristics or properties of some object for instruction, or an architect analyses the structural materials out of which a wall, an arch, or a floor is made, this appropriation is rather decontextualized, pedagogical, or objectivized.[3]

It is beyond the scope of this project to recontextualize these pedagogical objects – my examples, tapes, and transcriptions – but not beyond the scope of our interest in coming to develop a grounded theory of practice.

Represented objects as mediational means

Now that we have argued that ambient objects such as the hakata doll or, indeed, the room itself should be considered to be mediational means in the actions we are analyzing here, we can return to Example 44 in which M uses a painting of a boat on the wall to construct the characteristic pedagogical sequence: 'What's that? That's a boat.' This latter shows a baby-talk shift from TO to FO, that is, M is carrying out this M/B sequence through ventriloquation of the second half of the question/answer sequence. In this construal of the pedagogical sequence, M not only construes the sequence, she also obliterates the problem of representation. This is said to be a boat, not a painting. The mediational means is produced as a transparent instantiation of the object itself. This is juice, this is an apple, that is a doll, and that is a boat. Juice, apple, doll (all material), and boat (represented) are produced as being of equivalent ontological status.

This is how represented objects are construed throughout these data. The framework of representation is stripped away and hidden behind the direct equation of the sign and the object. Thus in Example 22 when B was (1:1.29) we have seen that B points to a picture of a balloon in a book and calls it a 'ball'. M semi-ratifies and corrects this as: 'Ball. Hm. That's balloon.' Again, this is not: 'No, book; picture of a balloon.'

At age 1:2.5 a week later in Example 24 we conducted our little discrimination test to see if, in fact, B was able to make anything out of black and white photographic representations of the most common objects in her world. As I have said, these photographs were made of the objects that we had attested that she would look to or recognize if queried the previous week. Her very poor performance in this task suggests to us that B did not, in fact, make the object–representation equation that is taken for granted in our adult prompts and construals. She did, however, show an acute interest in these photographs which, no doubt, suggests some degree of recognition, and it would be a study of considerable interest to probe further this separation of object and its representations at this age.

For our purposes here, it seems prudent to say that from B's point of view at this stage, represented objects remained undifferentiated. That painting of a boat was a boat, but what that is most likely to have meant is that any painting hanging on the wall of that color, shape, approximate design, and so forth might well have been a boat. This argues that as mediational means, at least at this stage, represented objects remain fused and unified material objects. We have seen, based on Piagetian analysis, how the self and the object become progressively distanced from each other. What remains for further study is how and when the object and its representations undergo an analogous separation and what sorts of mediational means are the result.

It is clear by Example 34 (1:7.23) that B is successful at pretending to represent the world in play. She makes pretend food with her sister and pretends to feed it to her toy horse. Again in Example 37 (1:8.14) they play at making sandbox cookies which they pretend to feed to M and which M pretends to eat. Thus we can say that by one year and eight months, the class or categorical characteristic of mediational means was well established in B's habitus as she was able to let sand and other objects stand in for cookies and other food.

If we then return to take a look at other more material and handleable objects such as the 'X', 'S', book, keys, coins/pennies, cassette tape, horsie, bear and other toys, her world was populated by representational objects which were first appropriated by B as mediational means in their purely material manifestations. Like the 'boat', the 'penny' or the 'S' (or as B insisted, the 'E') were material objects with names, and the representational potential was as yet entirely unrealized in her habitus.

In this I am reminded of our own daughter Rachel who in her third year lined up seven wooden blocks with letters and said that they spelled 'SCOLLON' (Scollon and Scollon 1981:62). These blocks did not spell 'Scollon' but she had worked out at least some part of the representational aspect of the mystery of the letters on her blocks. As we wrote about that:

> Rachel said, 'There's two kind of "o" [ou] [low slowly falling pitch] and [ou] [high rapidly falling pitch].' When her father wrote the letter 'O' she said it was [ou] [former]. The other she indicated intonationally was the 'Oh!' of surprise.
>
> (Scollon and Scollon 1981:89)

From this we can assume, perhaps, that representational mediational means – paintings, letters of the alphabet, and words themselves – begin first as undifferentiated material objects for which the representation aspects are not constituted in the habitus of the child. At least in a child like Rachel who was being inducted into a literate nexus of practice, by the second or perhaps third year, a kind of fission between the object as materiality and the object as representation takes place. We have studied this process in the case of our own daughter in the source just cited. Our study of B ended just as this process was beginning to occur and so, for the moment, I must simply infer that the representative mediational means becomes that through a process of gradual separation of the material object and what it represents, through the same process by which the crayon as object and the crayon as source of the color green have been incorporated in the habitus.

Summary

In this analysis of the ontogenesis of mediational means within the ontogenesis of the social practice of handing in the life of a one-year-old child perhaps I have done nothing more than to illustrate and elucidate the concept of the mediational means advanced by Wertsch. I believe, however, that this study clarifies several issues. I will summarize these below.

In the life of the child, mediational means predate the user. They arrive in her life as givens, as pre-existing material objects. To put this a bit more precisely, the objects which become represented as mediational means are represented as such in the habitus of her primary caregivers. The process of appropriating a mediational means begins in the behaviors in which she grasps an object, glances in a direction, or in some way shows a disposition to do something, and the objects involved are construed by caregivers as mediational means within the actions and practices also construed by the caregivers.

The mediational means is an historical and a categorical concept. I have argued that until an action (e.g. holding up the crayon) is construed as a social practice (handing), it is only an action. To call it a social practice is to construe it as an action in a recognizable and historical sequence of actions having taken place over time. Likewise, until something is construed as a mediational means, it is an object. A mediational means is the class of objects which can be appropriated within a practice as I have defined a practice as a very specific historical sequence of actions.

The mediational means arrives *through the agency of caregivers* who construe the objects in the life of the child as mediational means. While I have not argued the case here, I would now suggest that this is likely not to be much different for adults in the appropriation of any mediational means. In a somewhat paradoxical sense, it is the mediational means which appropriates the person, though the person may then use the mediational means in a host of quite specific, unique, and concrete actions.

This entails that we must make a *distinction between appropriation and use* because the mediational means is a category that arises over a sequence of uses. 'Appropriation' refers to the historical sequence of uses; 'use' refers to the specific, one-time-only, real-time instance in a social action.

Each use elaborates and complicates the structure of the mediational means and the habitus and therefore each use opens up the potential for more complex uses of objects as that mediational means.

In the life of the child there is a *separation first of the mediational means from the self* and then a *progressive separation of the object from its representations.*

Practice and mediational means: technologization and standardization

It may be terminologically useful to use the term 'technologization' for the processes of construal by which caregivers and others construct the mediational means. There is something about this pedagogization of the object as a mediational means which, while operating in practice, at the same time lifts it out of practice into a structural domain of analysis and objectivization. In the material I have studied here we have seen the highest levels of the construal of objects as mediational means in just those cases where M and others have been at pains to produce social performances. When M perceives the goal as getting B to say things, she appears to engage in the highest levels of pedagogization or, perhaps we should say, technologization. It would be putting far too much into our examples to argue that the institutions of schooling, literacy, and the standardizations of practice that accompany them all arise in such a simple straightforward manner from the technologization of practice. Nevertheless, this is a highly suggestive direction for further study, in my view.

The reciprocal process might be called standardization. That is, when the mediational means comes to exert pressure on practice so that actions not in line with the construed mediational means are disapproved for that reason, or the practices that are commensurable are valorized, we might want to speak of this as a sort of standardization or credentialization. Again, like the suggestion I have just made about technologization, it would go far beyond the scope of this body of research to do more than make the suggestion that these might be interesting avenues of study.

Discourse and mediational means: semiotic mediational means

Language is central to the construction of the mediational means of handing in the life of the one-year-old. I believe we can feel confident in this in the first place because throughout our analysis we see that handing is frequently, if not always, accompanied by some linguistic form. At the same time, as we have seen already, the linkage between what is said and the action itself is somewhat indirect and problematical. The language which accompanies handing in the first two years is not *about* handing. That is, it is not reflexive or meta-practical talk which is about the action or the practice in which the participants are engaged.

In my preceding discussion of the development of the child as a social actor – as a hander – I have argued that the central role of discourse is not in the construction of the practice of handing so much as in the construction of the social actor. That is to say, the focus of the discursive practice is meta-personal or meta-social; it is on the person as a social actor. I also argued that this meta-personal discourse was visible not in the separate actions in real time but as an aggregate of discursive practice over time. From that point of view, the relationship of the study of the discursive practice associated with handing and of the practice of handing itself is linked through the construction of the child as a particular kind of social actor – the hander. Perhaps this is simply another way of saying that we do not talk about our practices, we engage in them; but we do talk about ourselves as social actors of particular kinds and practice is implied to flow from those social actions.

Now in this analysis of mediational means, we have seen that discourse plays a major role in constructing the mediational means by which social actors take action in the world. From very early the objects in the child's world are construed as objects with which to take action. Crayons are to draw with, they are to be handed to sisters, they have colors. And what begins as caregiver discursive practice is soon picked up by the child as she hands the tape recorder to R and tells him to use it. Of course, because the habitus is aggregated in practice and through the use of mediational means (or as the use of mediational means), this role of discourse is central in the production of practice and habitus.

What is most striking to me in this is that discursive practice is itself not often construed as a mediational means. It is somehow almost entirely exempted from the discursive work of its own construction. We have seen very little meta-discursive discursive practice. It is true that early on M had commented: 'They want you to talk, Brenda. Say something' (Example 4). Later she said: 'Hear what you said? You said, "Chodai".' We are all aware that there is some meta-discursive commentary on the child's language, particularly in speaking to other adults in what I have called the WI register, that is, in talk that excludes the child or which treats the child as an object for discussion. Within the language used with the child, there is a surprisingly small amount of discourse about discursive practice, especially in these materials which were known to be specifically about her developing language use. The language which is used in these examples is about B as a social actor and about the mediational means; it is not about the language, either ours or hers. B is not much constructed as a speaker, nor is the language we are using constructed as a mediational means in that construction in spite of the fact that throughout, as we have seen, there is much work on the part of all the adults to get B to talk. This work is carried out almost entirely indirectly.

There is in this construction of discourse as a mediational means an interesting duality of function, perhaps even a paradoxicality. M says: 'What color is that? Green. Draw now', or 'Yellow crayon. Thank you.' But she does not say: 'Crayon. We teach language with that.' This discursive function of construing B as a social actor, and of construing objects as particular kinds of mediational means, is rarely called upon to construct language itself as a mediational means, nor is it used to construe speaking as a social practice, nor even to construe B as a speaker of language. We might almost want to say that this most representational of mediational means prefers to represent itself only in practice. Or to put it less agentively, it seems that language – discursive practice – enters the habitus as a mediational means almost entirely through practice and without being reflectively constructed in social interactions with others. In this it stands out as rather different in its ontogeny from the social practice of handing.

This latter comment needs to be looked at carefully. While it is the case in my data that language is rarely used to reflect on linguistic practices, this may well embed much about social practice within this particular nexus or community of practice which it would be a serious mistake to produce as a general statement about language or discursive development. Elsewhere we have argued that at least some children are socialized into a discourse which is to some considerable extent characterized by just these meta-discursive practices of discourse about discourse (Scollon and Scollon 1981). There we developed the idea of a discourse system (order of discourse, discursive formation, Discourse, nexus of practice – here the exact term is probably not consequential) of essayist literacy. We argued that in the case we examined of our own daughter, Rachel, we could argue that from the time she was between two and three years of age she had integrated in her habitus many of the social practices of literacy, and that without having developed the specific reading and writing skills so often thought of as literacy itself.

As I have pointed out above, between two and three years of age she used letter blocks to 'spell' out the name 'SCOLLON' and said that that was what she was doing. Later she 'wrote' stories, scribbles on scraps of paper which she read out to us. Near the end of that year we were camping in the mountains of Alberta in a place she had never been. I was putting jam on a cracker and she asked, 'What's this?' pointing to the jar with jam. I said, 'It's jam.' She said, 'No, what's *this*?' with emphasis. I said, 'You mean the jar?' She said, 'No, I mean what do they call it *here*?' It is clear that this is a level of meta-discursive discourse, that is, discourse about discursive practice as a mediational means. She had not yet developed the fully explicit means of handling this sort of question; she did not just say: 'What's the word for "jam" which is used by people who live in this area?' But she could be said to have known two things: (1) the names of objects change from place to place, and (2) you can find that out by asking that sort of question.

Thus in saying that in the data I have here I have very little evidence that discursive practice and the mediational means of discourse are themselves constructed as mediational means in the habitus of the child, I do not intend to suggest that this would never happen in the life of this child on the one hand nor that it does not happen in the lives of other children. Equally I do not want to suggest that the discursive practices that I have examined here would in any way be the same ones we would see in the analysis of other children of this same age in another universe of practice. I want to limit my comments to saying that *in this case* at which we have looked quite closely a child has come to be an adept user of the mediational means of handing, she has come to be construed as a social actor of this kind – a hander – and she engages in this practice in a way that is complexly linked to other language and discursive practices – naming, issuing directives, controlling conversational topics – without any apparent necessity of making those practices explicit in discourse and without making the discourses of these practices an explicit part of these practices.

Having said this, can we speak of language as a mediational means and what would this mean? Within the limits of the focus I have developed here, we can argue that the analysis of mediational means as isolated entities is an absurdity. It is very difficult to imagine what might be the result of positing crayons as a mediational means in some *a priori* fashion and then setting about to find out just how and when they might be used. I believe we would quickly find that the crayon is an object with specific characteristics, but is only a mediational means when it is appropriated within a specific practice by being used in a concrete social action. At that moment of intersection between its historical existence and its use in action we can see what sort of a mediational means it is. Within the data I have here the crayon would have to be analyzed as a mediational means for infant pedagogy; it is an object that can be colored green or yellow (and perhaps other colors as well), it is an object about which the function of drawing can be predicated, and it is an object that can be handed to one's sister. It would be a significant number of mediational means which could meet those criteria, not just the common crayon. Likewise, within an analysis of the practice of handing, the rice paddle is a certain kind of mediational means; in this case it is a noise-maker. To put it more succinctly, the analysis of the characteristics of objects in the world is not likely to lead very productively to the understanding of those objects as mediational means. This is because the mediational means, as I have argued here, is not an object but a class of objects positioned within a social practice which has both an external, material existence and an internal, psychological existence in the habitus.

More to the point would be to ask: in this or that social practice, is language or discourse constructed as a mediational means? If so, how is it constituted in the history of practice and in the habitus of the social actors who engage in this practice? Outside of this rather narrowed framework it seems an empty question to ask whether or not language is a mediational means.

NOTES

1 Provisionally we might want to talk about not just a sequence of practices that lead up to an action such as the purchasing transaction but, analogous to Goffman's 'funnel of betrayal' (Goffman 1961), we might want to examine a host of loosely connected preparatory practices which move in this direction; such as checking my wallet for money as I dress in the morning, scheduling a variety of minor office activities so as to have time for this purchase just before class; and so forth. We might call these the 'funnel of commitment' (to an action). It seems the closer we get to the crucial moment of uttering our order and paying up, the more difficult it is to turn back or to take another action.

2 Harris (1989) would use the term 'self' in this case.

3 We might say that all of the examples we have studied here have been objectivized for the purposes of this study in just this manner.

5   The nexus of practice

Identity and the morning cup of coffee

May I help you?
Yes, what's the difference between a *latte* and *café au lait*?
*****
May I help you?
Yes, I'd like a tall latte, please.
O.K.; $2.25.
*****
May I help you?
Yes, I'd like a tall latte, please.
Whole or skim?
Pardon me?
Whole milk or skim milk in that?
Uh, whole milk.

The three conversations I have reconstructed here recapitulate my induction into a world of coffee drinkers in late millennium America. I have used examples developed out of my own present coffee habit because they are fresh in my mind. A lifetime tea drinker finds it difficult in the US to locate a real cup of tea in public venues and so one strategy which I have adopted, now that somewhat improved varieties of coffees are more widely available, is to have coffee when I am out in the world and reserve my tea drinking for my life at home. Having lived in Asia for most of the last decade and in a small town in Alaska for the decade before that, when I returned to the US I found that an almost tropical variety and abundance of coffee was now available in most large cities but that I did not know any of the practices linked with this new coffee society.

In defense of my obvious ignorance of a central aspect of cosmopolitan world culture for the past 300 years I should point out that I had had coffee before this encounter on many occasions. Each of those public occasions was grounded solidly in practice. I had had what somebody else had. Normally that was the unmarked coffee of American coffee shops, restaurants, cafeterias, and other public venues, not the designer coffees of the new coffee society. In such venues, if my friend had *latte*, so did I. If *au lait*, that's what I had. As these cups of coffee were few and far between, in different shops and in different countries, the variability was so great that I had no empirical means of working out the differences among them.

As I approached the point of service in the first service encounter above I was not by any means ready to place my order. While I was being asked what I wanted, I was busily scanning the posted menus for a way to improve my knowledge of the practice so that I could order. Knowing that *latte* was Italian and *lait* was French was not enough to sort out which of these varieties of what I thought of as *coffee with milk* I wanted to order. My question, of course, placed me squarely outside of the society of regular customers at this shop; in fact it placed me outside of the society of customers at any of these specialist coffee shops. By asking it, however, I positioned myself as a novice, an apprentice, a learner. I positioned myself as one outside but wishing to come in.

This is the first point about identity which I will consider in this chapter: any action positions the social actor in relationship to others who are engaged in the practice. Poor performance in the practice might signal many things – novice status, cynical disdain of practice, temporary inattention, and a really indefinite number of other meanings. Likewise, good performance might signal an equally complex array of positionings. What is impossible is that no positioning occurs at all. The unmarked positioning when no attention is drawn at all to the action is that of the normal member of the group of people for whom this practice is embedded in the habitus. This is, then, the second point: how may we talk about such concepts as 'membership' or 'identity' on the one hand and the groups of people who have homologous habitus (Bourdieu 1990) on the other?

My second service encounter above shows me to have moved a bit further into the practice as I was able to simply step up and order what I wanted, or appeared to want, without hesitation on my part or confusion on the part of the server. As in all social actions, in this social action I make an implicit claim of identity in the coffee society, at least of this shop. That claim is ratified with 'O.K.' and further ratified when the price quoted is the one I have expected for a tall latte. In this case the word 'tall' has also served this business of claiming an identity as the word 'tall' has never been associated in my lexicon with 'the smallest one you have on sale', but that is its meaning in this particular shop.

A social practice is developed as practice through a sequence of social or mediated actions through which a person consolidates that practice in the habitus. Perhaps the real test of this historical-body (Nishida 1958) of action is whether it provides a basis for action across a variety of new or different situations. Of course this movement into new circumstances is always partial and always involves further adjustments and accommodations of the practice in the habitus to these new objective conditions. Thus when I went to a different coffee shop in the third example, I found that my newly constituted practice was as yet underdeveloped. There was a choice to be made between whole and skim milk about which I was wholly unaware, and so my claim of a normal identity failed as it could not be ratified in the first instance.

The problem which I will address in this chapter is the problem of identity as it is related to social action, practice, and habitus. As I have suggested here, one's actions produce one in the first place as a person who is competent or not in some social practice, and in the second place, they produce one as someone with an identity – a coffee shop habitué, a novice, or perhaps a stranger or foreigner. It is common to say that a child is being socialized into one or another social group, but this sort of statement is excessively teleological. It presumes either that one knows what social groups that child will become a member of as an adult, or that the child will simply become a member of whatever social groups his or her caregivers are members of. That is, it assumes an identity toward which the child is moving which is empirically, of course, impossible to do more than speculate about, or it assumes that a child will take on no identities but those of the caregivers.

Here I will, again, stick as close as possible to the empirical ground of the research I have already analyzed – the cases of B handing objects or receiving them from others. I have already argued that this practice of handing cannot be viewed *as a practice* in any single act of handing but that it must be understood as a history of such actions which are consolidated in the habitus as the practice of handing. I have also argued that this practice of handing is often linked, but not uniquely linked, to other practices, some of them discursive practices. Now I will argue that these linkages form what I will call a *nexus[1] of practice*. By that I mean to convey that a number of social practices intersect, never perfectly, never in any finalized matrix or latticework of regular patterns, but as a network which itself is the basis of the identities we produce and claim through our social actions.

Having argued on behalf of the concept of a *nexus of practice* I will then argue that the idea of a community of practice (or one of the now many alternative concepts), while problematical without further analysis, is best thought of as an objectified nexus of practice. That is, I will argue that there are many nexus of practice through which multiple practices are linked but only some of them become objectified by social actors as bounded communities into which one can gain access and membership, have that membership ratified, or be expelled from. In this the nexus of practice is like the habitus in being largely an unconscious linkage among practices but which may undergo processes of objectification.

The problem of communities of practice

Before I move directly to considering the data we have from B, first I need to briefly consider why we might need a concept of a community of practice (Lave and Wenger 1991; Wenger 1998; Hanks 1996); discourse community (Swales 1990, 1998), universe of practice (Bourdieu 1977, 1990), Discourse (Gee 1990, 1996), reality set (Scollon and Scollon 1979, 1981), or discourse system (Scollon and Scollon 1995), as well as the problems I find in using these for my analysis here. There have been rather different reasons for the proposal of such groups.

Bourdieu's *universe of practice* was not much developed when first introduced in 1977 and then not really reconsidered in the revision in 1990. As I have argued in

Chapter 2, Bourdieu at that time was ambiguous about whether habitus was to be thought of as located in separate persons or as located in social groups or social classes. He wrote of 'the objective homogenizing of group or class habitus which results from the homogeneity of the conditions of existence' (p. 80) as being 'the same' habitus in all members of that group or class, without being clear about whether we were to understand this as somehow a habitus which is distributed across biological individuals as members of social classes or what he was later to clarify as *homologous* habitus, that is, parallel structures of habitus in separate individuals which were the result of having that habitus constructed in the same objective social conditions. In this argument, Bourdieu simply presupposes that (1) people are members of the same group or class without further need for qualification – partial members, fledgling members, marginal members, (2) people are not members of multiple groups or classes, and (3) people do not move from group to group or from class to class. Within this rather rigid notion of sociopolitical structure he first (1977) introduced the notion of the *universe of practice* as the logical framework in which an objective condition might be interpreted by all the persons operating within that universe of practice.

In his 1990 revision Bourdieu seems to have substituted the concept of the *field* for the *universe of practice* and took it to be 'an arbitrary social construct, an artefact whose arbitrariness and artificiality are underlined by everything that defines its autonomy – explicit and specific rules, strictly delimited and extra-ordinary time and space' (p. 67). For him the *universe of practice* or the *field* is a conceptual structure formed by and in homologous habitus. Bearing in mind that for Bourdieu, the word 'practice' is most often used in the rather vague mass noun and general sense, the *universe of practice* or *field* seems little more than a terminological variant for homologous habitus of the members of a particular social class or social group. In any event, in Bourdieu's theorizing on practice one finds that groups and classes remain presupposed, autonomous, bounded, and non-overlapping analytical entities and his use of *universe of practice* or *field* seems little more than reterminologization of these presupposed entities.

Among sociologists and anthropologists until fairly recently there has been a tendency to think solely in terms of presupposed and bounded entities. It has been argued that this is logically and historically linked to the sociopolitical and ideological production of such entities as the nation-state in the modern period (Anderson 1991; Billig 1995, 1997; Harvey 1996) and is one of the ways in which a kind of genesis amnesia (Bourdieu 1977) has set in in scholarly analysis of social entities. On the whole Anderson and Billig argue that we have yet to develop robust theoretical frameworks to deal with social phenomena and practices which clearly are not contained nor are containable within the boundaries of the groups and classes we have grown accustomed to analyzing. We have forgotten that these entities are themselves sociopolitical constructs which carry ideological baggage that needs to be opened and examined.

Our own earlier work must be examined within this same critical perspective (Scollon and Scollon 1979, 1981). In trying to capture what we believed and still believe are important differences between what we called *Athabaskans* and *English speakers* – both highly problematical terms which we chose only after considerable qualification[2] – we argued that members of each of these groups held in common what we called a *reality set*; the first we called the 'bush consciousness' and the second we called the 'modern consciousness' after Berger, Berger, and Kellner (1973). Based in our ethnographic and discursive studies we argued, much along the lines of Bourdieu at about that same time, that members of these groups were predisposed through their experiences to see the world as a particular phenomenon or reality. We argued that a reality set was an internally consistent and self-regulating and ratifying set of interactions among worldview, socialization practices, forms of discourse, and social relationships.

There are problems with this concept of the reality set, however useful it might be in some ways. From the point of view I am taking here, the concept of the reality set is far too cognitive. To the extent reality set is thought of as a way of thinking – a consciousness – it privileges cognition and worldview as the organizing function of human society and social life and derives, at least by implication, the rest of the world, both cultural and material, from this concept. As Bourdieu would rightly argue, it takes an omniscient, objectivistic, and analytical view of the actions and material life of members of these groups and therefore ultimately is doomed to fail to capture the lived experience of social actors acting on the basis of the 'poor logic' (Bourdieu 1977, 1990) of habitus.

A second problem is that such a view of human social life too easily can be taken as an essentialist analysis which equates a person with the reality set of the group of which the person is a member. Like the field or universe of practice of Bourdieu, the reality set suggests, though we did not make this claim, that each person had or contained, as well as was governed by, this reality set as the motive engine, the interpretive key, and the perceptual filter of all reality. While in fact our specific argument was that many individuals participate in both of these reality sets (and perhaps others), and so we tried to argue that incommensurabilities were between reality sets, not between individual social actors, nevertheless, like Bourdieu, virtually all of our examples and arguments were based on simplified, homogeneous communities and individuals; one person–one reality set was the implicit model even though we somewhat paradoxically argued against this view.

When we returned to this idea (Scollon and Scollon 1995) we rephrased what it was we wanted to capture with the term *discourse system*. With that concept we wanted to capture two aspects which we believed were important in understanding discourse across boundaries, whether that discourse occurs as intercultural communication or more locally as communication between older and younger people, women and men, or professionals and service providers. The first aspect is the relatively stable nature of these systems of discourse which gives rise to both internal and external stereotyping. The second aspect is the multiple and often conflicting memberships we all express in our day-to-day communication. We argued that not only do we communicate as North Americans or Chinese, we communicate as women or men, as members of a senior generation or young people, as professionals or as laborers, as East Coasters or West Coasters, or as long-term residents or newcomers. In any one act of speaking I might make claims of identity as a man, a university professor, a father, and an American. No one of these and many other possible identities is *the* single identity which I produce in that act on the one hand, and some of those identities may well exist in a contradictory or paradoxical relationship with others. We argued that at a minimum, a discourse system could be analyzed as a set of genres, registers, or forms of discourse, practices of socialization to that discourse system, an ideology and worldview, and preferred practices of face-to-face or other interpersonal relationships.

Approaching from a different set of questions, Swales (1990) introduced the idea of the *discourse community*. For Swales what held the community together, its common thread or organizing principle, was a text or set of texts – genres, in fact. What was very useful about this idea was that a stamp collector in, say, Hong Kong, and another one in Denmark who might not, in fact, know each other or have any sort of social interactions with each other are nevertheless participants in a fairly large number of homologous practices. As Swales defined the discourse community, it was the stamps themselves which formed the link among these far-flung members of the 'same' community. As he developed the idea, anybody who had any dealings with these stamps was, in fact, a member of the discourse community as there was, in principle, no way of including the hobby collector but not his or her friend who passed on possibly interesting stamps or the postman who brought the stamps.

Swales more recently (1998) has given up this earlier notion of the discourse community as largely untenable or ultimately indefinable in favor of an idea of a community united by common place as in a workplace – the *place discourse community*. While there is something to be said for the idea that people who regularly work together form a kind of community, this sort of community is not likely to be organized in terms of common practice so much as diversity of practice linked to some common overall purpose, such as the computer service center Swales studies. As such, it seems the place discourse community is not a concept of particular relevance to the argument I am developing here. What I believe is important to capture from this work of Swales, however, is the idea that homologous habitus may exist in people who have no contact with or knowledge of each other and, more basic to my argument, a single practice may span multiple communities. A person in Hong Kong may engage in collecting stamps in a way that is virtually identical to a person in San Francisco, while those two people may in every other way engage as active members in very different social groups or classes.

Gee (1990, 1996, 1999; Gee, Hull, and Lankshear 1996) has preferred to use the term Discourse (with a capital 'D') as the term by which he positions and bounds social groupings. Originating his understanding of Discourses in the New Literacy Studies (Scollon and Scollon 1981; Heath 1983; Scribner and Cole 1981; Street 1984, 1995; Barton and Hamilton 1998) as well as his own work, for Gee a Discourse is:

Different ways in which we humans integrate language with non-language 'stuff', such as different ways of thinking, acting, interacting, valuing, feeling, believing, and using symbols, tools, and objects in the right places and at the right times so as to enact and recognize different identities and activities, give the material world certain meanings, distribute social goods in a certain way, make certain sorts of meaningful connections in our experience, and privilege certain symbol systems and ways of knowing over others.

(Gee 1999:13)

This congenially casual definition captures several important issues and covers much territory. For Gee a Discourse is both linguistic (discursive in the narrow sense) and non-linguistic, it involves power relationships, embeds an ideology, and privileges not only people and groups but their symbol systems as well. Central to a Discourse is the concern for the production of identities, both those established by and within a Discourse and the identities of those produced as others. In this Gee's Discourse is very much like our discourse system in its formulation, its extension, and its coverage.

One other term that has achieved recent currency in the lexicon of group analysis is the *community of practice* (Lave and Wenger 1991; Wenger 1998; Hanks 1996). I have found this term useful as a way of highlighting the learning and identity aspects of our production of ourselves as members of communities of practice (Scollon 1998). At the same time, it is a term that proves rather difficult to use with much assurance that one has not been pulled at least metaphorically back into presupposed and unexamined bounded social entities. Much of the writing about communities of practice has become absorbed in definitional matters of what is or is not such a community, what the structural criteria are for this classification, how membership is attained or rejected, and how big or small a community of practice should be regarded to be.

Beyond these problems with the term and perhaps confounded with these problems is the very great popularity of the term in non-academic areas of work. As Gee, Hull, and Lankshear (1996) note, the term is much used by management gurus of the new capitalism. A quick glance about the World Wide Web or the business section of book stores shows that it is a term which is taken as intuitively given and one of great utility, particularly to service providers who claim to offer *community of practice* membership to lonely individual computer users as part of the benefits of subscribing to their services.

Overall my goal here in this work is to try to come to understand the relationship between discourse and practice. If this were not the case, it would be quite satisfactory from my point of view to continue using either the idea of the discourse system or what I would regard as a terminological equivalent, Gee's capital 'D' Discourse, though I must say I am not particularly attracted by having to say 'capital "D" Discourse' or to write discourse as 'Discourse' if an alternative is readily available. But in this case where it is important not to confound social practices with the sub-class of social practices, discursive practices, I prefer to introduce, at least for the moment, the term *nexus of practice*.

Nexus as network of linked practices

A nexus of practice is a network of linked practices. I want to fix our attention on the word 'practice' with this term. What is significant are the linkages as well as the incommensurabilities (Calhoun 1995) and the loosely connected frameworks or nexus these linkages produce. The word leaves open the possibility of using it to refer to both the point of connection between practices as well as the overall set or pattern of connections. Elsewhere I have referred to the point of intersection or the moments in social action when two or more practices converge and are instantiated within and by a single action as a 'site of engagement' (Scollon 1998). Using this terminology, I would want to call the action in real time a site of engagement and the repeated coupling of two or more practices a linkage.

As I have tried to use the term 'practice', I am referring to a narrowly defined count-noun entity, not the loose, large, and ambiguous mass noun entity. To show the relationship between what I am speaking of here and what Bourdieu or, perhaps, Chouliaraki and Fairclough (1999) speak of as the 'practice of sheep farming' or the 'practice of teaching philosophy', I would call that sort of practice a nexus of practice. That is, I would argue that we recognize the 'practice' of teaching philosophy because of a large number of separate practices – lecturing, holding tutorials, setting exam questions, marking exams, giving reading assignments, assigning papers, certain modes of argument, and the like – which are linked together so that we recognize this as teaching philosophy as opposed to teaching driver education or sheep farming. Thus, 'nexus' is the comprehensive term and 'practice' is the specific, narrower term.

The question to which I will turn my attention now is this: how does B come to be identified and ultimately to claim an identity for herself as a social actor within a nexus or within multiple nexus of practice? For this I will turn to the data we have already examined to look at it from this point of view.

The nexus of practice in BRENDA

We saw in several early examples that the social practice that I have analyzed here, handing, is associated with or linked to a variety of other practices. For example in Example 3 B's motion of holding up a crayon was construed by M not only as handing but also as an opportunity for a practice we might call naming, though, of course, we have not carried out a comparable study of the practice of naming. We could identify several aspects of this practice from our experience with caregiver–infant talk. Naming is a practice in which the caregiver goes about producing the names of rather common objects in the world. Often this naming is prompted as in Example 44: 'What's that over there? That's a hakata doll.' In Example 44, naming is linked to another practice, pointing. Naming also occurs with handing throughout our examples. In Example 4, when B 'hands' her another crayon, M says: 'Yellow crayon. Give it to C.'

In our previous analysis we saw that these various discursive practices – naming, pointing, interacting, telling the function, nurturing – are not uniquely linked to the practice of handing. That is, in one case handing is linked to naming: M tells B that it is a crayon or some other object. In another case she tells B the color. She also tells her to give it to her sister (interacting) or tells her to draw with it (functioning). Each of these provides a separate point of linkage between and among this array or, in fact, nexus of practice.

There are yet other practices linked with handing. In Example 2 we saw what we might call cajoling. Handing was used to placate B and distract her from crying. Perhaps the most common practice which is linked to handing – one might argue that all the others including handing itself derive from this – is nurturing: 'Wan juice?', 'You want apple?'

Thus very early in B's social life, well before she can be attested to be able to engage in these social practices in an agentive way, various nexus of practice are constructed by M and other caregivers. We might want to talk at first about very minor nexus of practice. For example we might want to identify a nexus of practice which we could call CAREGIVING. Perhaps at the beginning it would look like this:

CAREGIVING: handing + interacting ('Mommy chodai') + cajoling + body care (washing, changing diapers and so forth) + nurturing.

We have examples of portions of this nexus in the data we have examined here and, of course, I have many examples of the other practices such as body care and nurturing (feeding) which I have not transcribed. What is important in this concept of the nexus of practice is to understand that just as we have seen in respect to handing, not all of these practices occur together simultaneously. Now it is these two linked in an action, again it is one of these linked with another. Now we have handing linked to cajoling, then we have handing linked to naming, then we have naming linked to nurturing, then nurturing linked to interacting. What forms the nexus is the multiple linkages among these different practices and the recurring production of such links in ever new and different combinations.

Within this nexus of CAREGIVING, B is construed as an infant in need of constant care and attention. Her identity, as constructed for her in these social interactions with M, is that of an infant whose primary interactions are with M.

A sketch of the CAREGIVING nexus of practice might be simplified to look like Figure 1. What I hope to capture with such a schematic diagram are several aspects of what we have seen in these data. First, there is no fixed linkage of any two practices such that if you have one you always have the other. Second, each practice is linked to other practices in ways that ultimately lead to a rather extended network of such linkages. One would not be able to, nor would one want to, say where the boundary of such a nexus is.

Third, Figure 1 represents an aggregation over time, not an analytical structure. Some of the nodes or points of intersection have been attested just once. Others have been attested many times. Ultimately the researcher would not know, could not know, which links have what frequency. And over time we begin to see that some practices, though not uniquely linked to others, are nevertheless

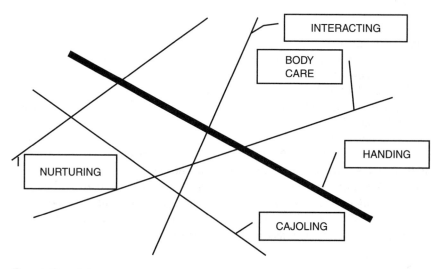

Figure 1 Caregiving

repeated frequently enough that it is not only the practice which enters into the habitus but the nexus of linkages as well.

As an example of this, the nurturing practice and the handing practice are acted out many times. Perhaps at first all cases of nurturing (feeding) B are linked to handing, but not all handing is linked to nurturing. Handing is also linked to naming. Not only is naming not uniquely linked to handing, but it is also linked to nurturing on the one hand and to pointing on the other. Thus what I am arguing is that it is not only practices that are constituted in the habitus over a history of social actions, but also the linkages are constituted in the habitus as well over a history in multiple sites of engagement.

Of course it would be futile to try to engage in the task of trying to decide how many nexus of practice have been constructed within the focal range of my data. In any event that number would be entirely an accident of the data I have at hand, as well as a systematic distortion caused by my focus throughout on the practice of handing and therefore only having visible cases of other practices which occur in linkage with handing or in the near vicinity. In addition to the CAREGIVING nexus of practice, we could identify very early in this material a nexus of practice we might want to call the PEDAGOGICAL nexus of practice. Example 44 is a linkage of pointing and naming: 'What's that over there? That's a hakata doll.' In Example 3 we have: 'What color is that? Green. Draw now.' In Example 4, 'They want you to talk.' Then just following that we have: 'Yellow crayon. Give it to C.' Here the nexus of practice links pointing, handing, naming, interacting into a nexus of practice within which B is produced in the identity of a language learner.

Notice that within this nexus of practice the identity that is produced for B is that of an active agent. She is not only told the names of things, she is asked if she knows them. She is told the function of objects and what to do with them. Her identity within this nexus is that of an active learner. This contrasts somewhat with her identity within the CAREGIVING nexus where she is constructed as an infant in need of unilateral care. Not surprisingly, over the year of data we have examined, these identities begin to shift. As the PEDAGOGICAL nexus identity takes, the CAREGIVING identity begins to become attenuated. As B is not only constructed as an agent in these social actions but herself shows what I have called 'agentive resistance', the CAREGIVING nexus becomes less often instantiated in actions and the PEDAGOGICAL nexus takes on new practices such as the 'book game'. By Example 22 (1:1.29) B is pointing at a picture of a balloon and saying 'Ball'. By the end of my data at about two years of age (2:0.12), conversations with B were often long sequences of her pointing to objects in the book and making comments about them. B's near soliloquy with her natural history book is an example of how developed her identity as a reader in the book game had become (a number followed by 'x' indicates the number of repetitions):

ladybug
butterfly
one butterfly (4x)
two (5x)
two (2x)
three (2x)
ladybug
two dems dere.
broke
dis can fix it up.
dey can fix it up.

B's reference here is to a picture of dinosaur bones as found in the matrix rock. The bones appeared scattered ('broke') in one picture, then in a later picture appeared assembled as a dinosaur skeleton on museum exhibit ('dey can fix it up').

A further point that needs to be made is that what is distinctive about a nexus of practice does not necessarily lie in any of the specific practices. The handing practice is linked to the practices which constitute the CAREGIVING nexus – notably but not only to nurturing – but it is also linked to the practices which constitute the PEDAGOGICAL nexus. Thus the identity of the infant needing care or of the learning child is not located in any specific practice but in the nexus of practice.

This parallels what we have said about the relationship between social action and practice itself. The practice does not lie in the action but in the historical sequence of actions out of which the practice is constituted in habitus. Likewise the nexus of practice and its produced identity are not found in any specific practice but in the nexus of practices.

Other nexus of practice

With the rather limited data I have considered it would be impossible to be more than suggestive about other nexus of practice which are developing in B's habitus. One that had begun, perhaps as one interlocked with the PEDAGOGICAL nexus of practice, might be called RESEARCH. I have argued that B had come to fully participate in our research agenda by the end of this series of recording sessions and visits. When we paused to eat ice cream it was B who brought the microphone and the note paper and the tape recorder and told us to get on with the business of recording her talk. This nexus of practice for us included such practices as notetaking, tape recording, and phototaking along with the discursive practices I have labelled WI baby talk, that is speaking about B in her presence as if she were an analytical object, not a participant in the discourse. By the end of these visits, B had clearly taken on agentive participation in some of these practices and had, therefore, joined the research project through these interlocking linkages among practices with us.

We might want to ask: is this a Japanese child? On the one hand we have seen that in a few cases M speaks to B using Japanese words and phrases. To be sure, some of these are quite limited ('Mommy chodai') but frequent, others very rare but rather insistent as in Example 24, the test of whether or not B could recognize common objects in her world from the black and white photographs. At the same time we cannot conclude from these data anything about what Japanese language might be used outside of these sessions, though as members of the family we know that within the home it is relatively rare for M to use much Japanese except when talking on the telephone to Japanese relatives and friends or when these people are in the home as visitors.

We might also want to identify Japanese objects and structures in the home. We have seen the hakata doll, a Japanese ornamental doll. The home is decorated and furnished in 'Japanese' style. That is, while there are sofas and chairs, there are also large floor spaces, low tables, and sitting/kneeling cushions, and most of the social interactions take place on the floor, not in the Western-style chairs and sofas. But this is a mixed décor. The kitchen and dining areas as well as the bedrooms are furnished Western-style with high tables and chairs in the kitchen and box spring and mattress beds in the bedrooms. In this the home is furnished and decorated much like many or even most of the homes in Honolulu in a mixed Japanese, Chinese, Western style.

Japanese food is prepared in the kitchen and served to the family and to guests. But this food is just part of the family's cuisine which also includes grilled cheese sandwiches, tacos, and gau.

But to make reference to Japanese words and phrases, or to Japanese artefacts, objects, and physical structures, or Japanese food, is not the same as coming to understand what are Japanese practices and some Japanese nexus of practice. Within the theoretical framework I am developing here, it would be senseless to speak of a 'Japanese child'. One locates personal identities within various nexus of practice. The questions to ask are two:

1   Which of the practices which this child is developing in the habitus might be homologous with practices developing in other children so that they (and others) might be able to engage in naturalized, out-of-awareness actions together? and

2   What practices might be linked in a commensurable way with other practices so that the child and others would come to recognize (Gee 1999) themselves as participating in some shared nexus of practice?

Handing *as linked to interacting and nurturing* ('Mommy chodai') is a good candidate for such a linkage. We have seen it occurring frequently. M asked B to hand her all kinds of objects, from an orange to peel to be given back to B (nurturing) or pieces of trash to be thrown away and thanked B for doing so (interacting). We saw another child in Example 43 and her M engaged in dealing with a piece of trash the child had picked up. In that case M said: 'Throw it away (4x). Slap your hand. Throw it away.' In this instance looking after the child's interests (nurturing?) was linked with threatening and the child's own action (throwing), not handing. The action was constructed not as a social exchange of the object nor as the mother's responsibility to look after the disposal of the object. Given just these two examples – and of course, these are far from sufficient to do more than suggest – we would guess that these two children are constructing rather different nexus of practice. B's, again guessing, is much more likely to be commensurate with other children who have Japanese mothers.

Thus it is more likely to be the nexus of practice, including, of course, the Japanese words but not at all dependent on them, that would be useful in producing the identity we might call *Japanese child*, not any isolated action or phrase in a particular language. As we have noted in Example 13, two years later S used 'chodai' in requesting (and receiving) an object from our own daughter, Rachel. Because this practice is so rare in Rachel's habitus and because it is not, in most cases, linked to nurturing or interacting, there is little reason to suggest that Rachel is developing this nexus of practice or that she could, based on this nexus, interact with B as children with homologous nexus of practice.

From this point of view it seems that we could find with further data that B is developing rather tenuous *Japanese* nexus of practice that might be to some extent homologous with those of other children in Japanese families. By the same token we know – this is only an assertion I am making based on the rather loose data of convenience of a family member – that she is also developing other nexus of practice that would more likely be linked to Hawaiian-Chinese nexus of practice. My concern here is not to locate B within any particular nexus of practice but rather simply to outline how such identities might be produced. To the extent that B can engage in linked practices with other social actors she can claim the identities of those nexus of practice. Her 'membership' is achieved to the extent others are willing to ratify those claims through accepting them at face value.

This latter point could use a bit more development. The terms 'claim' and 'ratify' are probably far too active for what I wish to convey here. As Bourdieu has argued, it is precisely to the extent that habitus develops a genesis amnesia that we recognize a person as a member of a group. That is to say, it is the taken-for-granted world that shows most clearly who we are. It is the practices in and through which we act without a second thought that most clearly reveal our habitus – the historical-body, as Nishida (1958) puts it, of our lives. So if a person hands an object to another person *and neither gives any thought to the matter of handing*, then we can say that this practice of handing is constituted in homologous habitus. By handing you an object without any thought of the matter I claim for myself and for you homologous habitus. In this act I claim that we are, in fact, a 'we' – two people who share enough habitus that we can bring off this social action without failing. By accepting the object you ratify this claim I have made for myself and this imputation I have made to you of this 'we' status. Thus it is in the most routine and unnoticed actions that claims and recognitions of homologous habitus are made.

Likewise I would argue that a nexus of practice comes to be recognized as that of a group to the extent that both the practices themselves *and their linkages* are recognized through this process of genesis amnesia, that is, through taking the nexus of practice entirely for granted as the naturalized life world. Such recognition is produced, not explicitly through commentary, but implicitly through nothing being noticed at all. It is these silent recognitions which are the culture (in the biological sense) within which the homologous habitus of a group or class grows. Identities in a nexus of practice are thus produced when nothing unusual is remarked.

This process of identity-making in silent recognition or through genesis amnesia is the basis for arguing, then, that one very significant nexus of practice (or perhaps more accurately multiple or complex networks of nexus of practice) is that of the middle-class American family. Heath's (1983) important ethnographic study of three segments of society in the town she calls 'Trackton' pointed out how significant literacy events with books are for the middle-class (and white) group she studied. Our own research at Fort Chipewyan and then again elsewhere in Northern Canada and Alaska (Scollon and Scollon 1979, 1981) argued that for a child being socialized to the practices of what we called 'essayist literacy' the 'book game' is a central nexus of practice. While we did not put it in the terms I have used here, we argued that the book game is a nexus constructed out of pointing ('what's this?'), naming ('ball'), interrogation (linking pointing with naming), representation (taking the represented object for the object without comment or confusion), and so forth.

While it goes beyond the scope of what I have argued here, I have in my data many instances of the book game in interactions between M and B, R or S and B, C and B, and often B by herself. This nexus of practice would be, I expect, entirely homologous with the children Heath studied and taken entirely for granted within this particular social class.

There are other nexus that could be identified for the middle-class American family. Drawing might be one of them. Not only is B's home populated with books of all kinds, particularly natural history books, but also there are abundant drawing and writing materials. There are the crayons we have seen, but also pens and papers of all kinds. These two children spend a lot of their time before going to school engaged in the representational practices of drawing (Kress and van Leeuwen 1998). These two nexus of practice together form a representational–semiotic nexus of practice which other research suggests is highly identifying of participation in the middle-class American family. These nexus of practice are supported by the objects cum mediational means – books, crayons, paper, pens – which the family has the income to provide on the one hand and the social practices to bring into engagement with the children. In just this representational/semiotic nexus we find some of the central materials out of which the middle-class American habitus is being constructed.

Community of practice as objectified nexus

Now that I have argued for the concept of the nexus of practice, I would like to return briefly to reconsider the idea of the community of practice, using the CAREGIVING nexus of practice as my example. As a community of practice it might be represented as in Figure 2.

Here we can immediately begin to see the difficulties which arise with the metaphor. As a nexus of practice, our focus was upon the practices. The point of view was the practices as constituted in the habitus of persons. The persons engaged in those practices varied around a center on B and within that around her practice of handing. That is to say, we considered handing whether it was to B or from B, whether the other person was M, C, R, or S (or, of course, someone else). In the same way the focus of interacting was B and the others with which she might interact. As the center of this orientation is the habitus of the person and the question is to what extent this habitus is shared, there are two places 'others' come into the nexus of practice. There are the others with whom B shares

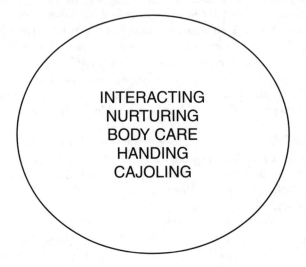

INTERACTING
NURTURING
BODY CARE
HANDING
CAJOLING

Figure 2 Caregiving community of practice, I

homologous habitus in regards to practices; that is, there are those with whom she hands, she interacts, who give her body care, and so forth. And there are those with whom B further shares homologous nexus; those who are engaged with her in more than just any one of the social actions or practices.

Figure 2 is very different in this respect. To draw a circle of a community of practice and locate within that circle the practices rather than a group of persons shows the power of the metaphor of the community. I believe I would be right in assuming that for most who use the concept of the community of practice, the elements of the community are the persons, not the practices, and this Figure 2 would seem idiosyncratic or inappropriate. This circle would contain the names or identities of persons. The questions then are focused on how these persons are related to each other, how they identify each other, how they become members and how they are legitimated as members, through their actions. Practice is very much marginalized as little more than the medium by which these persons construct their community of practice.

In saying this I do not want to suggest that we should therefore abandon entirely the idea of a community of practice because this idea has great currency at the unexamined level of common discourse; though of course, I also want to include the not-so-common discourses of anthropology, sociology, education, and management. On the contrary, what I want to suggest is that the community of practice is how the nexus of practice is objectified in discourse. We act within our nexus of practice but to the extent we begin to make these nexus explicit, formal, analytical, and above all objective and reified, we do so as communities of practice. This sort of objectification might look like Figure 3.

The large circle would represent the CAREGIVING community of practice, consisting (for simplicity here) of M the largest contained circle, C the larger of the 'child' circles, and B. The two circles overlapping are R and S who are to some extent within this caregiving community of practice but also to some extent only there peripherally. This focus on the persons allows us to highlight such things as the degrees of membership in the community – M is central and R and S are

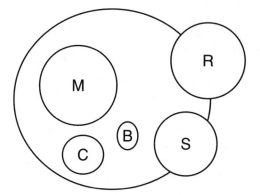

Figure 3 Caregiving community of practice, II

peripheral; C and B are central but still developing. It is structured in terms of inclusion and exclusion. Relationships beyond exclusion and inclusion are seen, as Bourdieu (1977, 1990) has pointed out, as communications: how M communicates with B, or B with R, and so forth.

As I have argued above, however, such a metaphor of inclusion and exclusion, of membership, apprenticeship, and alienness fails to capture or even to suggest the action of practice in this system. What is seen are the structural relationships among the participants; what is invisible are the practices engaged in through time and the constitution of the habitus of the individuals so represented. Furthermore, the focus on membership, inclusion, and exclusion obliterates the fact that some practices are homologous straight across such circles into other circles. Handing, the practice we have examined here, is likely to be virtually the same sort of homologous action within this CAREGIVING community of practice and in dozens or, really, thousands of other communities of practice.

What I would like to suggest here is that this is, in fact, just how we commonly objectivize our nexus of practice. We objectivize them as groups of persons, with inclusions and exclusions, criteria of membership, processes of credentialization, pre-membership socialization courses, and the rest. Doing so enables (or requires) us to organize social groups as bounded entities, not as nexus of practice. We name and technologize our practices, not as practices or as habitus, but as characteristics of human actors. In this view, actors *have* or *do not have* practices. Communities of practice value or do not value practices and therefore they value or do not value the people who are constructed by that community of practice as having them. The focus shifts to the development of practices *in individuals*, and along with that focus goes explicit forms of testing for the presence or absence of those practices, often through contrived sites of engagement and cultural tools designed specifically to test for them.

This view, of course, is not something which I can develop here as it goes much beyond the data that I have available. I can say how such a study would need to be made, however. On the one hand one would need a longitudinal study of practice and nexus of practice along the lines I have developed here. In that study one would focus on how actions become construed as practices over time and then how practices come to be recognized as homologous through genesis amnesia or naturalization. One would also want to focus on interactions or linkages among practices so that it would be possible to see how a nexus of practice is built up over time through such linkages.

Concurrent with that study, one would want to study the objectivization of practice which is occurring. What groups are being produced and what persons are being identified as members of those groups, with what participant statuses? Such studies would not be anything new to ethnographic analysis, of course. What would be new would be the study of the relationships among these productions – community and members – and the practices and nexus of practice which are the raw material of these technologizations and objectivizations.

Discourse and the nexus of practice

I am now in the position to return to a problem which I first raised in my analysis of the ontogenesis of the social practice of handing and which I have commented upon from time to time as I have proceeded with this study. What is the relationship between discourse and practice? More specifically, how can we respond to Chouliaraki and Fairclough's assertions that 'Discourse is always a significant moment because all practices are, as we have said, reflexive – constructions of that practice constitute part of a practice' (1999:23), or 'all practices have an irreducible discursive aspect, not only in the sense that all practices involve use of language to some degree' (1999:26).

I have argued that there is no unique link between a practice (as I have defined one) such as handing and a discourse, in the narrow sense of a discursive practice such as saying 'Mommy chodai' when asking the child to hand to M. I have now also argued that there is also no unique link between a practice such as handing and a Discourse (or discourse system) in that I have argued that a social practice may well be instantiated across many Discourses or, as I prefer to call them, nexus of practice. From the Discourse one would not be able to infer that there would always or ever be handing. From handing one would never be able to infer within what Discourse or nexus of practice it is being invoked.

What I have argued *is* important is the nexus of practice. I have not proved it by any means but I would suggest that a nexus of practice does always include linked discursive practices. While we can imagine a practice that is not discursive (handing, body care, etc.) it is very difficult to imagine a nexus of practice that does not include within the nexus some discursive practices. At the same time we cannot expect any unique linkage of a discursive practice with any other single practice (at the narrow level I have defined the term). What we can find is a historically produced and reproduced nexus of linkages of greater or lesser salience.

What does this mean for the analysis of discourse and social practice? In the first place, it means that a critical study of discourse and social practice cannot restrict itself to the study of discourse alone nor to practice alone because the significant meaning of both discourse practice and social practice lies in the linkages among them in the production of nexus of practice. It also means that, because practice is realized and recognized only across time, not in specific actions, that it must be analyzed across time as practice is constituted in habitus. A snapshot analysis of a social action, a text, or a mediational means used in the production of either of these can only address the question of potential. And since there is always the potential for practice to absorb an immense array of actions and mediational means, this potential analysis will always be highly speculative and indefinite.

That the link between discourse and practice lies in the nexus of practice also means that systematic relationships between nexus of practice and the objectivized communities of practice also need to be studied as a central aspect of understanding practice through discourse. The study of discourse and practice is thus inherently ethnographic.

The conclusion which I draw from this study, then, is that there is an inherent and irreducible link between discourse and practice, as Chouliaraki and Fairclough (1999) have argued, but to see that link as it works in practice requires studies which are fundamentally discursive-historical or longitudinal so that the workings of practice across a historical sequence of actions can be made visible. Such studies are also necessarily ethnographic so that constellations of practice, nexus of practice, can be made visible in order that the operations of both discourse (discursive practice) and practice (other, non-discursive practices) can be concretely seen as they develop in the habitus of the participants and in the nexus of practice which is produced homologously across participants. Finally, the production of communities of practice as bounded membership entities of inclusion and exclusion out of the nexus of practice must be studied to see how the transformation from practice, action, and habitus to person, characteristics, and identity is performed through discursive practices and other practices of technologization and objectivization. All of this, of course, is an empirical study which remains to be done.

NOTES

1 Nexus is both the singular and the plural form.
2 By Athabaskans we meant 'anyone who has been socialized to a set of communicative patterns which have their roots in the Athabaskan languages. These people are ethnically Athabaskan on the whole but may not speak any Athabaskan language' (Scollon and Scollon 1981:12,13). By 'speakers of English' we meant 'anyone whose communicative patterns are those of the dominant, mainstream American and Canadian English-speaking population' (1981:13). As our focus was on communication between people speaking out of these two positions, these definitions arose relatively naturally but can be seen to privilege cognition and communication in social structuring.

6 Mediated discourse as a nexus of practice

One last latte

If I may be forgiven for returning one last time to my morning coffee, we could look at the moment of purchase yet again to try to pin down what I mean by a mediated discourse analysis of such an action. Parallel to this, I would also like to return to a moment in the life of Brenda when she hands an orange to her mother, they drop it, but then Brenda gives it to her mother.

First, we can look at this moment of the opening of the coffee transaction.

Server: Hi, what would you like?
R: A tall latte, please.
Server: Cold enough?
R: *(handing $2.25 to the server)* Enough to suit me.
Server: *(ringing up sale)* Thanks.

Then, we can look at the moment in the handing of the orange from Example 14.

B: *(handing and dropping orange)*
M: Oiyo! Chodai. Chodai. Ah, thank you, thank you.

A mediated discourse analysis would talk about these little stretches of discourse as mediated actions. Each occurs at a site of engagement – 'at' is preferred to 'within' to avoid the notion of action within context; 'as a site of engagement' might be even more accurate.

From the point of view of mediated discourse analysis, the social action of purchasing a cup of coffee is the point of linkage of several social practices; that is, the social action produces that linkage of practices and is not just conditioned by them. Among the practices we can analyze here are *greeting* (or perhaps *service-greeting* as a sub-species of this practice), *handing, purchasing,* and, of course many others which are invisible in the transcript but which I have mentioned before, such as *queuing* and *menu reading*. The mediational means through which this action is taken are such things as *money, cash register, coffee, counter,* and invisible in the transcript, the *cold weather jackets* both the server and I are wearing.

A mediated discourse analysis sees the social action of M's requesting the orange and B's handing it to her also as the linkage of several social practices. Notable are *handing* and what I have called *interacting*. That is, there is a social practice – handing – and a discursive practice focused on the social interaction, saying 'thank you'.

From a mediated discourse point of view, what we are trying to understand here is how these social actions, these mediated actions, happen as human action. We want to know what enables the first action so that I can step up, order the coffee, shift footing into a conversation about the weather, and ultimately get my coffee. Our motivating interest is not, of course, just the purchase of a cup of coffee on the one hand, nor is it just the linguistic means by which this might be accomplished. Similarly, in my analysis of the developing of the social practice of handing, my interest was not just on the handing but also on the discursive practices – and there are several of them – which accompanied handing in the course of this year of study of this young child.

Now I would like to turn to the question: what is it that makes what I have done here in this book a mediated discourse analysis? Mediated discourse sees social practice and discursive practice as mutually constitutive. A mediated discourse analysis is not only interested in the linguistic-conversational-discursive action here, nor is it just interested in the purchasing or handing action. It would not even be correct to say that it is interested in both of these as one is the context for the other. The interest here is in developing an analysis of how the discursive business going on here mediates the purchasing or handing and as an integral part of this, how the purchasing and handing mediate the talk. That is, for a mediated discourse analysis these are neither social actions where discourse is simply an element, nor are they discursive actions – conversations – which rely upon the context for interpretation. This is mediated discourse analysis because we take discourse to always be mediated by social practice while simultaneously taking all social practice to be mediated by discourse. Social practice and discursive practice are mutually mediating; one is accomplished to a great extent through the other.

This brings me to the second point about mediated discourse analysis: a mediated action is seen within the history of that practice in the actor's habitus. As we have seen, in the first instances of handing and talk between B and M, there is no real reason to believe that any of the talk is understood, nor is there any evidence that the handing that takes place is any form of social action. As I have argued, B's movements are construed by M as being these actions and this construal has largely taken place simultaneously in action and in discourse. That is, when B holds up a crayon, M reaches to take it, thus construing it as handing, and she often also says something, thus construing it as some sort of discursive action. Also, as I have noted, there is nothing fixed or predictable about these discursive construals. At one moment it is construed as an occasion for naming and at another it is construed as the development of social graces, of saying 'thank you'.

A mediated discourse view of this morning coffee purchase would also argue, as I have suggested in the examples I have given before this, that we can only understand this action as we see it within the history of practice within the habitus of the participants in this action. There was a time not so long before the transaction here when I was not able to step up at the front of the queue and say, 'A tall latte, please'. As we have seen, this utterance has a history in habitus as I progressively was able to aggregate the contemporary coffee drinking/ordering practices along with the mediational means, 'tall', 'short', 'grande' cups, or differences between *latte* and *au lait, espresso*, and *regular brewed coffee*, between *milk*, and *steamed milk*. From this practice view of social action, the phrase 'a tall latte' embeds this history in the habitus in the same way that Brenda's handing of 'Mama's shoe' in Example 29 embeds the history of all these handings we have seen in the preceding 28 examples.

Mediated discourse sees discourse and practice as mutually constitutive in the social actions I have called sites of engagement. Secondly, these sites of engagement are interpreted historically as outcomes of the history of practice, the habitus, of the social actors. The third point that is crucial is the construction of the mediational means within practice. The tall latte which I have purchased in the example here was constructed over a history of morning purchases. In the first instance it was one of an array of possible objects listed on menus. In the instance above it has become 'my morning tall latte' – something which is no longer chosen against the paradigmatic array of menu choices with little clear understanding of the differences among various objects with different constituent coffees and milks. It is now constructed out of the history of lattes had in this coffee shop and others. It is judged not in terms of its differences with *au lait* or *regular with milk*, but against yesterday's latte or the one on Sunday in a different shop. The meaning of this object which has now become a mediational means is *for me* interpretable within this history.

Likewise we have seen in Example 14 that the 'orange' that B hands to her mother, while it may be the same material object for them both, is not easily construed as the same mediational means. This is very early in the period when B has achieved object permanency, as we saw in her following the orange's trajectory to the floor and then in her looking back at the floor after she had picked it up and given it to her mother. For B this orange is in large measure a mediational means by which she was working out such fundamental psychological concepts as object permanency. For M it is much more assimilated within her nurturing practice – it is something she is feeding to her baby.

Finally, the fourth point within a mediated discourse analysis is that practices come to form constellations of linkages which I have called nexus of practice. These nexus of practice are central sources of personal identity. When I am able to unproblematically buy my coffee – so unproblematically that the server and I can easily turn our attention away from this focal transaction to chat about the weather – we construct my identity to this small extent within a nexus of practice of contemporary coffee society. As we have seen in the case of the one-year-old, as she comes to produce herself agentively within practices rather than simply being construed by others as a social actor, she begins to construct herself (together with her caregivers) within nexus of practice. She is constructed as a child within a caregiving nexus of practice and as a learner within a pedagogical nexus of practice. She even makes a valiant attempt to construct herself within a research nexus of practice when she instructs me to use my tape recorder to tape her in Example 36.

To reiterate these four points, the mediated discourse analysis I have presented here has argued for these principles:

- Discourse and practice are mutually constitutive.
- Sites of engagement (the locus of mediated actions) are historical outcomes of the practices and habitus of social actors.
- Mediational means are constructed within practices.
- The linkage of discourse and practice is not direct but in nexus of practice; these are the source of the social identities of social actors.

The nexus of practice

There is much that is familiar in mediated discourse analysis to those who are working within the linked research frameworks that make up the nexus of practice of mediated discourse analysis. Beginning with the first research project with Brenda in the early 1970s, this research was based in what has now come to be thought of as interactional sociolinguistics or conversation analysis in other formulations. Among the concerns in this body of research has been coming to understand in the first place that social life is constituted at this micro-level of social interaction. There has been in this research tradition, therefore, a central focus on the interpretive and inferential processes by which social actors who are acting in real time are able to strategize their own actions within a negotiative process with other social actors to achieve their desired social meanings, including their identities, footings, alignments with others, and their positionings of themselves and others.

One might think of interactional sociolinguistics or conversation analysis as one line of practices within the mediated discourse nexus of practice. By this I mean that mediated discourse shares with this other research many of the same actual practices, such as using audio or videotape with transcriptions as methodological strategies for making concrete the ongoing inferential flow of conversations. There is also a central concern with the common and ordinary in day-to-day practice rather than the exceptional or high profile public discourses of various other research paradigms. In this aspect research in mediated discourse relies heavily on both methodological and theoretical work in these frameworks including the analysis of conversational inference, the emphasis on real-time processing in social interaction, the role of meta-communication, and the methodology of playback.

At the same time, mediated discourse rejects the privileging of conversation as a genre and of talk and discursive practice more generally that is often presupposed within conversation analysis and interactional sociolinguistic research. In this, mediated discourse analysis links another line of research to form an intersection with them – anthropological linguistics, or its sometime alternate, the ethnography of communication. A Deg Het'an (Northern Athabaskan, Holy Cross, Alaska) man once told me: 'The difference between me and you is probably that if you want to go hunting with a man, you'd want to play cards or get drunk with him to see if he was safe to go hunting with. I'd want to go hunting with him to see if he was safe to talk to.' I might not be able to articulate any better than this that the relative positioning of talk and practice (non-discursive) is far from a universal human valuation. The much celebrated inversion of Aristotle's theory and practice brought about by Marx and moved forward by writers such as Bourdieu remains firmly rooted in the discourses of theory and in the rather common privileging of discourse, particularly conversation, as the modal human form of social action. Of course this same centering upon discourse is characteristic of much work in critical discourse analysis as well, though more often there the focus is upon written discourse.

From the perspective of anthropological linguistics, it is an empirical question to be resolved by research where discourse and practice stand in relationship to each other. It must be independently established what is the role of conversation in a particular nexus of practice, and in this, mediated discourse relies on research in anthropological linguistics and the ethnography of communication which has provided abundant examples of the kaleidoscopic array of possibilities of linkages of discourse and practice throughout the world. From these disciplinary positions mediated discourse profits from what might be called 'inductive ethnoscience', that is, seeking to work out the conceptual frameworks developed within the habitus of the social actors in which one is interested. This, of course, relies on ethnographic methodology including participant-observation in fieldwork, particularistic analysis of concrete situations and actions, and at the same time rigorous comparative analysis.

If there is a tendency in interactional sociolinguistics, which is stronger yet in conversation analysis, to get almost obsessively taken up in the analysis of minute levels of social interaction in at least apparently trivial social encounters – who, after all, really cares *what I say* when I buy a cup of coffee or *what a mother says* when a baby hands her an orange? – there is a tendency in anthropological linguistic work to get caught up in providing concrete and sometimes equally minute and equally exotic counter-examples to the generalizations anybody would like to make about the social world. This arises naturally out of the rigorous comparative basis of anthropological linguistics which, as a reflex, cringes from making a generalization until the far corners of the world have been combed for possible exceptions. This extremely healthy impulse from the point of view of analytical honesty, however, can become debilitating in a research project which takes human social action as its focus, particularly a project which has as its driving interest the understanding of and achievement of social change.

Critical discourse analysis, in rather strong contradistinction to these research frameworks, has focused directly upon the big social issues of our contemporary world. Still, like the other research programs and frameworks I have mentioned, critical discourse analysis is far from being a unitary monolith. This is true whether we are speaking of its theoretical positions as outlined most recently in

Chouliaraki and Fairclough (1999) or of its methodological strategies. Nevertheless, mediated discourse finds in critical discourse analysis another strand of practices which make up the nexus of practice which is mediated discourse analysis.
These include the close analysis of the texts of public discourse – though hardly
an aspect of the project I have presented here, a close concern for social practice
in respect of public and social issues, and a critical or ideological analysis of social
process. In this, critical discourse analysis shares much with new literacy studies as
I have noted earlier. Perhaps most akin to the research I have presented here is the
work of the 'Vienna School' (Wodak and her colleagues) which they have called
discourse-historical critical discourse analysis. This work, as I have argued here,
takes it that the meaning of social action is produced historically along or through
a sequence of discursive (and social) practices, though that work takes institutional
process more than the actions of social actors as its focus of study.

Of course it is not clear to me whether or not it would make sense to try to treat
the practice theory of Bourdieu as a separate theoretical framework, as his work
and practice theory in general is so much part of the critical discourse analysis
project as well. Cole (1995) makes the cogent point that in practice the word
'activity' tends to be associated with psychological studies which historically derive
from the so-called 'Soviet psychologists', and 'practice' is more often associated
with studies deriving from Western Marxism or the Frankfurt School, even though
these two strands originate in the same historical/philosophical source of Marxist
writing. As I have argued earlier, practice theory also has a significant source quite
outside Marxism in the Buddhist philosophy of Nishida. In any event, it is clear
that practice theory is very much a bridge between the analysis of social and of
psychological processes.

Finally, as I have argued and tried to demonstrate here in this book, much
insight into social practice can be achieved through an ontogenetic analysis. In
this, mediated discourse owes much to activity theory from Vygotsky through
Michael Cole to the mediated action theory of James Wertsch. Mediated discourse analysis takes as its unit of analysis the same unit of analysis as Wertsch's
mediated action theory – the mediated action – though with the shift in focus to
highlight the dialectical relationship of discursive practice with social practice.

Nexus or Venn diagram?

One might try to schematically represent mediated discourse analysis as a Venn
diagram. Such a diagram would need to represent mediated discourse (MD) as
the central circle, as that is our focus here. Then the other contributing research
frameworks would be represented with their own circles – interactional
sociolinguistics/conversation analysis (IS/CA), anthropological linguistics/
ethnography of communication (AL/EOC), critical discourse analysis/new literacy studies (CDA/NLS), practice theory (PT), and mediated action/activity
theory (MA/AT). Such a diagram might look like Figure 4.

There are two problems with such a diagram, however. In the first place is the
question of whether or not mediated discourse should be represented as

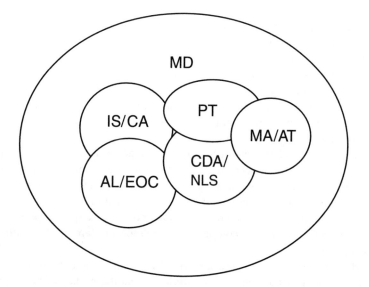

Figure 4 Mediated discourse as a colonizing Venn diagram

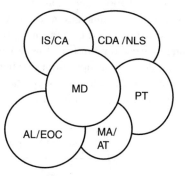

Figure 5 Mediated discourse as a mediating Venn diagram

encompassing all these other research traditions. This would certainly amount to a sort of self-aggrandizement – an attempt to colonize the significant work of others as being essentially little more than contributions to one's own grand scheme. I have no interest in such a project and would not want to represent such an idea, even by accident of the metaphor produced by the Venn diagram.

Alternatively, one would place mediated discourse in a still central position, but as a small circle which trades in aspects of the other frameworks as a kind of mediating position between or among them. Such a diagram might look like Figure 5. In my view this remains quite unsatisfactory in that it suggests, in the first place, that somehow mediated discourse is or could be in the position to do this mediation among scholars representing such a large range of institutions, histories, and practices.

The second problem is that it remains very difficult to know how many more or different circles would have to be made to make it clear just how much critical discourse analysis overlaps or not with new literacy studies and to what extent both or either of those overlap with anthropological linguistics on the one hand and with mediated action/activity theory on the other. Any set of circles would produce rather misleading and unrepresentative suggestions.

I prefer to represent mediated discourse as a nexus of practice though, to be sure, there are some representational problems with this sort of diagram as well. Such a nexus might be represented as in Figure 6.

Figure 6 represents mediated discourse analysis as a nexus of practice. This diagram goes against the grain of my own analysis here by representing something as complex as critical discourse analysis with a single line. It is only for convenience that I have not drawn separate lines for, say, 'text analysis', 'audio-tape recording', 'taking field notes', and so forth as separate actual and concrete specific practices which would reveal a much more complex set of relationships among and within this nexus of practice.

Nevertheless, what I hope to indicate with this diagram is that in a sense mediated discourse as a theoretical framework mirrors the social world that it hopes to analyze. That is, mediated discourse takes on an identity not through the production of boundaries nor through the mediation and communication between groups; it has taken on an identity through the linkages overall that are made through concrete actions and projects over time. That is to say, if we recall how I defined a nexus of practice in Chapter 5, we should not see this nexus of practice as a set of objectivized or structural relationships among different schools. On the contrary, these relationships exist only in and through concrete intersections of these practices in specific research projects. Thus one research

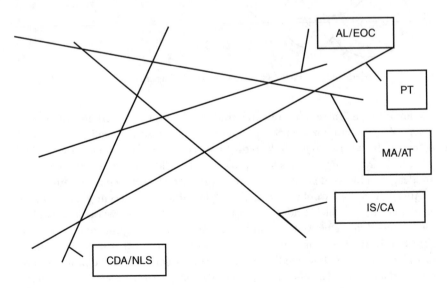

Figure 6 Mediated discourse as a nexus of practice

project might produce a linkage between interactional sociolinguistics and anthropological linguistics (IS/CA:AL/EOC), for example, our study of Athabaskan narrative (Scollon and Scollon 1979, 1981). Another study might produce a linkage between interactional sociolinguistics and activity theory (MA/AT), for example, my first study of this child, Brenda. In another case a study might link anthropological linguistics (AL/EOC) and critical discourse analysis (CDA/NLS). It is unlikely that any single project would link all of these groups or practices. What becomes the nexus of practice is the repeated linkage of practices over time. The identity of mediated discourse analysis, in that sense, is emergent in time through this history of linkages, not an objectivized set of either connections or of procedures.

Mediated discourse as change in the nexus of practice

I have argued that practices are most usefully seen as developing through time as a sequence of mediated actions. I have also argued that in this sense practice is always, to borrow Bakhtin's term, unfinalizable. A practice changes with each action as does the habitus of the social actor. I have also argued that a nexus of practice is a social structure which comes into existence over time as the intersections or linkages of specific practices in the sites of engagement of mediated actions. With the nexus of practice as with the specific practice and with the habitus, we do not look for the overarching vision of the structure nor for the reversible and transitive rules of structural relationships among elements in the structure. What we see is a view which emerges only in and through actions, which is always a rather poor vision of the structural whole because it is always and only seen from the point of view of the social actor, and which changes at least to some small extent through each new action.

Correspondingly, mediated discourse analysis, as a nexus of practice, could be said to have begun in early intersections of research practices such as those of longitudinal language development, interactional sociolinguistics or conversation analysis, anthropological linguistics, and new literacy studies, at least in my own view of it. In time some of those linkages have been made stronger through repeated research at those intersections and others weakened in neglect. Also new practices have been brought into intersection such as those of critical discourse analysis and Bourdieu's practice theory. As I have commented earlier, however, we can see that the lines of practice laid out in Bourdieu's sociological practice theory cover very much the same ground as those first traced in Nishida's Buddhist philosophy.

Habitus is not, of course, vision; neither Bourdieu nor Nishida tells us much about how to theorize a vector of directionality. In fact they would both argue against any form of teleologism which would see in today's action tomorrow's purpose. I do not wish to depart from this position as I would also argue that it is among the worst excesses of objectivism to produce structural rules on the basis of an objectivized and non-real-time view of a social structure and then to immediately return to real-time speculations about how those rules will certainly play out in tomorrow's social actions.

And so now I do not want to engage in any visionary or teleological analysis of what mediated discourse might become as it develops in time through research projects yet to be formulated. What I do want to organize here is a brief final digression on what I see as the most crucial problems now to be faced by mediated discourse analysis in attempting to come to understand human action, and therefore to understand social change. I see these as being of four major categories: (1) the problem of agency, (2) the problem of representation, (3) the problem of multimodal discourse, and (4) the problem of social structures – institutions, organizations, nations, cultures.

Agency

In my study of Brenda I observed that at one year of age it was very difficult to characterize her as taking action in respect, at least, to handing. However it was she acted, it was the action of handing only to the extent it was construed as that by the mother. I then spoke somewhat loosely of 'agentive resistance' developing over the period of her second year so that, as we got toward the end of it, we felt more comfortable with speaking of Brenda doing things. In this, however, I want to be careful not to simply cross over into positing the rationalistic, autonomous, willing individual as the concept of the agent underlying the term I have mostly tried to use – the social actor. I have tried to suggest with this term, following Bateson, that the actor of a mediated action is always a social actor. That is, I have wanted to conceive of the agent as constructed much like the mediational means is constructed, that is, through and in practice. At the same time Brenda is constructed within the social practice of handing, she is constructed as the social actor – a hander. From the point of view of this study, then, Brenda is this social actor, a hander, and about other characteristics she might have or about other sorts of social actions she is able to perform I can have little to say.

Further development of this nexus of practice, however, should address the issue of the nature of agency in the production and integration of the person as a social actor. Hutchins (1994) and, of course, many others have argued that cognition is distributed across human individuals (as well as their technologies). From the point of view of mediated discourse analysis, then, we would also want to say that Brenda's handing is distributed between her and her mother. In the beginning, it is the mother who carries the bulk of the activity of constructing this social action. By two years of age, Brenda is able to construct handing jointly. From a practice view, she should never be thought of as doing handing as a single agentive entity any more than Governor Patten in Chapter 2 was able to receive the flag from the Sergeant Major without a carefully managed, and in this case partially failed, joint work of construction. Nevertheless, there is an important psychological-sociological-anthropological research literature which indicates that from culture to culture, the person is constructed as a very different sort of entity (Hsu 1953, 1983, 1985; Miller, Potts, Fung, Hoogstra, and Mintz 1990; Miller, Mintz, Hoogstra, Fung, and Potts 1992; Fung 1994) and it would be valuable to develop research projects which would probe this problem.

Representation

The mediational means we have considered in this study have been minimal. In the study of Brenda we have seen oranges and crayons, juice bottles, and shoes. In the anecdotes about morning coffee we have seen coins and coffee and a few incidental aspects of the counters and other apparatus of a coffee shop. For the purposes of this analysis it has been useful to keep the perspective rather simple in order to outline the theoretical framework. Unfortunately, we have seen very little of the mediational means which are of greatest interest, the semiotic mediational means out of which the problems and crises of our social worlds are constructed – newspaper stories, television broadcasts, film images, and brand names and logos.

We could say by way of preparation for this study that semiotic mediational means are physical and conceptual residues of representational practices, but what are representational practices? I have argued that an infant is constructed as a social actor from the earliest days of life, but do we want to say that she is represented as such a social actor? As I have argued, this construction has more to do with the production of the baby-talk register and the social alignments as speaker/hearer than with explicit representation. In any event I am not ready to make the unprepared leap to asserting that a policy address by the Secretary of State is nothing but the residue of representational practices. Here I can only suggest that it is an important problem to mediated discourse analysis to come to a clear theorization of how such mediational means, from policy addresses to works of art, from newspaper editorials to advertising slogans, from brand names to municipal ordinances, are constructed in practice.

Equally problematical from the point of view of representation is to come to a clearer understanding of how these objects become mediational means within the practices of readers. How does the practice of reading a newspaper editorial work together with the representational structure of that editorial to become a mediational means in the action of the social actor – the reader? The study I have done here suggests that a close study of the development of reading habitus over time would be equally rewarding in helping to increase the resolution of our vision of the processes of the formation of political opinion.

Multimodal discourse

The problem of representation is increasingly becoming a problem of multiple modes of discourse. We had a glimpse of this in Chapter 3. In this analysis I have worked with a textual transcription of a set of examples. In order to elucidate *how* Brenda was being produced as a social actor I had to have recourse to descriptions of many factors that cannot easily be transcribed with a standard orthography. I have had to introduce descriptions of tone of voice, of faster than normal or slower than normal speed, or raised and lowered pitch. I have argued that the construction was done through these aspects of speech which are not easily represented orthographically.

Similarly, as the texts which are significant in our social lives are increasingly multimodal we feel the need to increase the theoretical scope of our analysis. Of course one reason our mediational means are progressively more complex combinations of text, image, sound, and color is that we have developed the representational technologies which allow us to produce such texts more easily than ever before. I believe we could argue that it was the development of the relatively inexpensive and portable tape recorder which opened linguistic analysis up to the studies of interactional sociolinguistics and conversation analysis in the late 1960s and early 1970s. Certainly the study we have examined here was predicated on the Sony TC110A, the first of the small, high quality portable cassette tape recorders. As we have seen it was small enough that a two-year-old could pick it up and bring it to me. This technology of representation opened up a kind of analysis that had been impossible before that. Now we could argue, by the same token, that new representational technologies are simultaneously producing new forms of representation and mediational means. Correspondingly, I believe this is a significant area into which mediated discourse analysis will move in seeking to achieve an understanding of human social action in our contemporary world.

Social structures

In Chapter 5 I gave the merest sketch of how a mediated discourse analysis may treat the social structures we have come to think of as essential for a critical analysis of human action. I suggested there that at the level of practice the organization of practice is as nexus of practice; that is, practices in the plural are linked never uniquely and never systematically into constellations or networks through the social actions in which these practices are instantiated in sites of engagement. I then went on to say that in some, perhaps many, cases, such nexus of practice become objectivized as structures – communities of practice. That is, they become constructed in practice and in discourses about that practice as structures. As such objectivized structures they are said to have structure, rules, and procedures. They are no longer organized around practice so much as around definitions, boundaries, membership, inclusion, and exclusion. As nexus of practice become objectivized they take on in the habitus of the social actors in those nexus the ontological position of being structural realities. To them the powers of causation are attributed and they come to be seen as prior both historically and ontologically to the social actors which are thereby constructed as dispensable 'members'.

In addition to these ontologically constructed structural entities, communities of practice begin to become identified with a range of objects which are constructed as the cultural tools of these communities of practice. Thus this process of objectivization when working on the nexus of practice produces a more or less bounded entity of members and others, while the same process of objectivization or technologization produces cultural tools out of the mediational means of practice.

This much can be suggested, but hardly argued successfully, from the data I have considered in this book. While I believe this analysis is promising, it remains for subsequent research projects to begin the study of the theorization of institutions and organizations within the nexus of practice of mediated discourse.

References

Allinson, Robert E. (1989) *Understanding the Chinese mind*. Hong Kong: Oxford University Press.

Anderson, Benedict (1991) *Imagined communities*. London: Verso.

Ang, Ien (1996) *Living room wars: Rethinking media audiences for a postmodern world*. London: Routledge.

Bakhtin, M. M. (1981 [1934–5]) *The dialogic imagination*. Austin: University of Texas Press.

Bakhtin, M. M. (1984 [1929]) *Problems of Dostoevsky's poetics*. (Caryl Emerson, ed. and tr. Minneapolis: University of Minnesota Press.

Barton, David and Mary Hamilton (1998) *Local literacies: Reading and writing in one community*. London: Routledge.

Bateson, Gregory (1972) *Steps to an ecology of mind*. New York: Ballantine.

Berger, Peter, Brigitte Berger, and Hansfried Kellner (1973) *The homeless mind, modernization, and consciousness*. New York: Random House.

Berlin, Brent and Paul Kay (1969) *Basic color terms: Their universality and evolution*. Berkeley: University of California Press.

Bhaskar, Roy (1989) *Reclaiming reality: A critical introduction to contemporary philosophy*. London: Verso.

Bhaskar, Roy (1997) *A realist theory of science*. London: Verso.

Billig, Michael (1995) *Banal nationalism*. London: Sage.

Billig, Michael (1997) 'Beyond the production and consumption of nationalism: A reply to Kim and Wertsch'. *Culture and Psychology* 3(4):485–491.

Bond, Michael Harris (1986) *The psychology of the Chinese people*. New York: Oxford University Press.

Bond, Michael Harris (1996) *The handbook of Chinese psychology*. Hong Kong: Oxford University Press.

Bourdieu, Pierre (1977) *Outline of a theory of practice*. 'Richard Nice,' tr. Cambridge: Cambridge University Press.

Bourdieu, Pierre (1990) *The logic of practice*. Stanford: Stanford University Press.

Bray, Francesca (1997) *Technology and gender: Fabrics of power in Late Imperial China*. Berkeley: University of California Press.

Bruner, Jerome S. (1966) 'On cognitive growth'. In J. S. Bruner, R. R. Olver, and Patricia Greenfield (eds), *Studies in cognitive growth*. New York: Wiley.

Calhoun, Craig (1995) *Critical social theory: Culture, history, and the challenge of difference*. Oxford: Blackwell.

Chouliaraki, Lilie and Norman Fairclough (1999) *Discourse in late modernity: Rethinking critical discourse analysis*. Edinburgh: Edinburgh University Press.

Cole, Michael (1995) 'The supra-individual envelope of development: Activity and practice, situation and context'. *New Directions for Child Development 67* (Spring 1995):105–118.

Cole, Michael and Jerome S. Bruner (1971) 'Cultural differences and inferences about psychological processes'. *American Psychologist* 26:867–876.

Cole, Michael and Peg Griffin (1980) 'Cultural amplifiers reconsidered'. In David R. Olson (ed.) *The social foundations of language and thought: Essays in honor of Jerome S. Bruner*. New York: W. W. Norton and Company.

Cook-Gumperz, Jenny (1986) *The social construction of literacy*. New York: Cambridge University Press.

Eco, Umberto (1995) 'Phenomena of this sort must also be included in any panorama of Italian design'. In Robert Lumley (ed.), *Apocalypse postponed (essays by Umberto Eco)*. London: Flamingo, 247–261.

Fairclough, Norman (1992) *Discourse and social change*. Cambridge: Polity Press.

Fairclough, Norman and Ruth Wodak (1997) 'Critical discourse analysis'. In Teun A. van Dijk (ed.), *Discourse as social interaction*. London: Sage, 258–284.

Fung, Heidi Han-Tih (1994) 'The socialization of shame in young Chinese children'. Doctoral dissertation, University of Chicago, Department of Psychology, Committee on Human Development.

Gee, James Paul (1990) 'Background to the "New Literacy Studies" '. In James Paul Gee, *Social linguistics and literacies: Ideology in discourse*. London: The Falmer Press.

Gee, James Paul (1996) *Social linguistics and literacies: Ideology in discourses* (Second edition). Bristol, PA: Taylor and Francis Inc.

Gee, James Paul (1999) *An introduction to discourse analysis: Theory and method*. London: Routledge.

Gee, James Paul, Glynda Hull, and Colin Lankshear (1996) *The new work order: Behind the language of the new capitalism*. Boulder, CO: Westview Press, Inc.

Goffman, Erving (1961) *Asylums*. New York: Anchor Books.

Goffman, Erving (1974) *Frame analysis*. New York: Harper and Row.

Goffman, Erving (1981) *Forms of talk*. Philadelphia: University of Pennsylvania Press.

Goody, Jack (1977) *The domestication of the savage mind*. New York: Cambridge University Press.

Goody, Jack (1987) *The interface between the written and the oral*. Cambridge: Cambridge University Press.

Goody, Jack and Ian Watt (1963) 'The consequences of literacy'. *Comparative Studies in Society and History* 5:304–345.

Gumperz, John (1977) 'Sociocultural knowledge in conversational inference'. In M. Saville-Troike (ed.), *28th Annual Round Table Monograph Series on Language and Linguistics*. Washington, DC: Georgetown University Press, 191–212.

Halliday, M. A. K. (1975) *Learning how to mean – explorations in the development of language*. *Explorations in Language Study*. London: Edward Arnold.

Halliday, M. A. K. (1978) *Language as social semiotic*. London: Edward Arnold.

Halliday, M. A. K. (1985) *An introduction to functional grammar*. London: Edward Arnold.

Hanks, William F. (1996) *Language and communicative practices*. Boulder, CO: Westview Press.

Harris, G. G. (1989) 'Concepts of individual, self, and person in description and analysis'. *American Anthropologist* 91:599–612.

Harvey, David (1996) *Justice, nature and the geography of difference*. Oxford: Blackwell.

Havelock, Eric A. (1986) *The muse learns to write*. New Haven: Yale University Press.

Heath, Shirley Brice (1983) *Ways with words*. New York: Cambridge University Press.

Hengst, Julie A. and Peggy J. Miller (1999) 'The heterogeneity of discourse genres: Implications for development'. *World Englishes* 18(3):325–341.

Hsu, Francis L. K. (1953) *Americans and Chinese: Passage to differences.* Honolulu: University Press of Hawaii.

Hsu, Francis L. K. (1983) *Rugged individualism reconsidered: Essays in psychological anthropology.* Knoxville: University of Tennessee Press.

Hsu, Francis L. K. (1985) 'The self in cross-cultural perspective'. In Anthony J. Marsella, Anthony J, George DeVos, and Francis L. K. Hsu (eds), *Culture and self: Asian and western perspectives.* New York: Tavistock Publications.

Hutchins, Edwin (1994) *Cognition in the wild.* Cambridge, MA: MIT Press.

Hymes, Dell (1966) 'Two types of linguistic relativity'. In William Bright (ed.), *Sociolinguistics.* The Hague: Mouton.

Keller-Cohen, Deborah (1993) *Literacy: Interdisciplinary conversations.* Cresskill, NJ: Hampton Press Inc.

Kress, Gunther and Theo van Leeuwen (1998) *Reading images: The grammar of visual design.* London: Routledge.

Kuhn, Thomas S. (1962) *The structure of scientific revolutions.* Chicago: University of Chicago Press.

Lave, Jean and Etienne Wenger (1991) *Situated learning: legitimate peripheral participation.* Cambridge: Cambridge University Press.

Lyra, Maria C. D. P. (1999) 'An excursion into the dynamics of dialogue: Elaborations upon the dialogical self'. *Culture and Psychology* 5(4):477–489.

Mehan, Hugh (1983) *Learning lessons: Social organization in the classroom.* Cambridge, MA: Harvard University Press.

Merritt, Marilyn (1976a) 'Resources for saying in service encounters'. Unpublished doctoral dissertation in linguistics, University of Pennsylvania, Philadelphia.

Merritt, Marilyn (1976b) 'On questions following questions (in service encounters)'. *Language in Society* 5:315–357.

Merritt, Marilyn (1978) 'On the use of "O.K." in service encounters'. *Sociolinguistic Working Paper,* 42. Southwest Educational Development Laboratory.

Miller, Peggy J., Judith Mintz, Lisa Hoogstra, Heidi Fung, and Randolph Potts (1992) 'The narrated self: Young children's construction of self in relation to others in conversational stories of personal experience'. *Merrill-Palmer Quarterly* 38(1):45–67.

Miller, Peggy J., Randolph Potts, Heidi Fung, Lisa Hoogstra, and Judy Mintz (1990) 'Narrative practices and the social construction of self in childhood'. *American Ethnologist* 17(2):292–311.

Miller, Peggy J., Angela R. Wiley, Heidi Fung, and Chung-Hui Liang (1997) 'Personal storytelling as a medium of socialization in Chinese and American families'. *Child Development* 68(3):557–568.

Nishida, Kitaroo (1958) *Intelligibility and the philosophy of nothingness.* Tokyo: Maruzen Co. Ltd.

Ochs, Elinor (1979) 'Transcription as theory'. In Elinor Ochs and Bambi B. Schieffelin (eds), *Developmental pragmatics.* New York: Academic Press, 43–72.

Okie, Susan (2000) 'The clout behind a cancer maverick'. http://washingtonpost.com/wp-dyn/health/A58316–2000Jan17.html

Ong, Walter J. (1982) *Orality and literacy.* New York: Methuen.

Piaget, Jean (1966 [1950]) *The psychology of intelligence.* Totowa, NJ: Littlefield, Adams & Company.

Piaget, Jean (1969 [1929]) *The child's conception of the world.* Totowa, NJ: Littlefield, Adams & Company.

Rogers, Carl (1951) *Client-centered therapy*. Boston: Houghton-Mifflin.

Schegloff, Emanuel (1972) 'Sequencing in conversational openings'. In John Gumperz and Dell Hymes (eds), *Directions in sociolinguistics*. New York: Holt, Rinehart and Winston, 346–380.

Schiffrin, Deborah (1987) *Discourse markers*. Cambridge: Cambridge University Press.

Scollon, Ron (1976) *Conversations with a one year old: a case study of the developmental foundation of syntax*. Honolulu: University Press of Hawaii.

Scollon, Ron (1979) 'A real early stage: An unzippered condensation of a dissertation on child language'. In Elinor Ochs and Bambi B. Schieffelin (eds), *Developmental pragmatics*. New York: Academic Press, 215–227.

Scollon, Ron (1997) 'Handbills, tissues, and condoms: A site of engagement for the construction of identity in public discourse'. *Journal of Sociolinguistics* 1(1):39–61.

Scollon, Ron (1998) *Mediated discourse as social interaction: A study of news discourse*. New York: Longman.

Scollon, Ron (1999) 'Mediated discourse and social interaction'. *Research on Language and Social Interaction* 32(1&2):149–154.

Scollon, Ron and Suzanne B. K. Scollon (1979) *Linguistic convergence: An ethnography of speaking at Fort Chipewyan, Alberta*. New York: Academic Press.

Scollon, Ron and Suzanne Scollon (1980) 'Literacy as focused interaction'. *Quarterly Newsletter of the Laboratory of Comparative Human Cognition*, Vol. 2(2):26–29.

Scollon, Ron and Suzanne Scollon (1981) *Narrative, literacy and face in interethnic communication*. Norwood, NJ: Ablex Publishing Corporation.

Scollon, Ron and Suzie Wong Scollon (1991) 'Topic confusion in English-Asian discourse'. *World Englishes* 10(2):113–125.

Scollon, Ron and Suzanne Wong Scollon (1995) *Intercultural communication: A discourse approach*. Oxford: Basil Blackwell.

Scollon, Ron and Suzanne Wong Scollon (2001) *Intercultural communication: A discourse approach* [Revised edition]. Oxford: Basil Blackwell.

Scollon, Suzanne (1982) 'Reality set, socialization, and linguistic convergence'. Unpublished doctoral dissertation, University of Hawaii, Honolulu.

Scollon, Suzanne (1996a) 'The commodification of the art of Taaigik Kyuhn (Taijiquan) in Hong Kong: A comparison of Sahn Wahn Pang Yau and organized classes'. Paper presented at the Conference on Consumer Culture in Hong Kong, Hong Kong University, 18–20 April 1996.

Scollon, Suzanne (1996b) 'The social construction of the somatic self: Learning Taijiquan'. Paper presented to the Public Discourse Research Group, Department of English, City University of Hong Kong, 11 March 1996.

Scollon, Suzanne (1998) 'Identity through the embodiment of authoritative gesture: The practice of taijiquan in Hong Kong'. In D. Ray Heisey and Wenxiang Gong (eds), *Communication and culture: China and the world entering the 21st century*. Amsterdam: Rodopi Editions, 181–204.

Scollon, Suzanne (1999a) 'Voice and authority: Positioning in taijiquan by interviewers/ editors in contemporary China'. Paper presented at the annual meetings of the National Oral History Association, Anchorage, 7 October.

Scollon, Suzanne (1999b) 'Pruning and grafting: The cultivation of identity through imagined genealogies'. Paper presented at the annual meetings of the American Anthropological Association, Chicago, 17 November.

Scollon, Suzanne (2000a) 'Whose side are you on? Mediation of national identity through positioning in public space in real time during the Taiwan missile crisis'. Paper presented at Sociolinguistics Symposium, University of Bristol, 27 April.

Scollon, Suzanne (2000b) 'Who do you think you are? Identity, cognition and pragmatics in a *taijiquan* group'. Paper presented in the panel 'Identity formation and social change' at the 7th International Pragmatics Association Conference, Budapest, 9–14 July 2000.

Scollon, Suzanne (2000c) 'Political and somatic alignment: Habitus, ideology and social practice'. Paper given at a workshop on Theory and Interdisciplinarity in Critical Discourse Analysis, Institute on Discourse, Identity and Politics, University of Vienna, 6–7 July 2000 as a pre-session to the 7th International Pragmatics Association Conference in Budapest (9–14 July 2000).

Scollon, Suzanne (In preparation) 'Pushing hands, pushing minds: Mediating transnational identity in a taijiquan group'. Georgetown University, Department of Linguistics, Asian Sociocultural Research Projects: Manuscript.

Scollon, Suzanne Wong and Huhua Ouyang (1998) 'Taijiquan as intellectual property: Secrecy, tradition, theory and practice'. Paper presented in the session 'Globalism in Hong Kong Public Discourse: Post-modern ideology and local resistance' at the annual meetings of the American Anthropological Association, Philadelphia, 2–6 December 1998.

Scribner, Sylvia and Michael Cole (1981) *The psychology of literacy*. Cambridge, MA: Harvard University Press.

Sinclair, John McH. and R. Malcolm Coulthard (1975) *Towards an analysis of discourse: The English used by teachers and pupils*. Oxford: Oxford University Press.

Street, Brian (1984) *Literacy in theory and practice*. New York: Cambridge University Press.

Street, Brian (1995) *Social literacies: Critical approaches to literacy in development, ethnography, and education*. London: Longman.

Swales, John M. (1990) *Genre analysis: English in academic and research settings*. Cambridge: Cambridge University Press.

Swales, John M. (1998) *Other floors, other voices: A textography of a small university building*. Mahwah, NJ: Lawrence Erlbaum Associates.

Tulviste, Peeter (1994) 'History taught at school versus history discovered at home: The case of Estonia'. *European Journal of Psychology of Education* IX(1):121–126.

Tulviste, Peeter and James V. Wertsch (1994) 'Official and unofficial histories: The case of Estonia'. *Journal of Narrative and Life History* 4(4):311–329.

Van Leeuwen, Theo (1996) 'The representation of social actors'. In Carmen Rosa Caldas-Coulthard and Malcolm Coulthard (eds), *Text and practices: Readings in critical discourse analysis*. London: Routledge.

Wenger, Etienne (1998) *Communities of practice: Learning, meaning, and identity*. Cambridge: Cambridge University Press.

Wertsch, James V. (1997) 'Narrative tools of history and identity'. *Culture and Psychology* 3(1):5–20.

Wertsch, James V. (1998) *Mind as action*. New York: Oxford University Press.

Wierzbicka, Anna (1985) 'Different cultures, different languages, different speech acts: Polish vs. English'. *Journal of Pragmatics* 9: 145–178.

Wierzbicka, Anna (1991) 'Japanese key words and core cultural values'. *Language in Society* 20:333–383.

Wierzbicka, Anna (1993) 'A conceptual basis for cultural psychology'. *Ethos* 21(2):205–231.

Wierzbicka, Anna (1994a) ' "Cultural scripts": A new approach to the study of cross-cultural communication'. In Martin Pütz (ed.), *Language contact and language conflict*. Amsterdam: John Benjamins Publishing Company.

Wierzbicka, Anna (1994b) ' "Cultural scripts" : A semantic approach to cultural analysis and cross-cultural communication'. *Pragmatics and Language Learning* 5:1–24.

Wierzbicka, Anna (1998) 'German "cultural scripts" : Public signs as a key to social attitudes and cultural values'. *Discourse and Society* 9(2):241–282.

Wittgenstein, Ludwig (1990 [1953]) *Philosophical Investigations*. Chicago: Encyclopaedia Britannica, Inc., 311–440.

Wortham, Stanton (In press [and 1999]). 'Interactionally situated cognition: A classroom example'. *Cognitive Science*. Also presented at the annual meeting of the American Anthropological Association, Chicago, November 1999.

Index